Science, Medicine, and the State in Germany

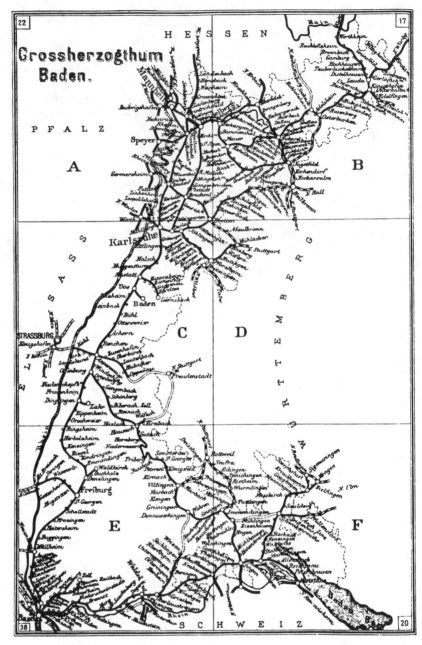

Map of Baden, Württemberg, and surroundings, 1853

Science, Medicine, and the State in Germany

The Case of Baden, 1815–1871

Arleen Marcia Tuchman
Vanderbilt University

New York   Oxford
OXFORD UNIVERSITY PRESS
1993

Oxford University Press

Oxford   New York   Toronto
Delhi   Bombay   Calcutta   Madras   Karachi
Kuala Lumpur   Singapore   Hong Kong   Tokyo
Nairobi   Dar es Salaam   Cape Town
Melbourne   Auckland   Madrid

and associated companies in
Berlin   Ibadan

Copyright © 1993 by Oxford University Press, Inc.

Published by Oxford University Press, Inc.
200 Madison Avenue, New York, New York 10016

Oxford is a registered trademark of Oxford University Press

Library of Congress Cataloging-in-Publication Data
Tuchman, Arleen.
Science, medicine, and the state in Germany : the case of Baden,
1815–1871 / Arleen Marcia Tuchman.
p. cm.   Includes bibliographical references and index.
ISBN 0-19-508047-5
1. Medicine—Research—Germany—Baden—History—19th century.
2. Research—Germany—Baden—History—19th century.   3. Universität
Heidelberg—History.
R511.B33T8   1993
610′.7′04346409034—dc20   92–23470

1 3 5 7 9 8 6 4 2

Printed in the United States of America
on acid-free paper

335904

For my mother
Dina Tuchman
in memoriam

Acknowledgments

I have accumulated many debts while writing this book, and it is with great pleasure that I now acknowledge them. The years spent on this project would have been more difficult and infinitely less pleasant were it not for the kindness and assistance of many librarians and archivists. I am especially indebted to the staff of the Institut für Geschichte der Medizin der Freien Universität Berlin, and foremost to its head librarian, Ailmut Kliesch, whose good will and tenacity frequently led her to track down sources for me long after I had accepted defeat. The Institut provided me with office space, strong coffee, and a challenging intellectual environment for which I am particularly grateful. I would also like to thank the staffs of the Badisches Generallandesarchiv Karlsruhe, the Handschriftenabteilung der Universitätsbibliothek Heidelberg, the Universitätsarchiv Heidelberg, the Universitätsarchiv Göttingen, the Handschriftenabteilung der Staatsbibliothek Preußischer Kulturbesitz, and the Geheimes Staatsarchiv Preußischer Kulturbesitz Merseburg.

Financial assistance from several organizations allowed me to spend extended periods of time in the German archives and libraries. The research for my dissertation, upon which this book is based, was funded by two years of support from the Fulbright Foundation and by a University of Wisconsin Richardson Fellowship in the History of Medicine. A summer grant from the American Philosophical Society and a Travel to Collections Grant from the National Endowment for the Humanities permitted me to return to the archives and complete the research. I also wish to thank the Vanderbilt University Research Council for its financial support of this publication.

Many people read parts, and in some cases, all, of the manuscript for this book. For their critical insights and helpful comments I would like to thank Michael Bess, Thomas Broman, Joyce Chaplin, James Epstein, Carole Fink, Gerald Geison, Frederic L. Holmes, Russell Maulitz, Matthew Ramsey, Guenter Risse, Charles Rosenberg, Barbara Rosenkrantz, and David Vampolla. Charles Rosenberg and Barbara Rosenkrantz played especially important roles in the publication of this manuscript. I am appreciative of Timothy Lenoir's many suggestions during the early stages of this project. Special thanks to Helmut Smith who found time during an extremely busy year to give my manuscript a meticulous reading. His suggestions, both conceptual and editorial, are gratefully acknowledged. I am also indebted to the previously anonymous reviewer, R. Steven Turner, whose suggestions for revisions, particularly his recommendation that I develop a comparative perspective, greatly improved this book. His reader's report, which was simultaneously critical and supportive, remains for me a model of its kind.

It is a very special pleasure to thank Johanna Bleker and Heinz-Peter Schmiedebach. They taught me much of what I know about nineteenth-century German medicine. The countless conversations we had during the many years I spent in Berlin contributed to the present work in more ways than I could ever adequately acknowledge. And the friendship and support they provided as I adjusted to a new city, a new language, and a new academic environment made all the difference in the world to someone who was very far from home.

Anyone who has written a book knows how much one relies on the good will and encouragement of friends and family. Sigrid Arnold, Alex Chelminsky, Brenda Hipshur, Susan Johnston, Morris Shooer, Deborah Smith, Chana Tropen, my father, Sam Tuchman, and my sister, Shendl Tuchman helped me through many difficult times during the past several years. Their unconditional support was and remains a gift for which I feel truly blessed.

Finally, my greatest debts are to two individuals whom I sorely miss. No one had a greater influence on my intellectual development than my thesis advisor and mentor, William Coleman. His has become the critical voice that I carry around with me as I do my own work. During the last years of his life, he also became a good friend. I only hope that he knew how much this meant to me.

My mother also died while I was working on this book. Yet in a fundamental way, she, more than anyone else, is responsible for its completion. In times of doubt, I remember her undaunted confidence in me and her own strength and spirit of determination. This book is dedicated to her.

Contents

Abbreviations

Acten	Acten der medizinischen Fakultät zu Heidelberg
Anzeige	*Anzeige der Vorlesungen auf der Großherzoglich Badischen Ruprecht Karolinischen Universität zu Heidelberg*
BGLA	Badisches Generallandesarchiv Karlsruhe
BB	*Badische Biographieen,* ed. Friedrich von Weech, 6 vols. (Heidelberg, 1875–1935)
BL	*Biographisches Lexikon der hervorragenden Ärzte aller Zeiten und Völker,* ed. August Hirsch, 6 vols. (Munich, 1962)
DSB	*Dictionary of Scientific Biography,* ed. Charles C. Gillespie, 14 vols. (New York, 1970–76)
Mittheilungen	*Mittheilungen des badischen ärztlichen Vereins*
RB	*Großherzoglich Badisches Staats- und Regierungsblatt*
SPK	Staatsbibliothek Preußischer Kulturbesitz, Handschriftenabteilung [Manuscript Division]
Verhandlungen	*Verhandlungen der Stände-Versammlung des Großherzogthums Baden*
GStA Merseburg	Geheimes Staatsarchiv Preußischer Kulturbesitz Merseburg

Science, Medicine, and the State in Germany

Introduction

"Knowledge is power," Hermann Helmholtz told an audience of students, faculty, and university administrators in May 1862. The occasion was his election to the office of rector at the University of Heidelberg, a major university in the southern German state of Baden. For his inaugural address, Helmholtz had chosen to speak on the relationship of the natural sciences to other branches of knowledge. Although intending to treat all branches equally, he ended up singing loudest the praises of the experimental sciences. Only they, he explained, permitted the control and manipulation of natural phenomena, allowing us to "exploit the powers of nature for our benefit and make them subservient to our will."[1]

Knowledge may be power, but the kind of knowledge western culture has deemed powerful has changed over time, shifting from spiritual or religious wisdom to classical, and then to scientific knowledge. This last transition is a relatively recent phenomenon, barely a few centuries old. Although the social value of scientific knowledge began to increase rapidly during the seventeenth century, scientific activity did not acquire professional status until two centuries later. At that time scientific research and the teaching of the scientific method to students, especially to medical students, became firmly established in the elite educational institutions of society, the universities. That scientists and physicians achieved this success well before they could fully realize the Baconian dream and transform scientific knowledge into direct material and therapeutic gains has long intrigued scholars.

This book studies the rise in status of scientific knowledge by looking at the multiple factors that influenced and directed increased support for science education in nineteenth-century Germany. During that century, Germany's university system fostered the rapid growth of scientific disciplines and scientific knowledge, quickly becoming the model for universities throughout Europe and the United States. The experimental sciences in particular began to flourish around 1850, and in the decades thereafter almost every university in each of the German states founded new faculty positions and expensive research institutes. Robert Bunsen's chemistry laboratory in Heidelberg and Carl Ludwig's physiology laboratory in Leipzig were just two of the many institutes built in the 1850s and 1860s that soon acquired international fame, attracting students from all over the world and turning Germany into the major center for scientific research and education in the second half of the nineteenth century.

Scholars have long been interested in the reasons for this remarkable proliferation of scientific activity, not least because the emergence of science-based industries during the last decades of the century helped transform Germany into one of the leading industrialized nations in Europe. Nevertheless, previous attempts to explain why the sciences flourished in mid-nineteenth-century Germany rarely considered the nature of the relationship between scientific knowledge and industrialization.[2] Instead these studies focussed on ideological factors, emphasizing the importance of the neohumanist notion of *Wissenschaft* for Wilhelm von Humboldt and other early nineteenth-century Prussian reformers.[3] For these reformers, education was a process in which the personal search for knowledge took precedence over the mere acquisition of information. This led, ultimately, to a higher estimation of the value of research, and expectations soon arose that a professor should be not only a good teacher but a renowned scholar as well. Yet as important as the notion of *Wissenschaft* may have been, this explanation could not account for the rapidity with which support for scientific activity spread throughout the various German states. Here historians have been influenced primarily by the work of the late sociologist Joseph Ben-David. In a series of articles written about thirty years ago, he argued that institutional factors must be considered as well. Attributing Germany's spectacular scientific development to the decentralized structure of its university system, he showed that this structural constellation created a competitive market that permitted professors to set conditions for their acceptance of academic appointments.[4] In the nineteenth century, as scientific research grew increasingly more dependent on sophisticated instruments, and as adequate laboratory space became a central demand of young scientists, state governments throughout Germany began to address these new needs. Pressured by the competitive market, concerned with the reputation of their universities, and interested in attracting the best scholars, they agreed to finance the construction of new research institutes. Thus for Ben-David, the full and rapid integration of laboratory training and research into the university curriculum was a consequence of what he termed "unintentional social evolution."

In later years other scholars built upon this model. R. Steven Turner, for one, emphasized the importance of the university's transition from a corporate structure to a state institution in the years following the Napoleonic wars.[5] Governments thus gained control of academic appointments, acquiring the power necessary to shift academic standards from collegiate to disciplinary criteria, and to redirect the emphasis from pedagogy and encyclopedic learning to independent research. Placing greater stress on the government's role in institutionalizing the research model than Ben-David, Turner also demonstrated more clearly the extent to which student demand influenced appointment decisions. He nevertheless did not abandon the general interpretive framework in which the government's primary motivations were based on a commitment to the ideology of *Wissenschaft* and a concern for national prestige. The general view thus persisted that the proliferation of institutes during the mid-century had little to do with developments that greatly altered the economy of the German states in the years prior to the 1880s and 1890s.

Although the notion of *Wissenschaft,* the decentralized structure of the university system, and government control of academic appointments all contributed fundamentally to the production of scientific knowledge, they alone cannot explain why Germany became the center of scientific research in the nineteenth century. By 1815 a competitive system that placed a high premium on *Wissenschaft* already existed, yet major laboratories did not appear until decades later. There was, moreover, an underlying tension between the holistic, anti-utilitarian emphasis implicit in the neohumanist definition of *Bildung*[6] and the kind of laboratory training provided in the latter half of the nineteenth century—training intended not for an elite group alone but for all students of the sciences and medicine. Scholars have failed to recognize that the increase in support for the natural sciences and research institutes began concurrently with an early and significant phase in Germany's economic development.[7] During the middle third of the nineteenth century, state governments pursued strategies that went beyond attempts to compete successfully in the academic market and gain control over professorial appointments; state officials also demonstrated an interest in providing students with the kind of education they believed would be necessary for tackling the problems of an industrializing economy.

Between 1830 and 1860 major developments in manufacture, trade, and transportation began to alter the German economy significantly. Construction and rapid expansion of the railroad, improved waterways, increased iron production, modernization of the spinning industry, the foundation of credit banks, and the establishment of the *Zollverein* (customs union) all marked the beginning of a long process that eventually transformed Germany into an industrial state. These developments depended to a great extent on the implementation of government reforms designed to help improve and modernize the economy. The abolition of serfdom and the weakening of guilds are classic examples of such measures, but of comparable significance were changes in the educational system that resulted in a greater emphasis on the natural sciences. Beginning in the 1820s and 1830s state governments throughout Germany founded technical institutes, trade schools, and non-classical secondary schools (*höhere Bürgerschulen*). The latter, an alternative to the traditional *Gymnasia*, provided an education in the *Realwissenschaften*—subjects such as mathematics, natural science, history, and the modern languages. Their purpose was to provide a general education for individuals who intended to dedicate themselves to a world of trade, commerce, and communication, rather than to a learned career. As the head of a government advisory committee in Baden informed his colleagues in parliament, the non-classical secondary schools were for the "productive citizens of the state," not for the "consumers."[8]

These changes also greatly influenced the content of university education; it was during this very period that the natural sciences began to thrive within university walls. This was no coincidence. The universities were state institutions, dependent on government appropriation of funds and thus constantly scrutinized by parliamentary representatives who had the needs of the state in mind as they voted on fiscal matters. Although not usually, these needs were occasionally perceived in utilitarian terms. Peter Borscheid, for example, in his study of the chemical industry in Baden, has demonstrated a direct link between the extent to which a state's economy suffered during the agricultural crises of the 1840s and the state's commitment to scientific research.[9] He has shown that the more serious the crisis, the more willing a government was to explore nontraditional methods for improving the quality of the soil. In Chapter 5 I deal with Borscheid's thesis in some detail. Its great significance rests, in my view, in its illustration of the intimate relationship between the institutionalization of research programs in the university system and the perception that these programs would yield practical returns—in this case Baden's belief that experimental chemistry would help alleviate the agricultural depression and prevent political unrest among its inhabitants.

Borscheid is not alone in his attempt to modify the dominant picture of nineteenth-century German universities as institutions dedicated solely to the pursuit of science for its own sake (*Wissenschaft um ihrer selbst willen*). Other scholars have also charted the universities' deviation from the pure Humboldtian model. Konrad Jarausch, for example, has argued that whether the universities contributed directly to industrialization or not, they definitely functioned as a forum for disseminating modern cultural values and social aspirations.[10] Taken together, these studies suggest that the universities were not immune from the forces that were gradually reshaping the German economic and political landscape.[11] My research supports this revisionist picture of the German university as well: it demonstrates that although government officials and educational reformers rarely viewed university education in strict utilitarian terms, they did consider it an ideal tool for generating a new approach to the analysis of problems deemed more appropriate for the emerging industrial order. My argument is that training in the exact method of the experimental sciences received institutional support in the German university system not simply because it had become the model for the way in which science should be done, but because it had come to signify the kind of "cultural education" (*geistige Bildung*) desired by a society trying to deal with the problems of a changing and growing economy. Like computers today, the scientific method in the nineteenth century provided an instrument for teaching school children and college students not only specific skills but also a particular way of approaching, defining, tackling, and solving problems.

To argue my point, I have written a case history, based on archival sources, of the events leading to the institutionalization of the experimental sciences, and specifically of experimental physiology, at the University of Heidelberg. The focus on Baden's major university is intended as a corrective to the Prussianization of German history. Most of what we know about German science (and German history, in general) is based on an exhaustive study of Prussian events. Yet developments elsewhere in Germany neither mimicked nor mirrored exactly what occurred in that single state. Without wishing to deny the central role played by Prussia in the history of Germany, I do wish to argue that the decisions made and paths chosen in other states reflected more than the blind following of the Prussian model. Even more to the point, the focus on Prussia has distorted our picture of the relationship between university, science, and the state, leading historians to view government interest in the sciences in the years preceding the unification of Germany as tepid at best. Yet Prussian developments in the 1850s, during which time that government sorely ignored its universities, did not reflect developments in all other German states; rather, at a time when Prussia devoted much of its energy to repressive political measures and military exploits, other states poured money into their universities.[12] In the 1850s, for example, Baden emerged as one of the strongest supporters of the experimental sciences, thereby setting an example that its northern neighbor would not follow until the 1870s and 1880s.

Borscheid believes that agricultural concerns catapulted Baden into this leadership role; yet I wish to argue that more was at play. Baden's brief but significant time in the limelight was also the result of its strong political tradition, dating back to the early *Vormärz* period, of political constitutionalism and liberalism. Up to now historians of German science have paid scant attention to the relationship between liberal ideology and science policy. But even a cursory perusal of the relevant literature suggests that in the years prior to the unification of Germany there was an undoubted connection. Science education flourished where and when liberal-minded ministers held important positions in the government: in Baden in the 1830s, when Ludwig Winter, the renowned liberal, headed the ministry of interior, and again in the late 1850s and 1860s, first under Franz Freiherr von Stengel and then August Lamey; in Saxony in the 1860s under Johann Paul Freiherr von Falkenstein; and in Prussia in the 1830s under Karl Freiherr von Stein zum Altenstein. Negative examples demonstrate this point as well: science education was never more neglected than during the years of reaction in Prussia, when Karl Otto von Raumer, a political conservative, headed the ministry of education.

To be sure, there is no inherent connection between the scientific method and liberalism. This method can be, and has been, associated with authoritarianism and totalitarianism as well. The desiderata of independent thought can be ignored; the technique alone can be emphasized. Nevertheless, in nineteenth-century Germany historical circumstances brought the scientific method and political liberalism together. This manifested itself most clearly in the liberals' conviction that an education in the natural sciences would better prepare the lower and middle classes for life in a modern economy: it would provide the former with skills and a "modern mentality" that would ease the transition from farm work to employment in small manufactories; and it would awaken in the latter an entrepreneurial spirit, inspiring in them a desire to participate in the economic and political affairs of a constitutional state. Without disregarding the value of a classical education, German liberals believed that an education in the *Realwissenschaften,* with its emphasis on the natural sciences, mathematics, modern languages, and geography, was ideally suited to these needs. As one member of the Baden parliament told his audience in 1831, these subjects would permit young people to take advantage "of the path now being taken by civilization as a whole."[13]

In addition to these specific benefits, liberals supported science education because it represented a powerful tool for attacking religious and political conservatives. There were strong parallels with the debates between "realists" and "humanists," which colored all discussions of educational reform in the mid-nineteenth century. The realists, while not denying the value of Latin and Greek, criticized these subjects for emphasizing memorization and obeyance while praising the *Realwissenschaften,* and especially the scientific method, for promoting independent thought.[14] Although the accuracy of this assessment can certainly be questioned, there is no denying the realists' conviction that only advantages would be gained from a hands-on approach to the study of nature. Advocating what could best be described as an "ideology of the practical,"[15] the realists argued that students who worked directly with the material in question, analyzing, dissecting, and manipulating the laws of nature, would learn to think for themselves. The emphasis on independent thought, added to the materialism often associated with the study of the natural sciences, frequently led religious and political conservatives to view the natural sciences with great scepticism. This may well explain the decision of several German governments in the aftermath of the revolutionary uprisings of 1848 to reduce the amount of time spent on the natural sciences in the *Gymnasia.*[16] It may also explain why the natural sciences flourished in Baden during this very same period. Baden's support for the sciences resulted, in my view, not only from the realization that measures had to be taken quickly to improve the productivity of the land, but also from a long tradition of political liberalism that both fostered a firm link between intellectual and material interests, and helped ease relations between the government and university during the difficult years of reaction.

II

The goal of this study, in the broadest sense, is to explore the social, political, and intellectual factors that contributed to the growth of scientific knowledge and to changes in the style of scientific research and teaching in the nineteenth-century German universities. Within this story there is also a more specific one that focuses on the history of the physiological sciences and their relationship to medicine. The book begins with the University of Heidelberg's appointment in 1815 of Friedrich Tiedemann as professor of anatomy, physiology, comparative anatomy, and zoology, and then traces the events leading to the emergence of experimental physiology as an autonomous discipline in 1858. At different periods during this forty-five year span, Tiedemann, Jacob Henle, Friedrich Arnold, and Hermann Helmholtz were responsible for teaching physiology at the University of Heidelberg, and each one tackled this responsibility with his own research style and pedagogical technique, and with different scientific facilities and instruments at his disposal. I trace these developments within physiology and place them within the broader context of changing state policy with regard to the university, science, and medicine.

The focus on physiology and medicine permits me to apply Borscheid's thesis to branches of scientific knowledge other than chemistry; it also allows me to refine his thesis, for I contend that the government's concern was not with agriculture alone, but with broader movements affecting the economic and social life of its citizens. Moreover, these concerns did not, as Borscheid argues, develop in the aftermath of 1848, but had their roots in the *Vormärz* period (the decades preceding the March revolution of 1848) when Baden was at the vanguard of political constitutionalism and liberalism.

These qualifications aside, I accept Borscheid's theory that the experimental sciences received institutional support because of their perceived utility. In this regard, I am directly challenging Ben-David and another sociologist, Avraham Zloczower.[17] In their studies of physiology, these two scholars have argued that the sciences flourished in Germany because of government acceptance of the principle of *Wissenschaft um ihrer selbst willen*. Their conclusion was based on separating the history of physiology from its medical context which, as I argue in Chapter 6, is a distorted view. The decision to finance new chairs and institutes for experimental physiology in the 1850s and 1860s rested to a great extent on the expectation that this science would raise standards within the medical profession and, ultimately, improve medical care.

This may seem a surprising claim. It has almost become a truism among historians of science that physiology made no direct contributions to medicine until the end of the nineteenth century. This is not, however, accurate. While therapeutics may not have benefited, other aspects of the medical field certainly did. For example, experimental scientists altered diagnostics through the invention of instruments, such as the ophthalmoscope, which helped increase the physician's knowledge of the organic signs and symptoms associated with disease. But physicians and medical advisors mentioned only occasionally these direct contributions to medicine; more important to them was the value of experimental physiology as a tool for teaching a particular way of analyzing and dissecting a disease complex. As the head of the Baden medical society wrote in 1852, the student who learned the exact method in the laboratory would have "so cultivated his sense for the proper way of looking at things . . . that the only task left would be to give instruction on how to direct his experience through the great labyrinth of pathology and therapy."[18] He was convinced, as were his fellow physicians, that the methods learned in the laboratory, under simplified conditions, would be directly applicable to an analysis of the complex factors governing the disease process.

This conviction needs explaining. By mid-century the use of the experimental method had greatly increased scientists' understanding of the laws governing chemical, physiological, and physical processes (even if this knowledge had only begun to demonstrate its profitability). As a result, the exact method of the experimental sciences had come to symbolize an approach to the study of nature that permitted extensive control and manipulation of the phenomena at hand. For this reason physicians viewed experimental physiology, more than pathological anatomy or the clinical sciences, as the cornerstone of scientific medicine. Helmholtz's rectoral address on knowledge and power was a classic expression of the perceived symbolic power of this method, and physicians well understood the message. For those struggling to fashion a science of medicine, the methods of analysis associated with experimental physiology represented the means through which they believed they would gain control over the disease process.

Although historians have occasionally acknowledged the link between experimental physiology and medical reform, their tendency has been to interpret physicians' interest in reform as little more than a desire to gain a monopoly over the medical market. While professional concerns were, to be sure, a primary focus in physicians' struggles for reform, this interpretation is simplistic. Physicians did not fight for changes that would simply bring them greater power and wealth; they fought for changes that would render them better health-care professionals, and thereby help them to control the medical field. In other words, physicians shared a conviction that medical care would indeed improve through the application of experimental methods to the study of health and disease. Many may have been driven by the personal benefits to be gained through their entry into the newly emerging scientific elite, but this only strengthened—it did not determine—their conviction that they had chosen the correct path. It is this conviction we must examine. That the absence of immediate therapeutic gains did not discourage them rested to a great extent on the strength of the faith in the experimental sciences shared by physicians, scientists, and government administrators alike in the mid-nineteenth century.

It was, moreover, faith in the power of scientific knowledge that fostered growth in support for science education and, especially, for laboratory training. My central argument is that this faith can only be understood if one considers the broader social and economic changes that ultimately transformed Germany into a modern industrial state. Within this context, laboratory training, once considered inappropriate for university studies, slowly increased in status, and dissatisfaction with the overly theoretical education traditionally offered by the universities began to grow. Professors and a small student elite had been engaging in scientific experiments since the early nineteenth century, but their work had been cast within a tradition that viewed research as the property of the chosen few. What marked the research institutes of the 1850s and 1860s was their inclusion of large laboratories, designed to introduce every student of science and medicine—even the "less gifted"—to the scientific method. To be sure, advanced research continued in these institutes, but the addition of routine instruction in scientific techniques for the average student distinguished the goals of these laboratories from the small office spaces, scientific cabinets, and museums of the early nineteenth-century.

III

The construction of large research institutes, financed by state governments, occurred before science and industry formed the link that came to define much of modern western culture, providing an essential, if not *the* essential, driving force for the economy. But there were individuals who, impressed by scientific research in such areas as electricity and chemistry, had visions of the power to be accrued from such a marriage. They included people in commerce and industry sitting in parliament, experimental scientists struggling for disciplinary autonomy, students of the technical institutes, and even government ministers. To take one example: with an eye on the rapid industrial developments occurring in England, the Baden minister of education fought for greater investment in the state's technical school. There, he argued, the student would learn to "see with his own eyes, examine, and contemplate . . . discovering thereby new truths that can find immediate profitable application in the area of production."[19]

Nebenius made this comment in 1833, almost a half century before his vision became a reality. But in the intervening decades German state governments were not idle; on the contrary, during these years they invested more and more heavily in science education and research laboratories, training large numbers of students in routine methods aimed at providing them with specific analytical skills. The investment eventually paid off; in the decades following the unification of Germany, science-based industries, staffed by many of these university-trained individuals, began to flourish. Chemical, pharmaceutical, optical, and electrical industries hired these young scientists to work in their laboratories and perform routine techniques. They also set up research laboratories in which accomplished scientists engaged in practical experiments, searching for new products that could be transformed into direct profit. In the last decades of the nineteenth century the long-awaited benefits of scientific research began to accrue. Salvarsan, chemical dyes, the development of anesthetics, and the synthetic production of ammonia, needed by Germany in World War I for making explosives, are just a few examples of discoveries that permitted Germany to corner a market in extremely profitable areas.

Thus, as I intend to demonstrate, the central role played by science-based industries in stimulating Germany's economic boom did not reflect a process of completely unintended social evolution. On the contrary, the marriage of science and industry, made possible by the availability of sufficient numbers of trained scientists to work in the industrial laboratories, was the result of a more complex social and political process in which state governments had gradually adapted their universities to the needs of an industrializing economy, shifting their allegiance from Latin and Greek to the scientific method as the best tool for training the critical faculties of the students' minds. This book is about that process.

Notes

1. Hermann Helmholtz, "Ueber das Verhältnis der Naturwissenschaften zur Gesamtheit der Wissenschaft," Akademische Festrede gehalten zu Heidelberg am 22 November 1862 bei Antritt des Prorectorats. In Helmholtz, *Vorträge und Reden*, 5th ed., 2 vols. (Braunschweig, 1903), vol.1, pp. 157–185.

2. I will return to this question later in the introduction.

3. See, for example, Helmut Schelsky, *Einsamkeit und Freiheit. Idee und Gestalt der deutschen Universität und ihrer Reformen,* 2nd ed. (Düsseldorf, 1971).

4. Joseph Ben-David, "Scientific Productivity and Academic Organization in Nineteenth Century Medicine," *American Sociological Review,* 25,2 (1960): 828–843; idem, "Review Article. Scientific Growth: A Sociological View," *Minerva,* 2,4 (1964): 455–476. See also his book *The Scientist's Role in Society: A Comparative Study,* with a new introduction (Chicago, 1984).

5. R. Steven Turner, "The Growth of Professorial Research in Prussia, 1818–1848—Causes and Context," *Historical Studies in the Physical Sciences,* 3 (1971): 137–182. See also idem, "Justus Liebig versus Prussian Chemistry: Reflections on Early Institute-Building in Germany," ibid., 13,1 (1982): 129–162, in which Turner expands his former argument to include the importance of student demand in the creation of institutes.

6. I discuss the various meanings of this term in Chapter 1.

7. Economic historians disagree over when, exactly, Germany began to industrialize. The most instructive assessment of this debate can be found in Frank B. Tipton, "The National Consensus in German Economic History," *Central European History,* 7,3 (1974): 195–224. Tipton emphasizes how relatively little we know about developments during the pre-1850 period. He also points out that historians have tended to neglect the great regional differences between and even within the various German states. For my purposes, it is less important to determine exactly when industrialization began than to acknowledge that the changes that ultimately transformed Germany into a modern industrial state represented a long, continual process.

8. Kröll, "Commissionsbericht über die Errichtung von höhern Bürger- und Gewerbeschulen," *Verhandlungen,* 2. Kammer, 66. Sitzung, 24 September 1833, Beilagenheft 5, pp. 235–251.

9. Peter Borscheid, *Naturwissenschaft, Staat und Industrie in Baden, 1848–1914* (Stuttgart, 1976).

10. Jarausch's central point is that the emergence of the modern state involved social changes that extended well beyond industrialization to such processes as rationalization, bureaucratization, and professionalization, and that while the universities may not have contributed directly to industrialization, they were definitely central to the development of the latter processes. See Konrad H. Jarausch, "Higher Education and Social Change," in Jarausch, ed., *The Transformation of Higher Learning, 1860–1930* (Stuttgart, 1982), pp. 9–36. See also Charles E. McClelland, *State, Society and University in Germany, 1700–1914* (Cambridge, 1980).

11. Among contemporary historians, Peter Lundgreen comes closest to viewing the universities as immune from broader economic and social developments. He argues, for example, that among all forms of higher education, only technical education contributed directly to industrialization. See Peter Lundgreen, *Bildung und Wirtschaftswachstum im Industrialisierungsprozess des 19. Jahrhunderts* (Berlin, 1973).

12. On Prussia's neglect of its universities during the 1850s, see McClelland, *State, Society and University,* chap. 6; and Max Lenz, *Geschichte der königlichen Friedrich-Wilhelms-Universität zu Berlin,* 4 vols. in 5 (Halle, 1910–1918), vol. 3.

13. Merk, *Verhandlungen,* 2. Kammer, 87. Sitzung, 2 September 1831, Protokollheft 21, p. 91.

14. Walter Schöler, *Geschichte des naturwissenschaftlichen Unterrichts im 17. bis 19. Jahrhundert* (Berlin, 1970), chap. 4.

15. I am grateful to R. Steven Turner for suggesting this phrase to me.

16. Schöler, *Geschichte des naturwissenschaftlichen Unterrichts,* chap. 4.

17. Avraham Zloczower, *Career Opportunities and the Growth of Scientific Disciplines in Nineteenth Century Germany* (New York, 1981). Surprisingly, Borscheid does not spell out the consequences of his argument for Ben-David's and Zloczower's thesis.

18. "Wie sollen die Aerzte gebildet werden?" in *Mittheilungen,* 12 May 1852 (Nr.9), pp. 65–69, here p. 66.

19. C. F. Nebenius, *Ueber technische Lehranstalten in ihrem Zusammenhange mit dem gesammten Unterrichtswesen und mit besonderer Rücksicht auf die polytechnische Schule zu Karlsruhe* (Karlsrhue, 1833), p. 52.

1

University Reform and Medical Education at the University of Heidelberg, 1815–1830

The German university system changed markedly during the nineteenth century. Apart from such exceptions as Göttingen and Halle, eighteenth-century universities were corporate structures, relatively free of state control and, for the most part, financially independent. Although they received some support from their respective governments, most of their income came from privately owned property and private endowments. Moreover, the emphasis on scientific and medical research that so characterized the nineteenth-century university had little counterpart in these earlier institutions. The latter fulfilled, rather, a predominantly pedagogical function, preparing students for entry into one of the professions through an education that focused on the classical works and classical languages. The student's possession of this knowledge marked him as a scholar (*Gelehrter*) and thus qualified him to become a lawyer, physician, clergyman, or civil servant. In this setting, the professor's primary function was to teach an already existing body of knowledge. Specialized research and the production of new knowledge were considered inappropriate for the university setting. Instead, the professor's scholarly pursuits centered on the publication of comprehensive textbooks and works of an encyclopedic nature, and he was rewarded for this work.[1]

The late nineteenth-century German universities looked drastically different. They were state institutions, marked by the presence of seminars, large teaching and research institutes, and modern teaching hospitals, and identified by their emphasis on original research and scholarship. Their pronounced goal was the pursuit of *Wissenschaft,* a difficult term to define not least because its meaning underwent several changes throughout the years.[2] Once identified closely with another nebulous term, *Bildung*, *Wissenschaft* originally signified the search for a holistic understanding of all knowledge aimed at cultivating the individual's personality by developing one's moral and intellectual sensitivities. In this earlier formulation, *Wissenschaft* had an inward focus, but as the century progressed, the focus turned outward and *Wissenschaft* came to refer to the production of new knowledge through in-depth scholarly work in a specialized area of research. Accompanying this transition was an increased appreciation of the importance of acquiring practical experience; by the late nineteenth century, at least in the sciences and medicine, the revered *Wissenschaftler* was one who could manipulate sophisticated instrumental apparatus and gain in this way control over laboratory conditions and, presumably, over nature.

The reforms responsible for this transition date from the early nineteenth century. Although universities throughout Germany had had their critics in the eighteenth century, and several of the changes historians associate with the nineteenth century actually began at this time, not until the Napoleonic Wars and the collapse of the Holy Roman Empire were these institutions significantly restructured and redefined.[3] The roughly thirty states that remained of the hundreds that had once belonged to the empire immediately began to reform the social and economic structure of their territories, and they included their universities (those that had them) in these reforms. Whether the goal was to emulate the French system of rule or develop a viable alternative, the various German governments sought, as part of these efforts, to gain control over university education and mold it to their new needs. Friedrich Wilhelm III's decision to create a new Prussian university in Berlin in 1810 in order to "replace intellectually what [the state] has lost physically"[4] is well known, but this was neither the first nor the only change in German higher education following the wars with France. Several other governments reformed their older universities; the goal was to end their corporate structure and convert them into state-financed institutions. One of the earliest examples occurred in 1803 at the University of Heidelberg in the southern German state of Baden.

Converting the University of Heidelberg into a State Institution

Baden had been one of a handful of German states to benefit from the wars with France and the subsequent restructuring of central Europe. Napoleon's intent had been to create several mid-sized states to act as a counterbalance to Prussia and Austria, and Baden had been among them. Between 1803 and 1805, largely as a result of the negotiating skills of Sigismund von Reitzenstein, Baden almost tripled in size from 3,900 to 14,000 square kilometers, and more than quintupled its population from 165,000 to 900,000 inhabitants.[5] One of its acquisitions was the east

Rhineland Pfalz, home of the University of Heidelberg. Since the university's founding in 1386 it had been a private institution, financing its needs partly through tithes, public taxes, and interest on loaned capital, but drawing its main income from the sale of natural products grown on privately owned property. This source of income had never been steady, and in the eighteenth century a series of crop failures brought the university into serious financial difficulties. The situation was further aggravated in 1792 when France occupied and eventually sequestered the university's most fertile farmland on the left bank of the Rhine. When the university was acquired by Baden in 1803, it was on the point of bankruptcy.[6]

Under these circumstances the government decided to transform the university into a state institution. Stabilizing the financial situation had been the primary concern, but the government also intended to redefine the goal of university education. To accomplish this, it totally restructured university governance, wresting control of educational affairs from the faculty senate, which previously had been the primary decision-making body.[7] In several statutes set down in 1803 and modified slightly during subsequent decades, the government placed the rectorship of the university in the hands of the Grand Duke of Baden, and assigned the actual control of university affairs to the ministry of interior. No decision could be made without the approval of the Grand Duke and the ministry, but the person who ran the daily affairs of the university, ensured that all rules and regulations were obeyed, and presided over all faculty meetings was the prorector, a member of the faculty elected by the *Ordinarien* (full professors). Although this suggests that the faculty had not been deprived of all its power, not until 1862 did a simple majority vote determine who would next assume office. Until then, the Grand Duke made the final decision, choosing the prorector from the three individuals who received the most votes. The government further circumscribed the power of the *Ordinarien,* who together formed the larger senate (*Grösserer Senat*), by placing above them a group, the smaller senate (*Engerer Senat*), which consisted of six individuals: the prorector, the ex-prorector, and the deans of the four faculties. The ministry of interior usually conferred with this group when making decisions, but it never relaxed its ultimate control. Moreover, not only were two members of the smaller senate (the prorector and ex-prorector) personally selected by the Grand Duke, but officially this group could do no more than debate and advise.

Having reduced the faculty's influence over university affairs, the government now had the power necessary to mold the university to fit its needs. Most government officials agreed that Baden's greatest challenge was to unify the recently acquired territories under one central government and establish the state on a firm financial basis. But agreement ended there. In Baden (as elsewhere) groups sympathetic to different educational philosophies fought during the first decades of the century over how best to meet the needs of the newly expanded state.[8] The issues they raised were reminiscent of similar debates fought during the previous century. One faction in the government, sympathetic to Enlightenment ideals, believed the universities could best help unify and strengthen the state by serving utilitarian ends, providing the younger generation with the specific knowledge and skills they would need as "future servants of the state and useful citizens (*Staatsdiener und nützliche Bürger*)."⁹ These individuals were critical of the university's traditional emphasis on the study, recitation, and memorization of classical texts. They fought instead for a curriculum that included modern history, geography, modern languages, mathematics, and the natural sciences. In their opinion, these subjects would help train qualified government officials, civil servants, lawyers, doctors, teachers, and clergymen—in short, the future leaders of civic life.

Opposing this group were individuals inspired by the neohumanist movement that had sprung up in several northern universities in the last decades of the eighteenth century. Göttingen had become the center of this movement, which retained the traditional emphasis on the classical works while seeking to infuse their study with a new spirit of philosophical inquiry based on a critical reading of the texts. Professors were to substitute the seminar for the lecture room, and attempt to cultivate in their students an aesthetic and moral appreciation of the classical works rather than encourage rote memorization. This focus on the student's inner development shifted attention away from the acquisition of useful knowledge and skills, creating a cleft between the *wissenschaftlichen* or more theoretical goals of the university and the practical aims of other educational institutes, such as the medical academies designed specifically to train physicians for the military. As Thomas Hoyt Broman has recently argued, university professors—particularly those ascribing to nature philosophy—emphasized this distinction between *Wissenschaft* and practice in response to Enlightenment critics who advocated either the abolition of the universities or their conversion into professional training schools.¹⁰ The nature philosophers hoped to justify the continued existence of their institutions by focusing on the differences between the utilitarian goals of vocational training, and the moral, spiritual, and intellectual enlightenment provided by a university education. The consequence, at least in medicine, was the gradual separation of the *wissenschaftlichen* interests of the university scholar from the practical interests of the physician.

The main advocate of neohumanism among Baden government officials was Reitzenstein—the "founder of the Baden state," according to Franz Schnabel, because of the territorial acquisitions he negotiated for Baden.¹¹ Although a member of the diplomatic service, Reitzenstein became involved in domestic affairs as well, entering the central government for a brief period later in his career. In all that he did, whether carrying out diplomatic, administrative, or educational reforms, Reitzenstein showed a proclivity for replacing old structures with new ones, convinced this was the best strategy for breaking traditional loyalties and generating allegiances to the new central government. In educational reforms, he drew his inspiration from Göttingen, where he had himself studied and cultivated a love for antiquity and the classics that persisted throughout his lifetime. In his early forties he even fulfilled a long-held wish and spent two years studying Greek, apparently achieving enough proficiency to engage in critical readings of the classics. Fearing that the Enlightenment reformers' emphasis on utilitarianism would "kill the free, living spirit"[12] in the university, Reitzenstein fought repeatedly to transform Heidelberg into the Göttingen of the south. He believed Baden's power among the German states, recently increased through its territorial acquisitions, would be enhanced further by its possession of a scholarly institution. Indeed, Reitzenstein had seriously contemplated the founding of a scientific academy, but decided instead to focus on turning the University of Heidelberg into a national center of education and scholarship, leaving Baden's other university in Freiburg to serve the local needs of the state.

But turning Heidelberg into a symbol of national pride was not all that Reitzenstein intended. For him, as for other early nineteenth-century reformers, such as Maximilian von Montgelas in Bavaria and Wilhelm von Humboldt in Prussia, the emphasis on *Bildung* and *Wissenschaft*—on the moral, aesthetic, and intellectual development of the individual's personality—was meant as well to awaken a new spirit in the nation.[13] The final collapse of the Holy Roman Empire demonstrated to these reform-minded individuals the dire need to change not only the economic and social structure of the state, but the mentality of its citizens as well. In their eyes, the embarrassing defeat of the German states at the hands of the French had resulted largely from the indifference felt by most Germans toward the absolutist regimes of the eighteenth century. Moreover, they witnessed how government officials and civil servants, trained to follow rules and regulations, had proven unable to respond creatively and successfully to situations for which they had not been prepared. All this suggested the need to invigorate the learning process by replacing the emphasis on rote memorization with an educational philosophy geared toward active participation of both professors and students in the pursuit of knowledge. *Wissenschaft* promised to do just that.

Throughout the first decade of the century Reitzenstein attempted to mold the university along neohumanist lines, but with little success. As a member of the diplomatic service, he traveled frequently, making it difficult for him to carry out his plans and influence faculty appointments. But the situation changed in the 1820s when he entered the central government and assumed control of university affairs. His first order of business was a series of appointments that substantially changed the makeup of the university staff. In the medical faculty alone this entailed five new appointments, all of them young and all of them actively engaged in scientific research.

Reforming the Medical Faculty

The structure of Heidelberg's medical faculty was typical of that of other German universities. It consisted of several *Ordinarien,* who loosely divided their teaching responsibilities into internal medicine and therapeutics; obstetrics and gynecology; anatomy, physiology, and surgery; and botany, pharmacology, and materia medica. However, the boundaries were extremely fluid. For example, Franz Karl Zuccarini, professor of botany at the time of Baden's acquisition of the university, also lectured occasionally on anatomy, surgery, and pathology; Franz Anton Mai, professor of obstetrics and gynecology, gave classes in pharmacology; and Jakob Fidelis Ackermann, professor of anatomy, physiology, and surgery, offered clinical instruction in the university's out-patient clinic.[14] In addition, most of these professors also had medical practices; indeed, a distinction between medical practitioners and professors of medicine hardly existed. On the contrary, professors trained in the eighteenth century typically began their careers as practitioners and retained their medical practices even after joining a university faculty.[15]

The men Reitzenstein hired in the second decade of the nineteenth century differed from their predecessors in two fundamental ways: except for the professors of clinical medicine, they no longer engaged in private practice, and they drew much sharper territorial boundaries between their respective subject areas. Both of these changes marked their participation in and commitment to the pursuit of *Wissenschaft*. As mentioned above, university professors had begun, already in the previous century, to distinguish their scholarly contributions to medicine from those of the practicing physician. Their goal, as they perceived it, was to study the phenomena of life in order better to understand, and ideally to uncover, the laws governing health and disease. Initially this scholarly work had been closely tied to a search for a unified conception of all knowledge, but as the decades wore on the goal of scientific activity gradually shifted to new discoveries and the production of new knowledge. As a result, scholars concentrated on increasingly more circumscribed areas of research, setting in motion a process of specialization that has persisted until today.

When Reitzenstein began searching for new faculty members in the 1810s, he sought professors who symbolized these recent changes. One of these appointments concerned a replacement for Ackermann, who, as mentioned above, had taught anatomy, physiology, and surgery, as well as providing clinical instruction. Neither Reitzenstein nor the ministry of interior showed any interest in the clinical abilities of Ackermann's successor. On the contrary, at the top of their list were Germany's most prestigious anatomists—Georg Friedrich Hildebrandt, Johann Friedrich Meckel, and Karl Rudolphi. However, as would so often happen during the university's history, Heidelberg had to modify its wishes because of inadequate funds. It turned, thus, to a pool of younger candidates, among whom two stood out: Johann Bernhard Wilbrand, a professor in Giessen, and Friedrich Tiedemann, who was teaching in Landshut. The ministry praised the former for his knowledge of anatomy, physiology, botany, natural history, and comparative anatomy, but it decided to offer Tiedemann the position. A number of considerations contributed to this selection, but most attention was paid to the people with whom he had studied and his scholarly achievements. Tiedemann had worked with Samuel Thomas Sömmering, "the greatest anatomist of our times," and with the famous French comparative anatomist Georges Cuvier; he had already demonstrated "extraordinary scholarly activity" through his research in anatomy, comparative anatomy, and zoology; and he had even won a prize for this work from the prestigious French *Académie des Sciences,* to which he also belonged.[16] These qualifications suggested that he embodied the spirit of *Wissenschaft,* and would, consequently, contribute to the prestige of the university, and thus to the state, and it was on these grounds that he was selected. Nowhere was there any mention of his abilities as a teacher of future medical practitioners. Tiedemann, who would eventually acquire a reputation as one of Europe's finest scientists, never taught microscopical or vivisectional techniques to his students, nor was he expected to do so. In the early nineteenth century, permission to engage in scientific studies was still considered the privilege of the chosen few.

Friedrich Tiedemann—An Early Proponent of "Wissenschaft"

Tiedemann's own education had prepared him superbly for a scholarly career. From an early age he studied both the classics and the natural sciences to an extent rarely seen in later generations.[17] Educated at home until the age of twelve, Tiedemann continued to receive private lessons even after enrolling in the local *Gymnasium* from both his father, a scholar of philosophy, Greek, and the classics, and from a family friend and professor of botany and chemistry. In 1798, at the age of eighteen, Tiedemann completed his *Gymnasium* studies and decided to study medicine and zoology at the University of Marburg. Nevertheless, as we will see, this did not mean a neglect of his classical training.

Throughout the nineteenth century it was typical for German medical students to attend several universities during the course of their studies. Tiedemann was no exception. In addition to studying at Marburg, he went to Bamberg and Würzburg to study clinical medicine before returning to Marburg to complete the M.D. with a dissertation on the polyps of the heart (*De cordis polyp*).[18] Tiedemann, more interested in medical theory and research than in practice, soon returned to Würzburg to attend Schelling's lectures on natural philosophy. The young doctor seems to have turned to the latter for an orientation in his own work, and it may be from Schelling that he first learned the virtues of a life devoted to *Wissenschaft,* but he soon grew disillusioned with the philosopher's speculative flights. Still searching for a mentor, Tiedemann moved on to Paris to study the relatively new science of comparative anatomy with Cuvier, making the acquaintance as well of Sömmering. This meeting resulted in mutual admiration and led the well-known anatomist to recommend Tiedemann for the position of professor of human anatomy, comparative anatomy, and zoology at the university in Landshut a few months later.

By the time Tiedemann arrived in Landshut in 1805 he had acquired a significant amount of knowledge in both clinical and theoretical medicine. More important, he had joined forces with a number of individuals intent on furthering the distinction between theoretical and practical medicine by redefining the science of anatomy so as to raise it to the level of a *Wissenschaft*. For most of its history anatomy had been little more than an information source for the advancement of surgical and obstetrical knowledge, but in the late eighteenth century the work of such people as Albrecht von Haller, Felix Vicq d'Azyr, John Hunter, Georges Cuvier, and Johann Christian Blumenbach had begun to change this.[19] What excited Tiedemann was the way these individuals went beyond the mere description of structure to the investigation of function as well, thus beginning to divorce anatomy from surgery and to provide it with its own set of questions.

Tiedemann was most directly influenced by Cuvier and Blumenbach, whose work provided a methodological framework for tackling the problems of organic form.[20] As Timothy Lenoir has argued, the central concerns of these functional anatomists was to demonstrate that despite life's unique qualities, the study of organic processes could be treated like other sciences. To accomplish this they incorporated both teleological and mechanical principles into their study of function. Drawing on the work of Immanuel Kant they argued that knowledge of the nature of life (specifically, whether it was material or immaterial) could never be acquired; rather, the study of life had to be restricted to an analysis of the phenomena. Vital phenomena obeyed the laws of chemistry and physics, and could thus be studied mechanically, but they could never be understood without recourse to an organizing principle (what they frequently referred to as the *Lebenskraft* or *Bildungskraft*). This was necessarily so, because the parts of organic bodies, unlike those of inorganic objects, could not be studied without considering the role they played in maintaining the organism as a whole, nor could the integrated organism be understood without reference to its parts. For these early "teleomechanists"—as Lenoir has labeled them—the study of life became the investigation of life's expression through the material changes of the organism.

The focus on material changes allowed Tiedemann and other teleomechanists to treat the study of life like other sciences, thus creating a framework for the emergence of an anatomical *Wissenschaft*. Within this framework, however, the specific techniques employed by anatomists and physiologists changed through time. Tiedemann, for example, began by using natural history and functional anatomy to organize mammals and birds into natural groups,[21] but he soon abandoned these approaches in favor of embryological studies. Not only did he and other German physiologists come to view developmental history as an ideal tool for studying life's expression, they also considered mastery of this technique a sure way to distinguish further the boundaries between anatomy and surgery, rescuing the former from its handmaiden status and rendering it a *Wissen-*

schaft comparable to other sciences. As Tiedemann explained, the more sophisticated anatomy's methodology, and the more functional its orientation, the more it could distance itself from its previous status as a merely descriptive science. He spelled this out most clearly in the preface to his work on the fetal brain:

> Certainly every intelligent anatomist, who does not consider the highest of all things to be mere anatomical descriptions, knowledge of organic structure, or the practical consequences or applications [of this knowledge] to medicine and surgery, will share the conviction that anatomy will only be able to lay claim to being a mature science when the developmental histories of organic forms and the laws governing their development are recognized.[22]

Anatomy would not acquire the status of a science until it became dynamic, shifting its focus from describing static structures to uncovering the laws governing developmental processes. Thus, in contrast to later battles fought to create clear disciplinary boundaries between anatomy and physiology, Tiedemann struggled to define anatomy as an independent science by adopting a physiological approach to the study of structure. The partial success that this strategy had attained by 1815 can be seen in Heidelberg's willingness to replace Ackermann, a man who had retained the unification of anatomy, surgery, and the clinic, and, consequently, of scientific research and medical practice, with Tiedemann—someone who had helped divorce these subjects by raising anatomy from the status of a "helping science" (*Hilfswissenschaft*) to that of a mature *Wissenschaft* in its own right.

Tiedemann's Years at Heidelberg

Reitzenstein had seen in Tiedemann a young talented scholar who embodied the new spirit of *Wissenschaft* and would help raise Heidelberg's status to that of an institute of scientific repute. The young professor did not disappoint him. In addition to teaching anatomy, physiology, comparative anatomy, pathological anatomy, and zoology, he dedicated a good deal of time to improving the facilities at the university.[23] By 1815 an important indication of a good medical department was the size and scope of its anatomical collection, and one of the first tasks Tiedemann set himself upon arrival was the improvement of the collection at Heidelberg.

In May 1816 Tiedemann submitted a lengthy report to the faculty senate praising the physical setup of the anatomy collection, but criticizing sharply the poor quality of its specimens and instruments. His statement that "the rooms of the institute are excellent and could be placed alongside any—even the most excellent—anatomical institute of any university" suggests how low standards were in 1816: the institute at that time consisted of the ground floor of an old Dominican cloister that housed not only anatomy, botany, and a small chemical laboratory, but the medical and obstetrical clinics as well. (To top it off, a surgical clinic was added in

1817.)[24] He was not, however, as satisfied with the equipment available, commenting that "the collection of anatomical specimens and the necessary instruments and utensils for work are unfortunately in miserable condition."[25] Tiedemann elaborated on the tools he needed: scalpels, pincers, instruments for injections, storage bins, and a microscope—in short, the needs of a functional anatomist. His requests, amounting to a total of 450 gulden, were filled within the month, along with the allocation of a yearly budget of 700 gulden.[26]

By 1818 Tiedemann had not only helped improve the university's reputation, he had also acquired enough of a scholarly reputation that Prussia showed interest in luring him to the medical faculty at the newly founded university in Bonn. Baden responded immediately and offered to meet Tiedemann's conditions for staying: a salary increase from 1800 to 2800 gulden. It feared losing the person who had raised the anatomical institute to one of the finest in Germany, and whose scholarly activities in comparative anatomy and zoology had placed him among the most talented men in Europe. This positive reinforcement from Baden's side, added to the poor state of the anatomical and zoological collections at Bonn, as well as the absence of an anatomical institute there, convinced Tiedemann to remain in Heidelberg.[27]

In the following years, Tiedemann's national and international reputation as a scientific scholar continued to increase, especially following his investigations of the process of material exchange during digestion. He pursued this research together with the young and talented chemist Leopold Gmelin, professor at the university and one of the five men hired as part of Rietzenstein's attempt to reform Heidelberg.[28] As early as 1820 they published a monograph on digestion; in 1823 they competed for an award question put forth by the Paris *Académie des Sciences,* in which the process of digestion was to be examined through a series of chemical and physiological experiments; and in 1826 they presented their completed research in a book entitled *Die Verdauung nach Versuchen.*[29] In all this work, Tiedemann and Gmelin demonstrated their skills in employing chemical, microscopical, and vivisectional techniques for examining the role played by saliva, bile, and the gastric, pancreatic, and intestinal juices in the breakdown of foodstuffs. In their experiments they extracted and then analyzed the digestive juices chemically, did some simulation of the digestion of foodstuffs in vitro, and examined the chemical composition of chyle in the digestive organs. Their procedures involved feeding the animals, killing them, and then analyzing the chyle, but vivisection was by no means absent. Drawing on clinical skills he had acquired during wartime,[30] Tiedemann created fistulas in the stomach and intestines for the extraction of digestive juices, blocked the bile duct to ascertain the importance of bile for digestion, and cut the pneumogastric nerves to determine their influence on the digestive activity of the stomach.[31]

As a result of this research Tiedemann acquired a reputation as one of the best experimenters in Germany. Students from abroad came to

Heidelberg to study with him, and in 1832 Prussia tried once again to lure him away from Baden by offering him the chair for anatomy and physiology in Berlin. As that university's philosophy faculty wrote:

> In anatomy and physiology a path to a higher goal has recently been prepared. Earlier, one had been satisfied with observing the phenomena. Now one attempts to create new phenomena through experiment. The men who are responsible for this new direction have earned a reputation in Europe. We already have an excellent observer. We would secure an experimenter in either Tiedemann or Müller.[32]

The interest that both Berlin and Heidelberg showed in Tiedemann's experimental skills focused on his talents in research. New discoveries, publications, membership in scientific societies, and European reputation were the criteria by which they defined excellence. The teaching of these skills to any but a small group of talented students was neither expected nor did it occur. Tiedemann did not offer courses in vivisectional or experimental techniques to his students. Although occasional demonstrations did accompany his lectures, the latter were often described as dogmatic, recitative, and stamped by exacting detail. The physician Adolf Kussmaul, a student in Heidelberg in 1840, described how Tiedemann would read his lectures

> page after page . . . clearly and deliberately in his somewhat nasal, ringing voice. Conscientiously, each muscle, even the smallest, was put to rights on the vertebral column, accurately described according to position and structure, attachment and apparent determination, not allowing the loss of even the most minute grain of this dry fodder. It was often boring to death.[33]

The fact that Tiedemann did not have elaborate laboratory space cannot provide an adequate explanation for the absence of experimental exercises among his courses, because he never petitioned the university to have an institute built. Nor can one argue that he believed experiments to be unimportant for medicine. In his physiological lectures, published in 1830, he listed the benefits, albeit scanty, already gained from physiological experimentation. These included "the doctrine of the healing of wounds, the closing of arteries upon ligature and the resultant expansion of nearby vessels, as well as the doctrine of the effect of poison and the means by which to remove these effects."[34] In addition, he attributed almost everything known about various functions, such as respiration, circulation, digestion, absorption, and muscle and nerve irritability, to experiments on living animals. There are two ways, he explained, of acquiring information about the properties of living organisms and the relations of these properties to one another and to nature. The one, observation, provides us with information about the phenomena immediately available to our senses. Through experiment, on the other hand, we can experience the behavior of the phenomena under artificially created circumstances. "In the former," he added we are eavesdropping on nature, in the latter we are asking for advice. More-over, experiments supply us with the most important facts in the explanation of phenomena, because we are penetrating all the more deeply into the nature of an object the more we demand multifarious and comprehensive know-ledge of its behavior in different states of nature.[35]

Tiedemann even held the aversion toward experimentation to be responsi-ble for the retrograde state of physiology in comparison to other physical sciences, and went so far as to favor animal experiments over observation of sick individuals as the basis for constructing a rational medicine. "Physiol-ogy," he wrote, "is not to be seen as a part or branch of medicine, as had earlier been believed. Rather, medicine consists much more in an applica-tion of physiology. . . . Medicine must, therefore, take its axioms from physiology if it wants to make claims to being a science."[36]

Thus Tiedemann's apparent indifference toward teaching experimen-tal techniques to students cannot be explained either by his failure to appreciate the importance of experimentation or his inability to master such techniques. Instead, we must accept a discrepancy between his re-search and teaching styles—one, moreover, that was by no means peculiar to him.[37] In the physiological sciences alone, Johannes Müller, Jan Evan-gelista Purkyne, and Johannes Schulze, to mention only the better known, were also using vivisectional, microscopical, and chemical techniques as early as the 1820s, and they were acquiring international fame because of it. Müller, for example, in one of his earliest studies, made use of vivisec-tional experiments to test whether the fetus breathes in the womb. He performed fifty experiments on rabbits, cats, and sheep, and was awarded a prize in 1821 for demonstrating the change in color of arterial and venous blood in the embryo.[38] Yet, like Tiedemann, Müller did not offer courses in these techniques; indeed, such courses did not become a standard part of the university curriculum until the late 1830s.[39] Since an explanation for this delay cannot be sought in the sad state of the scientific and medical disciplines themselves, the discrepancy that is all too obvious between the way these individuals did physiology and they way they taught it must have had its rationale in the assessment of the value of laboratory exercises in the education of physicians.

Scientific Training in the Early Nineteenth-Century German Universities

The near absence of any instruction in experimental procedures during the first decades of the nineteenth century does not mean that students were never introduced to microscopical, chemical, and vivisectional techniques. On the contrary, as early as the 1820s, professors began to embellish their lectures with experimental demonstrations, no longer spending the entire class period reciting from a text. Schulze, for example, began including demonstrations in his physiology course at the University of Freiburg in

1821; Purkyne did the same in Breslau in 1824; and Tiedemann followed suit one year later.[40] Indeed, most professors of the so-called basic sciences (botany, chemistry, physics, physiology) began, during this decade, to demonstrate the process of discovery to students. Most students did not, however, participate actively in this process, but were, rather, mere observers. Only a few talented and motivated students received an invitation to join their professors in cramped research quarters in order to learn investigative methods. But even here, the focus was never on acquiring proficiency in scientific techniques. True, the skilled experimentalist could force nature to reveal more secrets, but the avowed goal was a holistic understanding of nature's ways, not mastery of sophisticated instrumental techniques, which was more the sign of a technical than a university education.

This ambivalence toward "hands-on" training was equally evident in the university's attitude toward clinical exercises. Once again opportunities existed for the motivated student, but participation in such clinical courses was totally optional. For example, around the turn of the century almost all German universities founded either "polyclinics" or small stationary clinics.[41] The former functioned as dispensaries, providing out-patient medical services for the poor either at the clinic or in their homes, while the stationary clinics, usually with no more than twelve to sixteen beds, provided in-house care. More important, they functioned as educational institutions as well, providing advanced students the opportunity to examine and diagnose the sick, propose and discuss the proper therapeutic procedures, and prescribe medication. In addition, in the case of the polyclinic, the professor usually assigned the sick individual to one of the students, who thereafter had the responsibility of attending the person regularly in his or her home.[42]

When, for example, Jacob Henle attended the University of Heidelberg in 1830, he was impressed with the opportunities at hand for gaining practical experience at the bedside. Nevertheless, he explained clearly in letters to his parents that these opportunities did not exist during the semester, when the great number of students rendered clinical exercises useless.[43] The year Henle spent in Heidelberg, the director of the medical clinic, Friedrich August Benjamin Puchelt, reported an enrollment of eighty students in his clinical course in the summer semester, and another eighty-seven in the winter.[44] Obviously most students did little more than observe the professor's examination of the patient, just as they observed experimental demonstrations in their basic science classes. To remedy the situation, Henle stayed in Heidelberg during vacation time, when the number of students thinned out and he was able to work in the clinic, and even to take on responsibility for a city sector, inhabited mostly by the poor. Descriptions of the dissections he performed "on the unfortunate" are not missing from his letters home.

Henle was one of a small number of students motivated enough to take advantage of the available clinical opportunities. That so few did can most likely be attributed to the absence of incentives. In Baden, for example, neither clinical training nor dissection exercises were required courses or examination subjects. In fact, the requirements for obtaining a license to practice were extremely vague. As late as the 1830s the only stipulation was that candidates demonstrate a satisfactory knowledge of the natural sciences and theoretical medicine. Only after 1841 were two years of practice required before one could become a state-employed physician, but this did not pertain to physicians in private practice nor did it imply that practical experience was to be obtained in the university clinics, but rather "on the job." Not until 1858 did clinical subjects and laboratory experience become part of the state medical examination.[45]

Licensing requirements in other German states were somewhat more stringent. Prussia, for example, passed legislation as early as 1791 requiring all medical students to complete a three-month course of clinical instruction at the city's Charité hospital. Moreover, both Bavaria and Prussia required that students demonstrate their skills at examining and treating patients in the clinic before being granted a license to practice.[46] Thus Baden had clear models to follow when it began revamping its own educational and licensing requirements. Yet the strictness of the measures in the two larger German states should not be overexaggerated. The clinical course at the Charité, for example, drew roughly one hundred students at a time, thus raising doubts about the thoroughness of the practical instruction students received.[47] And the licensing examinations, although they included a small practical component, still focused largely on the students' knowledge of medical theory.

This greater emphasis on theory was consistent with the image of the physician as a "cultured" individual, knowledgeable of Latin, Greek, and the medical classics. It also reflected the higher respect accorded to theoretical over technical work implicit in the early nineteenth-century notion of *Wissenschaft*. As important, for example, as Tiedemann may have held experimental techniques to be for furthering physiological research, he did not believe the science of physiology was exhausted by these techniques alone. On the contrary, experimentation—whether vivisection, chemical analysis, or microscopical investigation—was merely one part of a comprehensive program aimed at studying organic function. According to him, the task of physiology was to describe and investigate the expressions of activity "which we call life," to discern the laws by which these expressions occur, and to study their interaction with one another and with the environment. This must, he added, be carried out through a combination of two methods: the "empirical-historical" and the "theoretical, dogmatic, or philosophical."[48] In the former the physiologist is involved in collecting information, and to this end makes use of experience, observation, and experiment. But this method, Tiedemann emphasized,

> supplies only the material, the stuff of physiology. It does not give us science. Before the multitude of facts about life acquired through sense perceptions and observations can be considered to form the essence of a science

> . . . order must be given to them through the reflective activity of the intel-
> lect, and the causal connection [between these facts] must be recognized. The
> main goal of physiology rests with the formation and substantiation of theory,
> that is, with the subordination of the phenomena and facts of life to general
> concepts, the investigation of general laws governing [these facts], and the
> explanation of their causes.[49]

Facts provide the foundation for constructing a science, but the scientific
or *"wissenschaftliche"* activity rests in linking these facts together into a
"whole, so logically subdivided and ordered that unity and coherence are
brought to the mass."[50] This whole would be a system in its form, the
science of physiology in its content.

Tiedemann stated explicitly that the contemplative activity of science
was not one in which all could participate; rather it required a certain
"intellectual (*geistige*)" quality. It was the "philosophical genius" who was
able to concentrate on the particulars without losing sight of the whole.[51]
It is worth noting that true to the Humboldtian ideal, Tiedemann did not
place emphasis on social origin or economic class, but rather on demonstrated talent. His humanistic bent is seen further in his conviction that the
way to exercise one's "reflective capabilities" in preparation for scientific
activity was through philosophy and mathematics, for these subjects
taught one to "experience properly, visualize clearly, comprehend cor-
rectly, and conclude and judge consistently."[52] The goal, in short, was a
holistic appreciation of life, and the emphasis was on the proper training of
the intellect (*Geist*).

Tiedemann's style of teaching, common in the beginning of the century, kept the process of discovery in the hands of the professors and a
select group of talented students. Although early nineteenth-century reformers, including Reitzenstein, had envisioned a more dynamic intellectual exchange between professors and students, for the majority of medical
students, education continued to take place predominantly in the lecture
hall, not in the seminar, laboratory, or clinic. The professor, standing at the
podium, recited from a textbook, usually his own, presenting the information in an orderly, packaged system. And the students, anticipating the
state examinations for licensure, did their best to absorb and retain this
material. Active student participation in the process of learning, except for
the talented and motivated few, was minimal.

Reitzenstein and others sympathetic to neohumanism had thus both
succeeded and failed in their attempt to institutionalize an educational
philosophy based on *Wissenschaft* and *Bildung*. By the third decade of the
century, most faculty members and government administrators professed a
commitment to these concepts, yet the majority of students attending the
university were not introduced to the virtues of the scholarly life. Nor,
however, were they being prepared for the world of practice. This had
been cause for complaint in the past; now, during the 1830s, the battle
resumed with new force. Political changes resulted in the election of a large
number of representatives to the Baden parliament who were critical once

again of what they considered to be an overly theoretical emphasis in university education. These criticisms reflected a concern that the state universities were not teaching skills necessary for keeping pace with the economic and social changes beginning to restructure European society in the early years of industrialization. On one level, the arguments had not changed much since the early years of the century—the advantages and disadvantages of a theoretical versus a practical education continued to define the parameters of the debate. Yet a subtle shift was occurring in what people meant by the words "theory" and "practice." Practical exercises, previously associated with direct utilitarian goals, gradually became a method for teaching students how to solve intellectual problems. The result was a blurring of the distinction between theory and practice and an ideological shift in the evaluation of practical experience from which the notion of *Wissenschaft* would not remain immune.

Notes

1. R. Steven Turner, "University Reformers and Professorial Scholarship in Germany, 1760–1806," in Lawrence Stone, ed., *The University in Society,* 2 vols. (Princeton, 1974), vol. 2, pp. 495–531; Thomas Hoyt Broman, "University Reform in Medical Thought at the End of the Eighteenth Century," in *Osiris,* 2nd series, 5 (1989): 36–53; Charles E. McClelland, *State, Society and University in Germany, 1700–1914* (Cambridge, 1980).

2. The literature on the role of *Wissenschaft* in the nineteenth-century German university system is extensive. The standard work is Helmut Schelsky, *Einsamkeit und Freiheit: Idee und Gestalt der deutschen Universität und ihrer Reformen,* 2nd ed. (Düsseldorf, 1971). For several more critical studies, see R. Steven Turner, "The Growth of Professorial Research in Prussia, 1818–1848—Causes and Context," *Historical Studies in the Physical Sciences,* 3 (1971): 137–182; idem, "University Reformers and Professorial Scholarship in Germany, 1760–1806;" and Broman, "University Reform in Medical Thought."

3. McClelland, *State, Society and University in Germany,* esp. chap. 4.

4. Cited in Frederick Gregory, "Kant, Schelling, and the Administration of Science in the Romantic Era," in *Osiris,* 2nd series, 5 (1989): 17–35, here p. 26.

5. Lothar Gall, "Gründung und politische Entwicklung des Großherzogtums bis 1848," in *Badische Geschichte. Vom Großherzogtum bis zur Gegenwart,* ed. Landeszentrale für politische Bildung Baden-Württemberg (Stuttgart, 1979), pp. 11–36, here pp. 15–16. Baden acquired these new territories as a result of the *Reichsdeputationshauptschluß* in 1803 and the Treaty of Pressburg in 1805.

6. Franz Schneider, *Geschichte der Universität Heidelberg im ersten Jahrzehnt nach der Reorganisation durch Karl Friedrich (1803–1813)* (Heidelberg, 1913), esp. pp. 4–7, 32–33. See also Gerhard Merkel, *Wirtschaftsgeschichte der Universität Heidelberg im 18. Jahrhundert* (Stuttgart, 1973).

7. The following is drawn from Eike Wolgast, *Die Universität Heidelberg, 1386–1986* (Berlin, 1986); Hermann Weisert, "Die Verfassung der Universität Heidelberg, Überblick 1386–1852," *Abhandlungen der Heidelberger Akademie der Wissenschaften. Philosophisch-historische Klasse,* 1974: 1–168, esp. pp. 84–94. The

government branch in charge of university affairs changed occasionally during the first decades of the nineteenth century, but most of the time the ministry of interior had responsibility, and after 1823 no additional changes occurred.

8. See Schneider, *Gesschichte der Universität Heidelberg;* Richard August Keller, *Geschichte der Universität Heidelberg im ersten Jahrzehnt nach der Reorganisation durch Karl Friedrich (1803–1813)* (Heidelberg, 1913). The titles of Schneider's and Keller's books are identical because they were both responses to the same prize question. For similar debates in other states, particularly Prussia, see McClelland, *State, Society and University in Germany,* esp. chap. 4.

9. Quoted in Keller, *Geschichte der Universität Heidelberg,* p. 50.

10. Broman, "University Reform in Medical Thought" and *The Transformation of Academic Medicine in Germany, 1780–1820* (Ph.D. dissertation, Princeton University, 1987). See also R. Steven Turner, "The Prussian Universities and the Concept of Research," *Internationales Archiv für Sozialgeschichte der deutschen Literatur,* 5 (1980): 68–93, here p. 80.

11. On Reitzenstein and his various responsibilities in the Baden government, see Franz Schnabel, *Sigismund von Reitzenstein. Der Begründer des badischen Staates* (Karlsruhe, 1927); Loyd E. Lee, *The Politics of Harmony. Civil Service, Liberalism, and Social Reform in Baden, 1800–1850* (Newark, 1980), chap. 1; Gall, "Gründung und politische Entwicklung des Großherzogtums bis 1848;" Willy Andreas, "Sigismund von Reitzenstein und der Neuaufbau der Universität Heidelberg," *Ruperto-Carola,* 9/10 (1955): 29–32; and "Sigismund Karl Johann Freiherr von Reitzenstein," *BB,* vol. 2, pp. 179–181.

12. Quoted in Schneider, *Geschichte der Universität Heidelberg,* p. 59.

13. McClelland, *State, Society, and University in Germany,* pp. 101–149.

14. Eberhard Stübler, *Geschichte der medizinischen Fakultät der Universität Heidelberg, 1326–1925* (Heidelberg, 1926), pp. 182–196; Werner Goth, *Zur Geschichte der Klinik in Heidelberg im 19. Jahrhundert* (Diss. Heidelberg, 1982), p. 54.

15. Broman, "University Reform in Medical Thought." As Broman argues, this is, however, something against which the nature philosophers fought.

16. "Die Wiederbesetzung der Lehrstellen der Anatomie und Physiologie," 6 December 1815, BGLA 235/3133.

17. Biographical information is from Theodor Bischoff, *Gedächtnißrede auf Friedrich Tiedemann. Vorgetragen in der öffentlichen Sitzung der königlichen Akademie der Wissenschaften am 28. November 1861* (Munich, 1861); Vladislav Kruta, "Friedrich Tiedemann," *DSB,* 13 (1976): 402–404; "Friedrich Tiedemann," in *BL,* 5 (1962): 586–587, and in *Allgemeine deutsche Biographie,* 56 vols. (Leipzig, 1875–1912), 38 (1895): 277–278.

18. I wish to point out that Tiedemann's educational experience challenges the traditional picture of early nineteenth-century German medical education as speculative and anti-practical. Tiedemann studied practical medicine with Adalbert Marcus in Bamberg, and with Kaspar von Siebold at the Julius hospital in Würzburg. Thus, although university lectures did emphasize theory, opportunities existed for gaining practical knowledge in some local hospitals and, more often, through the university polyclinics. Bamberg and Würzburg were, moreover, not the only universities to provide such opportunities. Johann Christian Reil in Halle, and Christian Hufeland, first in Jena and then in Berlin, offered similar clinics in which students were permitted to examine patients and even to visit them in their homes. See Wolfram Kaiser, Reinhard Mocek, *Johann Christian Reil* (Biographien hervorragender Naturwissenschaftler, Techniker und Mediziner, Band 41)

(Leipzig, 1979), chap. 2; C. W. Hufeland, "Nachrichten von der Medizinisch-Chirurgischen Krankenanstalt zu Jena, nebst einer Vergleichung der klinischen und Hospitalanstalten überhaupt," *Journal der practischen Arzneykunde und Wund-arzneykunst,* 3,1 (1797): 528–566.

19. Hans-Heinz Eulner, *Die Entwicklung der medizinischen Spezialfächer an den Universitäten des deutschen Sprachgebiets* (Stuttgart, 1970), p. 35. William Coleman, *Georges Cuvier, Zoologist. A Study in the History of Evolutionary Thought* (Cambridge, 1964), chap. 3. Timothy Lenoir, *The Strategy of Life. Teleology and Mechanics in Nineteenth-Century German Biology* (Studies in the History of Modern Science, 13) (Dordrecht, 1982), chap. 1.

20. Lenoir, *The Strategy of Life,* chap. 1. The following paragraphs are all drawn from this chapter.

21. Friedrich Tiedemann, *Zoologie* (Landshut, 1808, 1810, 1814).

22. Friedrich Tiedemann, *Anatomie und Bildungs-Geschichte des Gehirns im Foetus des Menschen, nebst einer vergleichenden Darstellung des Hirnbaues in den Thieren* (Nuremberg, 1816), p. v. See also the opening speech held by Tiedemann at the meeting of the Gesellschaft Deutscher Naturforscher und Ärzte in 1829 in the *Amtlicher Bericht über die Versammlung der Deutschen Naturforscher und Ärzte in Heidelberg,* September 1829, p. 23.

23. Tiedemann's courses are listed in *Anzeige,* 1822–1849. Unfortunately, printed accounts of courses being offered did not begin until 1822.

24. Goth, *Zur Geschichte der Klinik,* p. 77.

25. Report from Tiedemann to the faculty senate, 1 May 1816, BGLA 235/559.

A general description of the anatomical facilities at Heidelberg can be found in Stübler, *Geschichte der medizinischen Fakultät,* pp. 196–215. To my knowledge a more detailed description is not available. In general, not much is known about the exact layout of scientific institutes in the early part of the nineteenth century. A few scattered reports suggest, however, that other universities may have had better facilities than Heidelberg. See, for example, the description of the Breslau anatomical institute in A. W. Otto, *Einige geschichtliche Erinnerungen an das frühere Studium der Anatomie in Schlesien, nebst einer Beschreibung und Abbildung des jetzigen königlichen Anatomie-Instituts* (Breslau, 1823), and of the anatomy institute in Königsberg, in Timothy Lenoir, "Morphotypes and the historical-genetic method in Romantic biology," in Andrew Cunningham and Nicholas Jardine, eds., *Romanticism and the Sciences* (Cambridge, 1990), pp. 119–129.

26. Faculty senate to the ministry of interior, 30 May 1816, BGLA 235/559. Until 1858, one gulden equaled 0.67 taler or the equivalent of 2.01 marks. After 1858, one gulden equaled 0.56 taler or the equivalent of 1.68 marks. See Frank R. Pfetsch, *Zur Entwicklung der Wissenschaftspolitik in Deutschland, 1750–1914* (Berlin, 1974), p. 45.

The difficulty in finding information on institute budgets makes it hard to assess whether the money Tiedemann received from the Baden government was substantial. What seems to be significant is Baden's willingness to grant the money immediately.

27. Tiedemann to a "Freund und College in Bonn," 5 August 1818, Darmstaedter Collection, SPK 3K1830(2); Ministry of interior to the state ministry, 30 October 1818, BGLA 205/524.

28. For information on Gmelin, see Stübler, *Geschichte der medizinischen*

Fakultät, pp. 255–259, and Claude K. Deischer, "Leopold Gmelin," *DSB*, 5 (1972): 429–432.

29. Friedrich Tiedemann, Leopold Gmelin, *Versuch über die Wege, auf welchen Substanzen aus dem Magen und Darmkanal in's Blut gelangen, über die Verrichtung der Milz und die geheimen Harnwege* (Heidelberg, 1820); idem, *Die Verdauung nach Versuchen,* 2 vols. (Heidelberg, 1826).

30. In 1809, when the second Franco-Austrian war broke out, Tiedemann, then still at the university in Landshut, found himself in the middle of a battlefield. The Bavarian government immediately erected numerous hospitals, giving Tiedemann responsibility for several, including an obstetrical ward. There he had the opportunity to observe injuries, as well as to improve his surgical (or more likely dissectional) skills. See Bischoff, *Gedächtnißrede auf Friedrich Tiedemann,* pp. 8–10.

31. For an analysis of this work in the context of nineteenth-century studies of digestion, see Frederic L. Holmes, *Claude Bernard and Animal Chemistry* (Cambridge, 1974), pp. 149–159. See also Willi Mehlen, *Das Werk von Friedrich Tiedemann und Leopold Gmelin "Die Verdauung nach Versuchen"* (Diss. Bonn, 1976).

John Lesch, in his book *Science and Medicine in France. The Emergence of Experimental Physiology, 1790–1855* (Cambridge, 1984), has drawn attention to the importance of surgical training for the emergence of experimental physiology in the French medical schools. Instructed in dissectional and vivisectional techniques, the young French physiologists acquired skills that permitted them to intervene successfully in the life processes of the organism, performing controlled experiments whose results were easily reproducible. Lesch argues that this surgical training allowed an experimental tradition to develop in France in the early nineteenth century, whereas morphological/microscopical research dominated the German approach to the study of function. Tiedemann's experimental work may at first glance appear to contradict this argument, but he, as well as other Germans—Müller or Purkyne, for example—engaged in experimental research in the 1820s alone, soon abandoning such work and returning to morphological studies. This raises the interesting question whether the German's abandonment of physiological experimentation could be attributed to a lack of training in such techniques, rather than an ideological opposition to intervening in life's processes.

32. Prussia's interest in Tiedemann is discussed in Manfred Stürzbecher, "Zur Berufung Johannes Müllers an die Berliner Universität," *Jahrbuch für die Geschichte Mittel-und Ostdeutschlands,* 21 (1972): 184–226. The quotation is from p. 193.

33. Adolf Kussmaul, *Memoirs of an Old Physician,* transl. by the Journal Program for Scientific Translation (India, 1981), pp. 135–136. For a general discussion of teaching styles in nineteenth-century Germany, see Hans H. Simmer, "Principles and Problems of Medical Undergraduate Education in Germany during the Nineteenth and Early Twentieth Centuries," in *History of Medical Education,* ed. C. D. O'Mally (Berkeley, 1970), pp. 173–200, esp. p. 187. Also Theodor Billroth, *Ueber das Lehren und Lernen der medicinischen Wissenschaften an den Universitäten der Deutschen Nation* (Vienna, 1876).

34. Friedrich Tiedemann, *Physiologie,* 3 vols. (Darmstadt, 1830–1836), vol. 1 (1830), p. 13. Volume 2 was never published.

35. Ibid., p. 10.

36. Ibid., p. 44.

37. Paul Diepgen also points out the difference between research and teaching styles among early nineteenth-century German medical professors, but he does

not offer any explanation for the discrepancy. See Paul Diepgen, *Geschichte der Medizin,* 3 vols. in 2 (Berlin, 1951), vol. 2(1), p. 208.

38. See Gottfried Keller, *Das Leben des Biologen Johannes Müller, 1801–1858* (Grosse Naturforscher, Bd. 23) (Stuttgart, 1958), pp. 30–31. For Purkyne's experimental work, see Vladislav Kruta, "Jan Evangelista Purkyne," *DSB,* 11 (1975): 213–217; and William Coleman, "Prussian Pedagogy: Purkyne at Breslau, 1823–1839," in William Coleman and Frederic L. Holmes, ed., *The Investigative Enterprise. Experimental Physiology in Nineteenth-Century Medicine* (Berkeley, 1988), pp. 15–64.

39. On Müller's teaching style, see this book, Chapter 3. On the introduction of microscopical and clinical courses into the university curriculum, see Konrad Kläß, *Die Einführung besonderer Kurse für Mikroskopie und physikalische Diagnostik (Perkussion und Auskultation) in den medizinischen Unterricht an deutschen Universitäten im 19. Jahrhundert* (Diss. Göttingen, 1971).

40. On Schulze and Purkyne, see Coleman, "Prussian Pedagogy"; on Tiedemann, see *Anzeige,* 1825.

41. Theodor Puschmann, *A History of Medical Education* (facsimile of 1891 edition) (New York, 1966), p. 416.

42. See, for example, Hufeland, "Nachrichten von der Medizinisch-Chirurgischen Krankenanstalt zu Jena."

43. Hermann Hoepke, "Jakob Henles Briefe aus seiner Heidelberger Studentenzeit (26. April 1830–Januar 1831)," *Heidelberger Jahrbücher,* 11 (1967): 40–56, especially pp. 52–53.

44. Mentioned in Goth, *Zur Geschichte der Klinik,* pp. 87, 91.

45. *RB,* 5 August 1828 and 5 July 1841; *Mittheilungen,* 12 (1858): 17–20. The members of the medical faculty were not pleased with this laxity. As early as 1840 they requested that all students be required to spend an entire year in the clinics before being permitted to take the state medical examination. Nothing, however, came of this request. See the report written by the medical faculty to the ministry of interior, 18 April 1840, BGLA 236/4131.

46. Puschmann, *A History of Medical Education,* pp. 574–598.

47. Mentioned in a report from the Prussian minister Altenstein on 20 May 1828, in GStA, Merseburg, Ministerium der Geistlichen-, Unterrichts- und Medicinal Angelegenheiten, Rep. VIIIA, Nr.476.

48. Tiedemann, *Physiologie,* vol.1, pp. 6–9.

49. Ibid., pp. 18–19.

50. Ibid., pp. 27–28.

51. Ibid., pp. 19–21.

52. Ibid., pp. 31–32.

2

Political Changes and Educational Reforms in Baden, 1815–1848

In the 1830s the Baden parliament instituted reforms that increased government control over the educational system, thereby redefining the relationship between state, schools, and society. These measures were part of a larger attempt to alter the social and economic structure of the state. The elected representatives sitting in Baden's *Vormärz* parliament were only too well aware of the changes in manufacture, trade, and transportation that had been transforming European society since the turn of the century. Whether they turned their gaze to England, looked across their borders to Switzerland and the Alsace region, or focused on other more industrialized German regions, such as Saxony or the western parts of Prussia, they noticed the comparative backwardness of their own economy. All around them they saw signs of change: improvements in waterways and the canal system, the beginning of railroad construction, and the spread and modernization of the iron and spinning industries. Their dream was for Baden to be able to keep pace with these developments, and they believed that by following others in lifting restrictions on the economy they would best be able to achieve this goal.[1]

As a state lagging economically behind most of its neighbors, Baden had many models from which to choose—Switzerland and France (important because of their proximity), and above all Prussia. Thus Baden enacted measures to abolish the remaining restrictions on peasant freedom, end the tithes system, and weaken the stronghold guilds exerted over the manufacture and trade of goods.[2] Yet it did not adopt such measures uncritically. Indeed, knowledge, skills, and traditions are rarely transferred from one setting to another without undergoing changes as they are adapted to a new environment. Wolfram Fischer, for example, has demonstrated that although Baden modeled many of its economic and social reforms on Prussian measures, it also defined its own, less aggressive path toward a modern economy, marked most clearly by a reluctance to intervene directly in the process of industrialization. Thus where Prussia created state-owned factories as a way of actively fostering the mechanization of industry, Baden remained ambivalent toward rapid industrialization, showing greater concern for the plight of the small businessman, and preferring to influence economic growth through indirect measures.[3] Accordingly, the government favored educational reform as a way of bringing about change.

The goal of this chapter is not to argue that Baden placed greater importance on educational reforms than other German states, but to demonstrate that such reforms occurred within a context peculiar to Baden, and it was one defined not only by economic moderation, but by a strong tradition of political liberalism as well. The chapter begins with a discussion of this liberal tradition, focusing briefly on Grand Duke Karl's granting of a constitution in 1818 and subsequent developments in the political life of the state until 1830. The remainder of the chapter concentrates on the 1830s, when parliamentarians, working together with the Grand Duke and his ministers, enacted reforms that restructured the state's educational system. Their long-term goal was to provide the growing merchant and business class, and the displaced peasants and artisans, with skills that would permit them to partake in the modernization of the economy. However, the countless discussions over how best to accomplish this aim soon extended to debates over the reform of the classical *Gymnasia* and the universities in which a battle was fought once again between those with a more utilitarian bent and those who favored a humanist education. In the process, a major reorientation in the definition of *Wissenschaft* occurred.

The Creation of a Constitutional State

In 1818, Grand Duke Karl agreed to grant Baden a constitution as a strategy for integrating the heterogeneous territories his land had acquired when Napoleon restructured the German states. Earlier reform plans, written in the spirit of the Enlightenment and investing control almost exclusively in the Grand Duke and his ministers, had not proven successful in overcoming century-old loyalties to local administrations. Baden was, moreover, under constant pressure from Austria, Bavaria, and Württemberg—lands that maintained a persistant interest in regaining their lost territories—not to mention the threat from secessionist maneuvers within Baden itself. The Grand Duke and his advisors slowly came to the conclusion that popular support alone could guarantee the security of the state. On 22 August 1818, shortly before his death, Karl signed his name to one of the first constitutions in all of Germany. Clearly under the influence of

French constitutional liberalism, it gave Baden's citizens more influence in the political affairs of the state than any other German constitution.[4]

The author of the constitution, Karl Friedrich Nebenius (1784–1857), was the son of a Baden magistrate.[5] Broadly educated in Tübingen between 1802 and 1805, he majored in jurisprudence and economics, in addition to studying natural science and mathematics with Carl Friedrich Kielmeyer. After completing his degree in law, Nebenius entered the civil service and began advancing rapidly. By 1807 he was secretary of the ministry of finance, by 1811 a leading financial advisor. His talents soon became widely known in the government, and in 1818 Grand Duke Karl placed him in charge of a commission designated to draft the constitution for the state.

Nebenius's main goal was to limit the power of the nobility, which he accomplished in the following way. As part of the constitution a diet was called into being that consisted of two chambers: an upper house, occupied primarily by nobility, and a lower house, representing the towns and districts, composed of sixty-three elected members. In contrast to other German constitutions, which guaranteed the dominance of the upper over the lower house, Nebenius granted only the government and lower chamber the right to present financial bills, while forbidding the election of nobility to the lower chamber. The upper chamber could accept or reject these bills, but only in toto. In the event that a bill was rejected, the votes of both houses were combined, majority vote ruling. Given the greater number of elected representatives as compared to nobility, this measure succeeded in concentrating power in the lower house, thus making Baden the only German state whose constitution did not guarantee the domination of the aristocracy.[6]

The representatives sitting in the lower house, although elected, were, however, still a select group. Small property owners, less wealthy peasants, and farm laborers, for example, were kept from running for office by a stipulation that representatives receive an income or salary of at least 1,500 gulden (and pay some direct taxes) or pay taxes based on a taxable estate of 10,000 gulden per year. Moreover, only burghers and civil servants had the right to vote, thus excluding nobility, protected burghers, anyone who was not self-employed, mere residents, servants, and, of course, women. The result, not surprisingly, was a lower chamber composed largely of well-to-do burghers and civil servants.[7]

Ultimate power did not, however, rest with the diet, which had no legislative initiative or investigative powers, and could not meet on its own initiative. According to article 5 of the constitution the Grand Duke retained all rights of supreme power, although he agreed to "exercise them under the provisions established in . . . the constitution."[8] One can see how delicately the balance of power was poised between an enlightened monarchy and constitutional liberalism. While it may have been that taxes could not be levied without the diet's approval, only the Grand Duke could call the diet together or, as he saw fit, prorogue or dissolve it.

Thus, the political climate in Baden, although more dependent on the sentiment of parliamentary representatives than in any other German state, was still influenced greatly by the personality of the Grand Duke. This was immediately evident when less than four months after signing the constitution, Karl passed away and was succeeded by his nephew, Ludwig Wilhelm August. More conservative-minded than his uncle, Ludwig accepted the new constitution reluctantly, and in the twelve years of his rule (1818–1830) frequently took advantage of his power. In 1819, for example, he prorogued the diet, and in 1822 he dissolved it.[9] These acts were barely resisted. To understand this one must realize that the constitution had not come into being as a result of popular demand. Baden's constitution, like others in Germany, had been a gift from the government to the people, intended as a tool by which to inspire popular interest in the state. The awakening came, however, slowly, not least because older economic and social structures had remained essentially intact. The constitution, rather than replacing previous laws, existed alongside the older legal system, often standing in total contradiction to it.

In 1831, however, the tide began to change, and for several reasons. A young university-educated group schooled in liberal economics and constitutional thought began to dominate the state civil service. They had come to power in part because of the July Revolution's impact on elections. But of equal importance, Karl's son, Leopold, had become Grand Duke in 1830. Known as the *"Bürgerfreund,"* Leopold had attended the University of Heidelberg in 1806 where he had studied political science and political economy (*Staatswissenschaft* and *Staatswirthschaftslehre*). He thus shared a common education with many of his civil servants, a bond that helped them to work together in the 1830s to begin the slow process of reforming and modernizing the state.[10]

Leopold's interest in supporting the young civil servants led to a series of new appointments. With his ascendance to the throne, for example, he placed Ludwig Winter (1778–1839), a civil servant known for his liberal views, at the head of the ministry of interior.[11] This was the first time in Baden's history that someone from outside the nobility held such a high position in the government. The son of a poor Lutheran pastor, Winter was raised by a family friend, Emmanual Meier, after his father's untimely death. Meier was a civil servant and determined to prepare his young protégé for a government career. To this end Winter went to Göttingen (1797–1800) and studied jurisprudence, political science, and history, after which he entered the civil service, holding a number of different positions before joining the ministry of interior in 1815. When the first provincial diet (*Landtag*) met in 1819 Winter was present in a double capacity—as government commissioner and as elected representative of Durlach, a town just southeast of Karlsruhe. Yet despite his government connection he quickly became one of the leading figures fighting for reform, and remained so throughout his life. He also became a close friend of the Grand Duke, so that Leopold's decision to promote him to head of the

ministry of interior did not come as a surprise. Winter remained the leading government representative to the diet until his death in 1839.

The actual day-to-day work of the ministry rested, however, not with
the head but with the director, and in 1831 Winter appointed Nebenius to
this position. A good friend of Winter, Nebenius had already joined the
ministry of interior in 1823 at which time he had begun to fight for
improvements in technical education. Although he had had little contact
with the diet in the 1820s, his liberal views, as evidenced foremost by his
authorship of the constitution, were well known to the government. With
his promotion in 1831 Nebenius was also given responsibility for supervis-
ing the educational branch of the ministry of interior.[12]

These were the people who worked together with a diet dominated by
Heidelberg graduates to set in motion the reforms responsible for altering
the economic and social structure of the state. Between 1831 and 1839
liberal-minded representatives governed with minimal opposition and had
thus the opportunity to complete many of the reform measures begun in
the first few decades of the century. This is not to say they all shared
common interests and goals. As the parliamentary proceedings demonstrate, and as James Sheehan, Lothar Gall, and other historians of German
liberalism have argued, a unified liberal party program did not exist
anywhere in Germany in the *Vormärz* period.[13] On the contrary, self-
proclaimed liberals differed on a host of issues, including the balance of
power between government and parliament, the question of who should
be granted suffrage, and the extent to which economic restrictions should
be removed. Nevertheless, historians agree that despite these differences,
Vormärz liberals shared a commitment to replacing bureaucratic absolutism with a constitutional state that guaranteed fundamental rights to the
individual, such as freedom of expression and the press, trial by jury, and
political participation in all affairs of the state. Moreover, they shared a
conviction that the future and success of a constitutional state rested in the
creation of a strong middle class (*Mittelstand*), dedicated to the principles
of political liberalism, skilled in the modern means of production, and
capable of and committed to competing economically with the middle class
of other industrializing nations. Baden's parliamentary proceedings attest
to this general picture; they also demonstrate an acute awareness that
before substantial changes could be expected in the economic and social
structure of the state, people had to begin thinking differently, and this
meant changes in the kind of education being provided to the future
citizens of the state.[14]

Political Interests and Educational Reform in the 1830s

Between 1831 and 1837 the Baden government and diet worked together
to completely reorganize the state's educational system. The first move in
this direction came in 1834 in a government decree regulating the organi-

zation and curricula of the primary and Sunday schools. The fundamental concern was to guarantee that all children acquire basic knowledge of the 4 R's: reading, writing, arithmetic, and religion. A few months later the decision followed to found two new types of educational establishments. The first, trade schools, were intended for those in the artisan class who, for economic reasons, had to begin working at the age of fourteen and could not therefore attain an education beyond that provided by the primary schools. Baden made attendance in these schools compulsory, being one of the first German states to do so.[15] The children attended classes during the evenings and weekends for four hours per week, six months of the year, during which time they received instruction in arithmetic, German, natural science, mechanics, drawing, and agriculture. The second type of school that was established—non-classical secondary schools (*höhere Bürgerschulen*)—had a more sophisticated clientele in mind and offered an alternative to the *Gymnasia* for those who intended to be active in the private or commercial sphere of the economy. While not ignoring the importance of a classical education, these schools placed greater emphasis on such subjects as mathematics, natural science, history, and modern languages that were of immediate importance for a life in the world of commerce and trade.[16]

The last major educational reform came in 1837 and involved the reorganization of the classical secondary schools: the *Lyceen, Gymnasia,* and *Pädagogien.* The state placed all three under the supervision of a board of education (*Oberstudienrat*), established a fixed curriculum and examination procedures, and made the final school examination (the *Abitur*) a prerequisite for acceptance to the universities.[17]

In formalizing and enacting these educational reforms, Baden drew much inspiration from Prussia, where trade schools and non-classical secondary schools had been established a decade earlier. Peter Beuth, director of the Prussian department for trade and industry (*Abteilung für Handel und Gewerbe*), had ordered each administrative district to establish a trade school. This ordinance reflected his conviction that economic modernization depended on state support of vocational training. Although most of these schools remained small and poorly subsidized, the ones in the more industrialized Rhine provinces, and especially the trade institute (*Gewerbeinstitut*) founded in Berlin in 1824, became models for many other German states.[18]

Nebenius shared Beuth's conviction that economic modernization had to begin with educational reforms. Indeed, he viewed Prussian developments as proof that where governments fostered public education, material progress was bound to occur.[19] He and other liberal reformers believed this because they viewed the schools as vehicles for introducing young people not only to useful information, but to new ideas and techniques as well. One way in which the schools did this was by familiarizing the youth with machines, helping them to lose their fear of mechanization. As Franz

Schnabel has argued, it was a matter of "making a nation of peasants and artisans, within a short period of time, capable of adapting modern techniques and industry to the life of the nation."[20]

But Nebenius and other liberals sitting in parliament had more than skilled factory workers in mind as they reformed the school system. They also wished to encourage the growth of a powerful middle class who would help create a new social and economic order while becoming that order's most ardent defendant. This sentiment may have been particularly strong in Baden, where almost two-fifths of the parliamentary representatives in 1831 were engaged in some kind of economic activity.[21] For them, the granting of a constitution had been one powerful means of awakening a new spirit in the land, but as the parliamentarians never ceased to emphasize, it was one thing to bring new laws into existence and another to change the way people think. The latter could only be accomplished through education. Thus *Vormärz* liberals viewed educational reform not only as a way to expand the amount and kind of information at the disposal of the emerging working and commercial classes; its aim also had to be the creation of a new type of citizen. "Freedom and true constitutionalism," wrote Baden's finance committee in its report on the education budget in 1831, "can never exist where education and knowledge are the property of a single class."[22] Schools other than the classical *Gymnasia* had to exist for those individuals desiring higher education but intent on pursuing a livelihood in commerce and trade, rather than in one of the professions (*Berufe*). Only in this way, *Vormärz* liberals argued, could they hope to find a replacement for a degenerate guild system that they viewed as more of a hindrance than a help for production. Drawing on the writings of Adam Smith, they spoke critically of the use of prohibitive measures and high tariffs for the promotion of manufacture and trade. Although most *Vormärz* liberals stopped short of urging the abolishment of guilds, they did advocate weakening the guilds' stronghold and limiting state involvement in business enterprises. What they favored was a gradual transition to a free-market economy, in which improvements in the means of production would eventually be accomplished through the establishment of an open system based on the free flow of quality ideas. "Knowledge," argued Winter, "knows no guilds . . . only freedom."[23]

In the reports and discussions on educational reform in the parliamentary proceedings, the representatives defended a particular pedagogical method that, clearly in the tradition of such Enlightenment pedagogues as Johann Heinrich Pestalozzi, placed great emphasis on a combination of theory and practice.[24] Nebenius presented this method in exemplary form in an essay on the place of technical institutes in the educational system— an essay cited extensively in parliament. In this work Nebenius emphasized the importance of these schools in training the student to "see with his own eyes, examine, and contemplate." By offering the opportunity for thorough instruction, he added, the government finally places [the members of] this class [of producers] in the position to make their own proper observations at the workplace, reflect on what they have observed as well as on phenomena accidentally noticed, and perform well-directed experiments, discovering thereby new truths that can find immediate profitable application in the area of production.[25]

The belief that this kind of education would ultimately lead to the attainment of knowledge that could be used to stimulate and improve the means of production provided much of the inspiration for these reforms. But the method by which these ideas were to be acquired was anything but the simple transmission of technical information. These schools were instead meant to create environments where students would learn, through active participation, to think for themselves and develop new ideas. The focus on the individual's creative potential, and more so, on the importance of providing an educational environment aimed at stimulating this potential, is fully consistent with the humanist conception of *Bildung*. The difference, of course, is the focus on practical exercises as the pedagogical method through which this self-expression would come to fulfillment. Twenty years later this model would receive an institutional setting within the universities as well.

In the 1830s, however, it was not yet possible to introduce a practical orientation into the universities. This is evidenced by the attempt of a small group within parliament to reform the universities in this very fashion. Although the diet did not, as it had in the case of the primary and secondary schools, propose an official government decree on the reform of the universities, it did express much dissatisfaction with the kind of education being offered at these higher institutions of learning. The main complaints came from a group of men centered around the factory owner, Franz Buhl,[26] and the district councilor Adolf Sander. They argued that the universities (Baden had two—one in Heidelberg and the other in Freiburg) ignored important needs of the state and that part of their endowment would be better spent on a civic (*bürgerlich*) university that would concern itself primarily with the practical aspects of state life.[27]

Baden had, in fact, already founded a polytechnic school in Karlsruhe in 1825. It was the third such school in a German-speaking country, the first being in Prague (1806) and the second in Vienna (1815). They were all modeled on the Paris *École Polytechnique,* which had been founded in 1794 to provide a basic education in mathematics and the natural sciences for those individuals intending to study later at one of France's specialized institutes for the sciences and technology. Like the *École,* which sought to combine theoretical studies and practical applications, the polytechnic school in Karlsruhe provided general courses in the natural sciences and mathematics, and specific training in engineering, architecture, trade, forestry, and business.[28] But in the early years of its existence the school fared poorly in comparison with the universities. Funding was limited, attendance was low, and its social standing in the educational hierarchy left much to be desired. In 1831, amid discussions on ways to improve the situation of the school, a number of representatives came out strongly in support of moving the institute from Karlsruhe to Freiburg. Their main argument was that the natural resources in the Black Forest region provided a more suitable setting than the state capital for technical training, but it is clear that they also hoped to improve the school's status by establishing connections to the university. In their fight they received support from two Freiburg professors, Karl von Rotteck and Karl Welcker, famous for their liberal views through their editorship of one of the most successful liberal encyclopedias of the *Vormärz* period, the *Staatslexikon*.[29] Rotteck and Welcker even went so far as to favor combining the university with the polytechnic school. Not only, they argued, would it be easier to provide students at the polytechnic school with a theoretical education, but there would be no harm done to the university were it to begin considering practical applications of scientific knowledge. The head of the ministry of interior, however, would hear nothing of this. "The polytechnic institute can never be moved to a place where there is a university," responded Winter, "because the purpose is totally different. One has a scientific (*wissenschaftlich*) goal, and the other a purely practical goal."[30]

Buhl could not have been in more agreement with Winter that a union of the polytechnic school and the university would never work. But he turned the argument completely on its head. Reasoning that two universities for the "so-called higher sciences" were too much for a state as small as Baden, which had, furthermore, more civil servants than it could use, he proposed a total transformation of the University of Freiburg into a polytechnic academy. His opposition to unification rested, as it had with Winter, on the great difference in teaching methods. But he praised rather than scorned the integration of theory and practice that characterized the lessons in the technical institutions. As he explained, the kind of lesson ridiculed by Schiller in the parody "He who studies metaphysics/ Knows, that he who burns does not freeze" does not suffice for vocational schools. On the contrary, he added, there

> we must learn to investigate the richness of the powers contained in the elements, and to apply them to good use. For such a lesson it is absolutely necessary that practice and theory be combined. The former must demonstrate the correctness of the latter through tests.[31]

Friedrich August Walchner, director of the polytechnic school, used the same argument two years later in an attempt to justify increased funding for technical education. Here, he claimed, "it is a question not only of theoretical but also of practical lessons. For the latter, where students must engage in different manipulations, exercises, and handwork themselves, laboratories, workshops, and instruments are necessary."[32]

Twenty years later it would no longer be possible to use this criterion to differentiate a polytechnic school from a university, but in the early 1830s laboratory work did not yet form an integral part of a scholarly education. This does not mean that changes had not yet begun. On the contrary, as early as 1833, Karl (Joseph Anton) Mittermaier, professor of law at the University of Heidelberg, claimed that the growth in financial support for the natural sciences and medicine was largely responsible for the higher endowments being requested by the universities. Earlier, he explained, people believed philosophical, philological, or historical knowledge alone made a good scholar, and that the universities could totally ignore practical concerns. But, he added, that had fortunately changed, and the universities were taking care that they possess excellent natural science collections and medical institutes.[33]

We have already seen confirmation of Mittermaier's statement in Tiedemann's improvements of the anatomical collection. Moreover, as early as 1818 Heidelberg had upgraded its clinical facilities, moving the medical, surgical, and obstetrical clinics out of the old Dominican cloister, which they had shared with anatomy, chemistry, and botany, and into their own building (Marstallhof). Through this arrangement the university had hoped to compete with Berlin. In the new building, a dissection room, auditorium, and administration offices occupied the first floor; the medical clinic, with a total of forty beds by 1828, occupied the second floor; and the surgical and obstetrical clinics shared the third floor. In 1830, partly because of lack of space, but largely because of the persistence of puerperal fever, the university had added a wing to the building expressly for obstetrics. Thereafter surgery took over the entire third floor, with a total of eighteen beds.[34]

In 1835 Nebenius met with the medical faculty to discuss once again expansion of the university's medical and clinical facilities.[35] They had heard that the state's psychiatric asylum, then housed in a former Jesuit college in Heidelberg, would be moving within the next couple of years to the town of Illenau, about fifty kilometers southwest of Karlsruhe, and Nebenius, together with the members of the medical faculty, proposed that the university purchase and renovate the building to permit improvement of the scientific and clinical facilities. The specific plan was to move the medical and surgical clinics into the renovated building, thus permitting obstetrics to take over most of the Marstallhof, which all the clinics were then sharing. Zoology and the models collection could then occupy the remainder of the old clinic, which would grant anatomy and chemistry more room for their collections and instruments in the old Dominican cloister. Expected costs came to roughly 5000 gulden.

Everything, however, depended upon the psychiatric asylum's move, and this did not occur until 1843. Thus the scientific and clinical facilities remained as they were for almost another decade. I wish to point out, moreover, that despite these proposed improvements, a gap existed between the kind of research going on at the universities and the practice-oriented science demanded by Buhl and Walchner. The latter saw laboratory work as a pedagogical tool for training students, whereas in the universities scientific investigations remained in the hands of an elite—the university professors and their assistants. Moreover, these investigations had little to do with the kind of technical laboratory work being advocated by Buhl and Walchner. The approach taken by men such as Tiedemann, Müller, and Purkyne in their physiological studies, although based on such techniques as chemical analysis and microscopy, grew out of a neohumanist definition of *Wissenschaft*. By no means did these men harbor an antagonism toward detailed work, but they believed exact studies could never be an end in themselves. Rather the purpose of scientific research rested in its contribution to a process whose goal was the pursuit of an integrated, holistic view of life.

The transition within the universities from this nontechnological, holistic research method to the kind of laboratory-based scientific activity described previously would come about through a slow process that would take about thirty years to reach its mature form. This transition, however, would not occur because the universities eventually acknowledged a utilitarian approach to scientific research, but because active participation in problem-solving, exemplified by the laboratory setting, became the model for the way in which scientific research should be done. But more important, familiarity with the exact method of the experimental sciences came to represent the kind of "intellectual cultivation" (*geistige Bildung*) desired by a society trying to provide the next generation with the necessary mentality and intellectual skills for dealing with the problems of modernization.

In the 1830s this transition, like the industrialization of Germany, was still in its infancy, but throughout the *Vormärz* period signs of tension and change increased steadily. This was mirrored nowhere more clearly than in the debates between humanists and realists (the *Humanismus/Realismus* debates) that accompanied discussions on reform of the secondary schools.[36] The controversy focused less on the importance of the *Realwissenschaften* per se—which no one denied—than on their importance for a general education. In concrete terms, the issue was whether mathematics, natural science, and modern language should be given greater emphasis in the predominantly philologically oriented *Gymnasia*.

The "Humanismus/Realismus" Debate

In 1831 a special committee, headed by the civil servant and financial advisor Franz Anton Regenauer, reviewed the situation in the classical secondary schools. "Your commission," he told parliament, "is of the conviction that too much time is spent in our schools on the learned languages [Greek, Latin]."[37] Regenauer went on to assure his audience of the commission's appreciation of the importance of Latin and Greek for the learned professions, but he did not believe it necessary to require nine or more years of language study. There are, he emphasized, other subjects that are at least as valuable for the formal education of the intellect.

The majority of the representatives present at this meeting agreed with this analysis. Although most had attended the classical school system, they anticipated that a classical education omitting the *Realwissenschaften* would slowly become anachronistic in a society experiencing the changes brought about by railroads, steamships, and power-driven mills. During the discussions, the supreme court judge Josef Merk captured a common sentiment when he requested that school instruction be directed more toward the needs of the day. "By the future drafting of a school plan," he elaborated,

> one must especially not forget that the means of communication between people do not lie in the higher sciences, as they had till now in the Republic of Letters. Rather they are to be found in the general participation of people in a political cosmopolitanism. . . . Therefore knowledge of the modern languages and of that which is of true general welfare will provide the means of young people to take advantage both of this general communication and of the path now being taken by civilization on the whole.[38]

A shared vision did not, however, mean a common understanding of the way to achieve this goal. In the early 1830s, the central question was whether these reforms should be carried out in the *Gymnasia,* or whether special schools should be founded expressly for teaching the *Realwissenschaften.* In 1833 a special commission, headed by the representative Kröll, dedicated a lengthy report to the advantages of the latter arrangement. By the tone of the report it is apparent that the commission was waging a war against the philologists. These schools, Kröll argued, would provide a general citizen's education (*"Menschen- und Bürgerbildung"*) rather than the highly specialized classical training found in the *Gymnasia.* They would be responsible for completing the transition from absolutism to constitutionalism by offering an education that would prepare future citizens for active participation in the affairs of the state.[39]

Throughout the report and in the ensuing discussion, Kröll and other parliamentary representatives attempted to redefine the content of a well-rounded education. In contrast to the neohumanist claim that the study of the classics best developed an individual's intellectual and moral character, they argued that the near exclusive focus on Latin and Greek characteristic of the *Gymnasia* served only the specialized needs of a privileged group destined for an academic career. As in 1831, their argument focused on the changing times, expanding population, growth in industry, and increased worldwide connections that together created greater challenges for the businessman and made it necessary for him to prepare more thoroughly for the tasks ahead. Special *Bürgerschulen,* they argued, that emphasized the *Realwissenschaften* without neglecting the classics, would teach those subjects of importance for the "productive citizens of the state," not for the "consumers." They would, in short, provide a more general *bürgerliche* education for those whose professional activities contributed directly to the material interests of the state.[40]

The enemy here was by no means Latin and Greek—subjects that the commission highly praised—but rather philologists who insisted that knowledge of the classics was the sole mark of cultivation and scholarly learning. To enter the details of this debate would go beyond the scope of this book. The conflict, by no means restricted to Baden, went far beyond differences of opinion regarding the value of the sciences and had much to do with the protection of, or conversely the attack on, class and professional interests.[41] Of importance here is parliament's explicit recognition of the new needs of the state and its decision to meet those needs. On 20 June 1834 non-classical secondary schools, designed to offer the emerging middle class an education in the *Realwissenschaften* and modern languages, were founded by government decree.[42] There is no doubt that the motivation was in part to end the debate between humanists and realists. Thereafter the *Gymnasia* would be for those "who want to dedicate themselves to a learned profession."[43] But the creation of schools specifically for the teaching of mathematics, natural science, and modern languages reflected much more the recognition that promotion of the material interests of the state would best be met through improved educational opportunities. In an article on Baden, which appeared in 1838 in the popular Brockhaus encyclopedia, *Conversations-Lexikon der Gegenwart,* the author praised the parliament of this small land for keeping in mind both material and intellectual interests "more than any other diet in Germany."[44] As Table 2.1 demonstrates, the Baden parliament did not hesitate to convert this conviction into concrete funding. Throughout the *Vormärz* period it committed itself more and more to those educational institutions that offered preparation for a nonacademic life, whether it be in trade, commerce, or industry. Furthermore, as columns Va, VIa, and Figure 2.1 show, the rate of growth in funds allocated for the *Realwissenschaften* far surpassed that for the education budget on the whole.[45]

Significantly, the creation of schools specifically for the teaching of the *Realwissenschaften* did not mean that the *Gymnasia* remained unaffected by the reform concerns of the previous years. In a report on the classical secondary schools read before parliament in 1833, the representative Albert Ludwig Grimm began by expressing his conviction that the *Gymnasia* should keep their philological character, but he quickly added that this was merely the general direction that should be followed in these schools. It is necessary, he went on.

> to appreciate that general education had begun to take on another direction, and that the classical schools, where our clerics and state officials of all kinds receive their preparatory education, cannot totally disregard this direction if their pupils are not to remain behind the times.[46]

Thus, despite the creation of non-classical secondary schools, the *Gymnasia* intended to offer courses in the *Realwissenschaften*. In 1837 the government went one step further and issued an official decree guaranteeing that this indeed occur. As part of a general ordinance on the reorganization of the classical secondary schools—an ordinance designed to standardize administrative and curricular affairs—Baden established natural history, natural philosphy, and mathematics as fixed courses in the curriculum.[47]

Table 2.1   State Expenditure for Science Education

Year	I	II	III	IV	V	Va	VI	VIa
1831/32	41,240				41,240	1.0	498,438	1.0
1833/34	41,600	12,000			53,600	1.3	536,488	1.1
1835/36	59,727	14,400			74,327	1.8	551,694	1.1
1837/38	58,700	14,000		10,725	83,425	2.0	634,067	1.3
1839/40	51,700	14,221		21,592	87,513	2.1	629,553	1.3
1842/43	60,213	16,087		23,750	100,050	2.4	683,711	1.4
1844/45	66,254	16,784		29,332	112,370	2.7	702,579	1.4
1846/47	67,784	18,709	17,522	34,250	138,365	3.4	880,393	1.8

I	= Polytechnic school	V	= Total (columns I–IV)
II	= Trade schools	Va	= Rate of growth (column V)
III	= Agricultural education	VI	= Total budget for education
IV	= Non-classical secondary schools	VIa	= Rate of growth (column VI)
	(*höhere Bürgerschulen*)		

Source: "Vergleichung der Budgets-Sätze mit den Rechnungs-Resultaten für die Etats-Jahre 1831 bis 1847," in *Verhandlungen*, 2. Kammer (usually, but not always, in Beilagenheft 2).

In short, once the government guaranteed the *Gymnasia* the right to retain their philological character, it had little difficulty ensuring that the *Realwissenschaften* would become an integral part of the classical curriculum.

A comparison with developments in other German states highlights the significance of this measure. Bavaria, for one, banned the natural sciences from the *Gymnasia* in 1830, shortly after the conservative-minded

Figure 2.1   Graphical Representation of Columns Va and VIa.

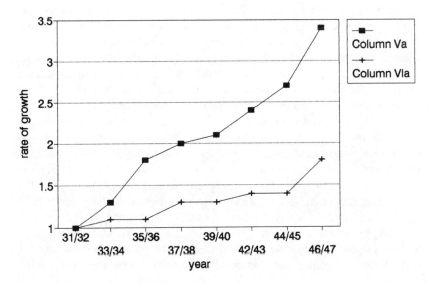

Ludwig I took the throne.[48] In Saxony, a battle began in 1831 shortly after the King established a constitutional monarchy in his land. The newly created parliament immediately raised the issue of school reform. "The absence," it lamented,

> of a proper introduction to the study of the *Realwissenschaften,* and consequently our failure to prepare and instruct the youth for the demands that life will make on them, continues to be a shortcoming of the majority of our learned schools.[49]

Support for educational reform in Saxony's parliament was considerable, but not enough to counter the opposition. Drawing on the government's fear of revolution, opponents of educational reform linked the study of nature with the spirit of the Paris *École Polytechnique* and, by association, with the July Revolution of 1830. As the superintendent of Leipzig's schools argued, the study of the *Realwissenschaften* had fomented "the spirit of unrest," whereas the study of the classics had proven itself to be "an essential pillar of order."[50] Such arguments led to a ban on the natural sciences in 1834 which was not removed for over a decade.

Even in Prussia, defendants of a purely classical education almost succeeded in banning the natural sciences in 1837, but they proved unable to overpower Johannes Schulze, minister of education and cultural affairs, and others in the ministry who had long fought to integrate science education into the classical *Gymnasia*.[51] Only in Hessen and Nassau did events resemble those in Baden; without much difficulty, the governments enacted legislation establishing the natural sciences as an integral part of a classical education.[52]

Although the absence of detailed case studies makes it difficult to determine precisely why these debates had different outcomes in the various states, it seems that where parliaments existed and political liberalism was strongest (Baden, Hessen, Nassau), governments had the least trouble challenging traditional seats of power and instituting reforms. Prussia, which eventually integrated the natural sciences into the curriculum of the *Gymnasia,* may seem to be the exception that breaks the rule, but despite its politically conservative nature, it far outshined all other states in economic liberalism. Moreover, the absence of a functional parliament placed all the more power in the hands of the ministers, and in the 1830s Prussian ministers had a decidedly liberal bent. Their support, however, was never as firmly rooted as in a state like Baden, where an elected parliament influenced government affairs. This may help to explain why Schulze's opponents almost proved successful in 1837 in banning the natural sciences from the *Gymnasia*. Their failure, however, was only temporary. In 1854, during the height of the reactionary era, they finally had their way.[53]

The ease with which Baden reformed secondary higher education thus reflected the extent to which political liberalism flourished in parliament and the government ministries. It indicated that a broader basis of support existed for challenging old traditions and enacting new legislation. This does not mean *Vormärz* liberals never acted conservatively. On the contrary, they often showed a marked proclivity for slow and controlled change, especially in southern Germany where small towns and farms continued to dominate the way of life much more so than in the more industrial north. Nevertheless, their vision of the ideal society differed markedly from the one in which they lived, and they believed the best way to guarantee gradual change was through education.

Changing Definitions of Wissenschaft

Legislation dictating that the natural sciences be taught in the *Gymnasia* did not mean that advocates of a humanist education acknowledged they were advancing a more utilitarian approach to education. On the contrary, throughout the *Vormärz* period they maintained that they continued "to lay the foundation for a well-rounded humanist education."[54] What had changed was their willingness to grant the natural sciences a place in such an education. As the representative Christian Friedrich Platz pointed out in 1837, the practical sciences had become "all the more qualified as a formal tool for education (*Bildungsmittel*), the more they had advanced in the course of time."[55] Six years later, the principal of Heidelberg's *Lyceum* made an even stronger statement. In a two-part article published in the local newspaper, the *Heidelberger Journal,* he praised mathematics and physics above all other subjects. The method of these subjects, he wrote,

> contributes just as much to forming the intellect in a formal sense, as it provides the intellect with the most useful and most indispensable concrete information (*Realkenntnisse*). Such a teaching method, which forces the student in general to think and discover for himself, cannot remain without a very significant benefit for all other sciences. It alone is qualified to ban forever the wavering and insecurity in the operations of reason. . . .[56]

Thus the government ordinance in 1837 establishing the *Realwissenschaften* as an integral part of the curriculum of the *Gymnasia* signified not so much a shift in attitude toward utilitarianism as toward the natural sciences themselves. It marked a growing appreciation of the pedagogical value of the scientific method as a tool for training the critical faculties of the mind. A transition was taking shape wherein scientific knowledge and practical exercises slowly became divorced from their association with utilitarian ends and began to be more closely aligned with a *wissenschaftlichen* education. By the early 1840s the method of the natural sciences was becoming an integral part of the humanist notion of *Wissenschaft,* but not without eliciting a change in the notion itself; by then the image of *Wissenschaft* as pure research untainted by practical work was beginning to disappear. This occurred at a time when the call for greater attention to the *Realwissenschaften* and for a combination of theory and practice appeared often in the popular literature, whether in newspapers, encyclopedias, parliamentary proceedings, or medical journals. And it did not leave the uni-

50 Science, Medicine, and the State in Germany

versities untouched. As we will see in the following chapter this was the decade when teaching style changed so as to engage the students more in the learning process, when looking through the microscope became a part of medical education, and most important, when new institutes for medicine and the natural sciences came into being. Between 1847 and 1849 the Baden parliament granted almost 75,000 gulden for the construction of a new anatomy and zoology building, and in 1846 plans began for a natural science institute that would include physics, chemistry, mineralogy, technology, and archaeology.[57] Baden's interests, however, went beyond the desire to improve the quality of instruction in the universities, for this building was intended as a public institute as well. The scientific collections were not to serve the teaching needs of professors alone, but were also to be available for public display. Baden was embarking on a plan to bring science to its citizens.

Notes

1. Wolfram Fischer, *Der Staat und die Anfänge der Industrialisierung in Baden 1800–1850. Vol. 1: Die staatliche Gewerbepolitik* (Berlin, 1962); Loyd E. Lee, *The Politics of Harmony. Civil Service, Liberalism, and Social Reform in Baden, 1800–1850* (Newark, 1980), chap. 5; F.-W. Henning, *Die Industrialisierung in Deutschland, 1800–1914* (Paderborn, 1973), pp. 35–111; Thomas Nipperdey, *Deutsche Geschichte, 1800–1866. Bürgerwelt und starker Staat* (Munich, 1984), pp. 178–210.

2. Lee, *The Politics of Harmony.* Although Baden enacted measures to weaken the guilds, it did not abolish them and declare the right for anyone to pursue any trade until 1862. See Fischer, *Der Staat and die Anfänge der Industrialisierung in Baden,* p. 34.

3. Fischer, *Der Staat und die Anfänge der Industrialisierung in Baden.*

4. Wolfram Fischer, "Staat und Gesellschaft Badens im Vormärz," in *Staat und Gesellschaft im deutschen Vormärz, 1818–1848,* ed. Werner Conze (Stuttgart, 1962), pp. 143–172; Lothar Gall, "Gründung und politische Entwicklung des Großherzogtums bis 1848," in *Badische Geschichte,* ed. Landeszentrale für politische Bildung Baden-Württemberg (Stuttgart, 1979), pp. 11–36.

5. "Karl Friedrich Nebenius," *BB,* 2: 99–105. See also Lee, *The Politics of Harmony,* pp. 42–43.

6. James J. Sheehan, *German Liberalism in the Nineteenth Century* (Chicago, 1978), p. 10; Lee, *The Politics of Harmony,* pp. 52–56. The first chamber consisted of the princes of the house, the nine peers, eight representatives of the manorial lords, the head Roman Catholic bishop, one representative for each of the universities (Freiburg and Heidelberg), and no more than eight representatives appointed by the Grand Duke.

7. Lee, *The Politics of Harmony,* pp. 54, 86.

8. Ibid., p. 52.

9. Ibid., chap. 4.

10. Ibid., pp. 133–134; "Friedrich Daniel Bassermann," *BB,* 1: 39, and "Karl Leopold Friedrich, Großherzog von Baden," *BB,* 1: 23.

11. "Ludwig Georg Winter," *BB,* 2: 493–510; and Lee, *The Politics of Harmony,* pp. 44–45.

12. Lee, *The Politics of Harmony,* p. 154.

13. See Lothar Gall, "Liberalismus und 'bürgerliche Gesellschaft'—zu Charakter und Entwicklung der liberalen Bewegung in Deutschland," *Historische Zeitschrift,* 220 (1975): 324–356; James J. Sheehan, "Liberalism and Society in Germany, 1815–48," *Modern History,* 45 (1973): 583–604; idem, *German Liberalism in the Nineteenth Century,* chap. 1; Nipperdey, *Deutsche Geschichte,* esp. p. 290; Dieter Langewiesche, *Liberalismus in Deutschland* (Frankfurt am Main, 1988).

14. See Nebenius in *Verhandlungen,* 2. Kammer, 137. Sitzung, 17 November 1831, Protokollheft 30, pp. 234–241; Winter (a representative, not the state minister) in ibid., pp. 262–263; Welcker in the 18. Sitzung, 16 May 1835, Protokollheft 1, p. 272; von Itzenstein in the 67. Sitzung, 26 July 1837, Protokollheft 8, p. 54. See also Lee, *The Politics of Harmony,* chap. 5.

15. Fischer, *Der Staat und die Anfänge der Industrialisierung,* pp. 168–169.

16. *RB,* 25 (1834): 177–200; 26 (1834): 201–226. See also Nebenius in *Verhandlungen,* 2. Kammer, 77. Sitzung, 9 October 1833, Protokollheft 16, p. 192; Ludwig in ibid., 20. Sitzung, 19 May 1835, Protokollheft 1, pp. 39–40. See also Lee, *The Politics of Harmony,* p. 156.

17. *RB,* 8 (1837): 53–64.

18. Franz Schnabel, *Deutsche Geschichte im 19. Jahrhundert,* 3rd ed., 3 vols. (Freiburg, 1934), vol. 3: Erfahrungswissenschaften und Technik, pp. 292–319; Gert Schubring, "The Rise and Decline of the Bonn Natural Sciences Seminar," in *Osiris,* 2nd series, 5 (1989): 57–93, esp. pp. 60, 70.

19. C. F. Nebenius, *Ueber technische Lehranstalten in ihrem Zusammenhange mit dem gesammten Unterrichtswesen und mit besonderer Rücksicht auf die polytechnische Schule zu Karlsruhe* (Karlsruhe, 1833), p. 51. For a discussion of this point, see Frank R. Pfetsch, *Zur Entwicklung der Wissenschaftspolitik in Deutschland, 1750–1914* (Berlin, 1974), p. 137.

20. Schnabel, *Deutsche Geschichte,* vol. 3, pp. 292–301. The quotation is on p. 292. See also Grimm, "Commissionsbericht über die Mittelschulen," *Verhandlungen,* 2. Kammer, 67. Sitzung, 26 September 1833, Beilagenheft 5, pp. 303–343, esp. p. 343; and Nipperdey, *Deutsche Geschichte,* pp. 183–189.

21. Sheehan, *German Liberalism in the Nineteenth Century,* p. 22.

22. Budget for the ministry of interior, *Verhandlungen,* 2. Kammer, 1831, Beilagenheft 10, p. 219.

23. Cited in Lee, *The Politics of Harmony,* p. 115. For a discussion of the guild system, see Representative Kröll, "Commissionsbericht über die Errichtung von höheren Bürger- und Gewerbeschulen," *Verhandlungen,* 2. Kammer, 66. Sitzung, 24 September 1833, Beilagenheft 5, pp. 235–261, esp. pp. 251–254.

24. For Pestalozzi's influence on early nineteenth-century educational reformers, see Friedrich Paulsen, *Geschichte des gelehrten Unterrichts auf den deutschen Schulen und Universitäten,* 2 vols. (Leipzig, 1897), vol. 2, p. 278.

25. Nebenius, *Ueber technische Lehranstalten,* p. 52. This passage is also cited in Rep. Kröll, "Commissionsbericht," pp. 252–254.

26. The Buhl family was extremely influential politically and commercially. See Fischer, *Der Staat und die Anfänge der Industrialisierung,* pp. 210–211. Also *BB,* 2: 141–143.

27. See the discussions in *Verhandlungen,* 2. Kammer, 133. und 137. Sitzung, 10 and 17 November 1831, Protokollheft 29 and 30.

28. Karl Heinz Manegold, *Universität, Technische Hochschule und Industrie* (Berlin, 1970), pp. 18–39; Schnabel, *Deutsche Geschichte,* pp. 305–307; Reinhard

Riese, *Die Hochschule auf dem Wege zum wissenschaftlichen Großbetrieb* (Stuttgart, 1977), pp. 294–308.

29. Koppel S. Pinson, *Modern Germany. Its History and Civilization,* 2nd ed. (New York, 1966), p. 60. See Hans Zehntner, *Das Staatslexikon von Rotteck und Welcker. Eine Studie zur Geschichte des deutschen Frühliberalismus* (Jena, 1929).

30. Winter, *Verhandlungen,* 2. Kammer, 137. Sitzung, 17 November 1831, Protokollheft 30, p. 253; Welcker, ibid., p. 252; von Rotteck, ibid., pp. 265–266. For a discussion of the tension between universities and technical schools in Germany in the first half of the nineteenth century, see Manegold, *Universität, Technische Hochschule und Industrie,* pp. 26–54.

31. Buhl, *Verhandlungen,* 2. Kammer, 137. Sitzung, 17 November 1831, Protokollheft 30, pp. 246–247. See also Buhl, ibid., 133. Sitzung, 10 November 1831, Protokollheft 29, pp. 323–324. The desire to keep the universities and technical schools separate was shared by many advocates of a technical education in Baden and elsewhere. See Manegold, *Universität, Technische Hochschule und Industrie,* pp. 34–43.

32. Walchner, *Verhandlungen,* 2. Kammer, 85. Sitzung, 18 October 1833, Protokollheft 18, p. 16.

33. Mittermaier, *Verhandlungen,* 2. Kammer, 81. Sitzung, 14 October 1833, Protokollheft 17, p. 147.

34. Eberhard Stübler, *Geschichte der medizinischen Fakultät der Universität Heidelberg, 1326–1925* (Heidelberg, 1926), pp. 217–222.

35. The protocol of this meeting was written on 29 November 1835, in BGLA 235/676.

36. These debates were carried out throughout Germany. See Walter Schöler, *Geschichte des naturwissenschaftlichen Unterrichts im 17. bis 19. Jahrhundert* (Berlin, 1970), esp. pp. 72–132; and Manegold, *Universität, Technische Hochschule und Industrie,* pp. 43–54.

37. Regenauer, "Commissionsbericht über die Adresse der ersten Kammer, die Revision der Mittelschulen betreffend," in *Verhandlungen,* 2. Kammer, 65. Sitzung, 25 July 1831, Beilagenheft 6, pp. 77–106, here p. 91.

38. Merk, *Verhandlungen,* 2. Kammer, 87. Sitzung, 2 September 1831, Protokollheft 21, p. 91. See also Lee, *The Politics of Harmony,* p. 135.

39. Kröll, "Commissionsbericht," pp. 242, 246.

40. Winter (representative), *Verhandlungen,* 2. Kammer, 77. Sitzung, 9 October 1833, Protokollheft 16, pp. 170–171; Kröll, "Commissionsbericht," pp. 235–246.

41. See Lenore O'Boyle, "Klassische Bildung und soziale Struktur in Deutschland zwischen 1800 und 1848," *Historische Zeitschrift,* 207 (1968): 584–608; Paulsen, *Geschichte des gelehrten Unterrichts,* pp. 313–353, 539–570; Schöler, *Geschichte des naturwissenschaftlichen Unterrichts.*

42. *RB,* 8 (1837): 53–64.

43. Ibid., p. 53.

44. "Baden," in F. A. Brockhaus, *Conversations-Lexikon der Gegenwart,* 4 vols. (Leipzig, 1838–41), 1838, vol. I, pp. 295–309. [The *Conversations-Lexikon der Gegenwart* is a supplement to the 8th edition of the larger Brockhaus *Conversations-Lexikon,* 12 vols. (Leipzig, 1833–39).]

45. Financial statistics are from the "Vergleichung der Budgets-Sätze mit den Rechnungs-Resultäten für die Etats-Jahre 1831 bis 1847," in *Verhandlungen,* 2. Kammer (usually, but not always, in Beilagenheft 2). Rate of growth was calcu-

lated by setting the value for the first year at one and dividing each successive year by the first year's value.

46. Grimm, "Commissionsbericht über die Mittelschulen," pp. 310–311. See also Nebenius, *Verhandlungen,* 2. Kammer, 77. Sitzung, 9 October 1833, Protokollheft 16, p. 219.

47. *RB,* 8 (1837): 54.

48. Schöler, *Geschichte des naturwissenschaftlichen Unterrichts,* p. 108.

49. Cited in ibid., p. 116.

50. Cited in ibid., p. 117.

51. Ibid., pp. 117–121.

52. Ibid., pp. 121–122.

53. Ibid., pp. 93, 115–122, 295 (note 84). Also, see Chapter 5 of this book.

54. Platz, *Verhandlungen,* 2. Kammer, 66. Sitzung, 25 July 1837, Protokollheft 8, p. 43. See also the discussions in ibid., 1841/42, Protokollheft 3, pp. 272–275; 1844, Protokollheft 9, pp. 222–243; 1846, Protokollheft 6, p. 24.

55. Platz, *Verhandlungen,* 2. Kammer, 66. Sitzung, 25 July 1837, Protokollheft 8, p. 43.

56. C. Schmetzer, "Erinnerungen an die letzte Prüfung im Lyceum zu Heidelberg," *Heidelberger Journal,* 15 and 16 October 1843.

57. See Chapter 4.

3

Scientific Medicine: The Development of the Program

On 21 November 1843 Franz Freiherr von Stengel, a member of Baden's ministry of interior responsible for educational affairs, announced that new talent was needed if the reputation of the medical faculty at the University of Heidelberg was to be saved.[1] The professor of special pathology and therapy, Friedrich Christian Sebastian, had passed away in 1840, and several of the remaining five senior professors were close to the age of retirement. In addition, Tiedemann, who had once contributed so prominently to Heidelberg's reputation, had been slowly withdrawing from university and scientific affairs. In 1835 he had handed over his courses in physiology and pathological anatomy to the *Privatdozent* Theodor Bischoff, and in 1837 had requested a leave of absence for a year and a half. The death of three children, serious eye problems, and repeated attacks on the university by the lower chamber of parliament had been largely responsible for this withdrawal, but, according to Bischoff, "the enormous stimulus that physiology received through the use of the microscope and through the ever expanding application of physics and chemistry" contributed as well.[2] Tiedemann, already taxed by other problems, did not have the energy to keep abreast of the latest scientific developments.

In his report, sent to the state ministry, von Stengel referred to the decreasing student enrollment brought about by the unpopularity of the medical faculty.

> Privy Councilor Tiedemann is on in years and wishes an easier load. Privy Councilor Puchelt, as much as he distinguishes himself as an honorable scholar and writer, is not very popular as a clinical teacher and many students are

leaving the University of Heidelberg because they prefer to attend practical courses in internal medicine at other universities.[3]

Students were indeed choosing other universities. In 1830 Heidelberg had attracted ten percent (225 students) of all German medical students, but by 1840 this had fallen to seven percent (140 students) and there was no indication that this decline would cease. In fact, in the fall of 1843 attendance hit the lowest point in twenty years, with only thirty-two local and seventy-eight foreign students enrolled.[4] Von Stengel, together with the university administration, began seriously to reevaluate the situation. Yet their goal was not simply to promote what was fashionable in order to increase enrollments. In searching for replacements, they showed an interest in individuals who represented a particular direction in research and teaching. The concerns von Stengel had expressed in his report demonstrated his awareness that a practical emphasis in medical education was growing in importance. A protégé of Ludwig Winter and, along with Carl Nebenius, Alexander von Dusch, Johann Bekk, and Karl Mathy, one of Baden's leading liberal ministers in the 1840s, von Stengel shared his colleagues' belief that science education, modernization, and political liberalization all went hand in hand. As we will see in Chapter 4, this inspired him to help draw up plans to expand the university's scientific and clinical facilities; it also led him to support the appointment of several young *Privatdozenten* who offered instruction in auscultation, percussion, and microscopy. As part, moreover, of this overall strategy, von Stengel, supported by the majority of the faculty senate, created two new positions—one in anatomy and physiology and the other in the clinical sciences—and offered them to Jacob Henle and Karl Pfeufer. These two individuals, whose education and early careers form the focus of this chapter, excelled not only as scholars but as teachers of modern scientific techniques as well. In contrast to Tiedemann and Müller before them, Henle and Pfeufer brought their research instruments—the microscope and stethoscope respectively—into the classroom, instructing large numbers of students in their use. Such pedagogical innovations were, moreover, part and parcel of a broader attempt to reform medicine by creating a medical science in which scientific theories learned in the laboratory would inform medical practice at the bedside. Henle and Pfeufer, who taught together at the University of Zurich for four years before coming to Heidelberg, perceived of themselves as a team whose goal was to forge a bridge between theory and practice.

Jacob Henle (1809–1885)

In 1827 Henle began his medical studies at the University of Bonn under the tutelage of Johannes Müller. Indeed, Müller was partly responsible for Henle's decision to forego an earlier interest in the ministry and pursue instead a career in medicine.[5] The young protégé remained in Bonn three years before moving to Heidelberg to continue his studies. What he had learned from Müller he took with him, particularly the conviction that only through a thorough understanding of theory could one hope to acquire independence from authority. Writing home to his parents in the spring of 1830, he praised the skills of the clinicians at the University of Heidelberg, but elaborated on the dangers of teaching practical courses without providing a theoretical basis. "The consequences will present themselves," he wrote, "when the guiding hand of the teacher is absent one time." Only by studying the cause and foundation of disease, he added, "can one succeed in achieving something free and independent, and not have to follow blindly the first best thing that comes from experience."[6]

In 1831 Henle returned to Bonn to take his examinations for the doctorate. The year turned out to be an important one for him. He and Müller searched around for dissertation topics, neither able to determine whether an anatomical or medical emphasis would provide a better strategic advantage in the field. A chance discovery by Henle led them to choose the pupil membrane and blood vessels within the eye. One year later the young protégé received the M.D. and decided to abandon medical practice and pursue an academic career. As he explained in a letter to his parents, he had come to this decision because of his love for anatomy, his talent in research and drawing, his desire for independence, his attraction to the academic life style, and very important, Müller's promise of support and protection, without which success in the competitive academic field would not have been possible.[7]

Upon completion of his doctorate Henle went to Berlin to take the state medical examination. One year later, in 1833, Müller received a call to Berlin as professor of anatomy and physiology, and true to his word he offered Henle the job of prosector in the anatomical institute and the editorship of the *Archiv für Anatomie, Physiologie und wissenschaftliche Medizin*. Henle accepted immediately, and by 1837 had completed a habilitation on the epithelium of the intestinal villi. Within a year the university promoted him to *Privatdozent* and he began offering courses in general pathology and general anatomy.

In the anatomy course Henle broke with tradition and brought the microscope into the classroom, instructing students in how to use the instrument. The very first semester the class drew sixty students, a number that surprised even Henle. This may have been one of the earliest cases of microscopical technique being taught to medical students, although it is not likely that Henle was alone. Unfortunately, little is known about the exact nature of scientific instruction in the early nineteenth century. When university course listings advertised an anatomy or physiology lecture accompanied by "microscopical demonstrations" or "microscopical investigations"—and these were common by the late 1830s—it is not clear to what extent students were actively involved in using the instrument. By 1839, however, at least two individuals other than Henle (August Meyer in Bonn and Wilhelm Grube in Tübingen) were providing "instruction in the use of the microscope," and there were probably a few more. Henle, for example, did not state explicitly in his course description that he would be showing students how to work with the microscope. There is, therefore, every reason to believe that individuals at other universities were also beginning to introduce students to microscopical techniques. Few, however, acquired as much of a national reputation for their microscopical skills as Henle.[8]

Henle's decision to make the microscope an essential pedagogical tool had benefited from recent developments in the construction of the instrument that had improved its quality and reduced its costs.[9] A central problem in early nineteenth-century microscope building had been how to reduce the chromatic aberration caused by dispersion. Early attempts at the construction of achromatic microscopes had suffered because of the difficulty of achieving satisfactory resolution at high magnifications. In 1824 the Frenchman Charles Chevalier succeeded in solving this problem by inserting a biconcave lens between several achromatic lenses. The instrument attained immediate popularity, inspiring other microscope builders, such as Jean Baptista Amici in Modena, Italy, to produce modified copies of this model. As the demand for achromatic microscopes grew, the number of producers increased as well. By 1830 Georg Oberhäuser in Paris, Simon Plössl in Vienna, and Philipp Heinrich Pistor and F. W. Schiek in Berlin were manufacturing good microscopes, at greatly reduced costs. "Those were the happiest days," wrote Henle in 1882, "for which the present generation may well envy us, as the factories of Plössl in Vienna and Pistor and Schiek in Berlin produced the first good, usable microscopes at reasonable prices, affordable out of a student's allowance."[10]

Nevertheless, as late as 1834 the University of Berlin owned only one microscope.[11] As much as Müller may have promoted use of the instrument in scientific research, there is no indication that he, any more than his contemporary Tiedemann, saw its importance for medical education. Friedrich Bidder, for example, prosector at the University in Dorpat, came to Berlin in 1834 to learn the new research techniques, but was soon disappointed. As he wrote in his memoirs,

> I expected that the man who had, in such an outstanding way, attempted to give physiological principles an empirical foundation, would also present such experiences and the method of their acquisition in a more concrete way to his students. That was, however, not the case. The students and others in the audience still had to be content with theoretical explanations.[12]

Bidder went on to describe how Müller would be alert for any student who demonstrated talent during the dissection exercises—exercises that went totally unsupervised with ten to twenty students hacking away at a single corpse—whom he would then invite to his private study with the explanation that one "could work better there away from this confusion."[13] Research, though important, remained an activity for the chosen few.

Henle's innovation was to turn the microscope into a significant pedagogical tool. Albert Kölliker, later to become Henle's prosector in Zurich,
described his experience in Henle's course in 1839, crediting his teacher
with being the first to direct his attention to the microscopical structure of
the body.

> I still see the narrow, long hallway in the university building next to the
> auditorium where Henle, for lack of another room for demonstrations,
> showed us and explained the simplest things, so awe inspiring in their novelty,
> with scarcely five or six microscopes: epithelia, skin scales, cilia cells, blood
> corpuscles, pus cells, semen, then teased-out preparations from muscles, liga-
> ments, nerves, sections from cartilage, cuts of bones, etc.[14]

As mentioned earlier, this would not have been possible without the
inexpensive production of good microscopes, but it is obvious from a
comparison of Henle's and Müller's teaching styles that availability of the
instrument and the ability to use it—two conditions that applied equally
well to both men—did not suffice to create an appreciation of the pedagogical significance of the microscope. One had also to believe that practical experience was important for all students, not merely for a small elite.
They—the average students—were now to receive training in simple microscopical and chemical techniques. Scientific research remained, to be
sure, the domain of the professors and talented students, but students at
large were beginning to be introduced to routine laboratory methods as
well.

In a society starting to develop an interest in modernization, technical
culture, and practical experience, Henle's strategy found much acclaim.
This is not to say that introducing the microscope into the classroom
represented a calculated effort on his part. It may or may not have—the
documents available provide no clue as to his motives. His writings suggest, however, that he firmly believed, as did others of his generation
interested in liberal politics and medical reform, that introducing students
to scientific instruments and the scientific method would help them learn
to think independently. Still, the strongly competitive university system in
which Henle wished to establish himself may also have provided incentive
and, indeed, have made it necessary to develop new strategies. Henle had
written home to his parents more than once complaining about the competition among the *Privatdozenten*, his frustration with the university's policy
of dividing up newly vacated positions among many individuals, and his
concern that he be able to dedicate himself fully to academic pursuits
without having to supplement his income through private practice. The
microscope gave Henle the competitive edge he needed.[15]

As mentioned above, Henle's anatomy course found great popularity
among the students, but it had the unfortunate side effect of arousing
Müller's suspicions. In a short while relations grew so tense that Henle lost
his prosectorship and the editorship of the *Archiv,* which meant the loss of
his salary of 700 taler. In 1840 he wrote to his friend A. Schöll: "Müller

had long ago divided this money among individuals whom he hoped to mother and from whom he hoped he would have less to fear." Furthermore, he explained: "From then on I was closed out of the anatomy [institute] and had to fear remaining so the more I could justify being entitled to using it through the success of my lectures."[16]

Henle's reaction was to shift emphasis to his lecture course on pathology, but this situation was by no means satisfactory and in 1839 he applied for the chair of pathology in Berlin, made available by the death of Christian Hufeland. That a person trained in anatomy and physiology would apply for this position was somewhat unusual, but not only was Henle anxious to secure a better position, he was convinced that recent developments in these areas were of potential medical significance. In a letter to the state ministry, he argued that his decision to apply was inspired not by the desire to take advantage of an opening in the system but rather by his

> conviction of the intimate connection that anatomy and physiology have to the science of the phenomena of disease. The task of a rational medicine cannot be any other than to comprehend disease symptoms as consequences of the original typical organization of the body and the influences which have an effect upon [the organization]. A combination of both disciplines, however, may be all the more opportune at this moment, because our knowledge of the healthy organism has so increased in the last few years through so many discoveries, particularly microscopical ones, and [our knowledge] is waiting to be applied to pathological processes. In part it has already been applied with some success.[17]

These were not empty words, and much of the proof for these assertions came out of the research going on in Müller's anatomical institute, where, in addition to Henle, Theodor Schwann was working as an assistant. Just one year prior to Henle's application for Hufeland's position, Schwann had announced his "cell theory." Inspired by Matthias Jacob Schleiden's demonstration that the cell was the ultimate structural unit of all plants, Schwann had carried out investigations that convinced him that all animal and plant tissues derive from cells. The importance of this discovery for the biological sciences cannot be underestimated. Although "cells" had been described in the seventeenth century, and extensive studies of "cellular" structures had, because of improvements in microscopy, become popular in the 1830s, much confusion had persisted as to the exact nature of these structures. The significance of Schwann's and Schleiden's discovery rests in the identification of a common form of development for all cells, and their demonstration, through numerous microscopical investigations, that the cells, and not the tissues, were the ultimate units of structure, and probably function.[18]

Henle, who had already carried out extensive research on the formation of epithelial cells, recognized the importance of Schwann's work and applied it immediately to questions of pathological significance. Indeed, just a few months after Schwann published his findings, Henle incorporated the cell theory into a paper on the formation of mucus and pus.[19] In this study, he demonstrated the commonality in developmental pattern not only of these two "abnormal" elements, but of normal epithelial cells as well. Specifically, he argued that all three originated from common primary cells (*primäre Zellen*). Henle was very pleased with this work, for it demonstrated to him that the products or symptoms of disease developed *within* the organism through a process that could not be distinguished in pattern from normal development.

Henle combined the results of this research into a larger synthetic work entitled *Pathologische Untersuchungen,* which he submitted along with his application for Hufeland's position as evidence of his commitment to problems of medical concern. The book contained four separate essays that together were meant to form "a system of general pathology."[20] The first essay, "On Miasma and Contagia, and on the Miasmatic-Contagious Diseases," has received most attention from historians because of the conclusion, derived forty years before the bacteriological revolution, that microscopical organisms are the cause of many epidemic diseases.[21] However, of far greater importance for Henle's later work was the third essay, "On the Course and Periodicity of Disease," for it is here that he began to work out his ideas on the central precondition of a scientific or rational medicine—the notion of disease as a physiological process.

Disease as a Physiological Process

This notion did not originate with Henle. Throughout history two concepts of disease—one physiological, the other ontological—appeared repeatedly.[22] The latter viewed disease as an entity that invaded the healthy organism and followed its own peculiar course of development. The view drew its greatest strength from observations of epidemics, where relatively clear disease patterns were discernible and external agents appeared to be responsible for the onset of disease. In the early nineteenth century, the advent of large city hospitals, where comparisons of thousands of cases could be made, facilitated the establishment of disease patterns and thus further strengthened this notion. Not surprisingly, the Paris clinical school became one of its most fervent advocates.

Critics of this ontological definition of disease pointed out that diseases could not be distinguished and classified as easily as plants and animal species. Individuals were often afflicted by more than one disease at a time, producing complex groups of symptoms. Moreover, one disease often developed into another, obscuring boundaries. But the greatest objection was that the object of medical care was never an abstract complex of symptoms, but always a sick person with all the idiosyncrasies peculiar to the individual case. The physiological notion of disease stressed the uniqueness of each person's illness, defining the illness as the consequence of an alteration of the normal organic functions. Symptoms were not the signs of an alien disease entity living out its own life cycle within the sick individual, but rather the result of a disturbance of the body's normal physiological processes.

This notion of disease had many proponents, some of the most outspoken being John Brown, Louis Broussais, and the authors of the Corpus Hippocraticum. The revival of the concept in Germany in the late 1830s and 1840s differed, however, from these earlier notions through its affiliation with a program aimed at providing a deterministic explanation of disease.[23] The demand for a "physiological," "rational," or "scientific" medicine was at the same time the command that medicine become a causal science based on knowledge of the natural laws governing organic disfunction. Implicit in this program was a firm belief in the regularity and predictability of the phenomena of life and disease. Given this conviction, an ontological notion had to be rejected, for it maintained that an entity could exist within the sick individual, following its own course of development and inducing the host organs to function contrary to their nature. This is the argument that Henle presented in the third essay of the *Pathologische Untersuchungen,* and it is evident that he, like Tiedemann before him, was working completely within the teleomechanical tradition.[24]

Central to Henle's discussion of the mechanism by which an organism becomes ill was the notion of an organizing principle. The "type," like the teleomechanist's *Lebenskraft,* determined the lawful development and, consequently, the particular form of an organism.[25] Subject to the laws of physics and chemistry, the type was nevertheless responsible for the outcome that the semiautonomous structures and organs of the body functioned together to form an integrated whole. Like Tiedemann and the teleomechanists, moreover, Henle did not define life merely as the expression of the type but emphasized the role played by the environment in providing the materials, such as nutrients, oxygen, and heat, necessary for the development and maintenance of the organism's activities. It was through the interaction of the type with its environment that life came into being and continued to exist.

Through this interaction the organism could, moreover, also become ill. In fact it was because of the dependence of the organism on the environment that disease was at all possible. As Henle explained,

> If the organism, the germ, were to carry within itself all the conditions for developing according to its idea [that is, type], then deviations would not be possible. But since these conditions are in part external and independent of it, the possibility exists that it will deviate from the idea, and this is the most general concept of disease.[26]

Given that disease resulted from the interaction of the type with the environment, there should be, logically speaking, two mechanisms whereby deviations could occur. Either the type could respond abnormally to stimuli or the external stimuli could be responsible for the deviations. But Henle denied the first option, arguing that a *"Typus irregularis"* would be a *"contradicto in adjecto."*[27] The type, by definition, determined the lawful expression of life's activities. Without this assumption of lawfulness, the entire teleomechanical framework would in fact collapse, because if the phenomena of life followed no rules, then a scientific approach to the study of these phenomena would be impossible. Similarly, the science of pathology depended on the predictability of the disease process, and this was guaranteed by a definition of disease as the response of the "typically organized body" to abnormal conditions, where the lawfulness of the type is given.

> What degree of mechanical or chemical stimulation a being can tolerate without danger, how it is changed through these [stimulations], how long it takes for the normal structure and composition—as far as it is possible—to become healthy again, all this depends upon the original organization of the being and thus, leaving out the breadth of individual fluctuations, upon the type. If, however, the reactions are typical, then so are diseases, because disease is founded . . . in the altered formative activities of the organism in consequence of external influences that the body cannot keep in control.[28]

A parasitic notion of disease, where the pathological symptoms would be seen as the expression of a distinct disease entity or, worse yet, as an entity itself, must be denied if one accepts the lawfulness of the type.[29] The idea of a foreign entity carrying out its own life's functions within the affected organism cannot be made consistent with the belief in order and purpose implicit in the notion of the type. This is not to deny that contagions or miasmas could cause disease. The first essay in the *Pathologische Untersuchungen* argued this very point. But they would only be the stimuli for a set of physiological reactions, not the disease itself. The latter was, and could only be, the normal physiological reactions of an organism confronted by abnormal external conditions. As Henle would point out in a later work, "either this principle is correct, or scientific medicine is a chimera."[30]

In his letter to the state ministry, Henle suggested the advantage of this definition of disease. It permitted one to apply the knowledge acquired from anatomy and physiology to the study of the phenomena of disease, thereby helping to bridge the gap between the theoretical and clinical sciences. Furthermore, Henle stated explicitly that this should be done through the use of the microscope. Having demonstrated its value in the study of life's normal functions, this instrument would now be used in pathology, allowing one to probe beneath the symptoms to investigate the disturbed organic function.

Henle did not get Hufeland's position, but in 1840 was offered the chair of anatomy in Zurich.[31] Although he would have preferred to remain in Berlin, it had become clear to him that relying on lectures without being "a full professor" would not lead anywhere. But Henle had ambitions and in a letter to his friend, A. Schöll, he wrote frankly that he saw this position as temporary. His aspirations were to return to Germany, and preferably to Berlin, and he expressed confidence that "the time is not so far away when we will both be rather 'desirable objects' for every university and will, to some extent, have our pick."[32] Henle's prognosis, at least for himself, was correct. In 1842 Tübingen offered him a position, in 1844 Heidelberg, in 1852 Göttingen, and in 1858 Berlin. His success relied on his reputation as a good scientist, an excellent teacher, and a leader in microscopical research and medical reform, and it was a reputation that he, through pedagogy and polemic, had helped to popularize.

Henle's Years in Zurich, 1840–1844

Henle began teaching at the University of Zurich in the winter semester of 1840. In the four years he spent there he continued to promote microscopical studies among his students. This included courses in microscopical investigations as well as prize questions that required use of the instrument. In his own research he also continued to emphasize the microscope. This came out clearly in this first textbook, *Allgemeine Anatomie,* completed in 1841. "General anatomy," he wrote, "is today primarily microscopical anatomy," and the subject of its study is the tissue.[33] This certainly did not mean that Henle viewed the tissue as an anatomical structure alone, but rather as a functional unit as well. Here one can see Henle's allegiance to the histological tradition of the French scientist Xavier Bichat. But Henle's book, as a contemporary reviewer pointed out, differed from Bichat's in both the amount of information and "in the starting points, in the methods, and in the tools for research. Bichat had made use of the knife and chemical reagents, but Henle had applied the microscope, thus being able to go beyond Bichat's 21 tissues to an analysis of the structure of these organic forms."[34]

The text consisted of two parts. The first, on the fluid components of the human organism, was primarily a summary of the textbooks of Jöns Jacob Berzelius, C. J. Loewig, and F. Simon on organic chemistry, although Henle occasionally corrected the chemical knowledge through microscopical investigations. The second and major section of the book focused on the solid parts of the body. After a brief introduction to the history of histology, Henle offered a manual for the use of the microscope in which he described new developments in the construction of the instrument, discussed different combinations of lenses and various sources of lighting for attaining optimal effects, explained how to identify and avoid optical illusions, and offered advice on the preparation of samples, on chemical and microscopical experiments, and on micrometers.[35]

In this textbook Henle used the microscope to reinterpret organic form and development in light of the recent cell theory, bringing isolated discoveries together into a rational system. With this as his goal, he analyzed all the tissues of the body, offering for each a description of its structure and function, a comparative study of its presence in the animal kingdom, and a critical history of research done on the tissues to date. As a comprehensive histological compendium, this text surpassed all previous works. Moreover, it went beyond the study of healthy tissues and included references to the pathology of these structures as well. As Henle explained in the introduction:

> The physiology of the tissue provides the foundation for a general or rational pathology that seeks to understand disease processes and symptoms as the lawful reactions of organic matter endowed with specific and intrinsic [*eigenthümliche und unveräußerliche*] forces toward abnormal external influences. I have not let any opportunity pass to indicate, albeit only briefly, the consequences that follow from the principles developed here for the understanding of diseased processes.[36]

By considering the physiology of the tissue as the foundation of a general pathology, Henle was seeking to contribute to recent attempts at a "pathological physiology." The expression, appearing for the first time in the writings of the French anatomist Antoine Portal, had acquired popularity through the work of Xavier Bichat, Jean Corvisart, and François Magendie.[37] Localizing the disease process in the tissues of the organism, these physiologists had gone beyond pathological anatomy to a study of the structural and functional changes thàt described the pathological process. Popular in France in the 1820s and 1830s, pathological physiology began to flourish in Germany one decade later, finding its most vocal advocates in Henle, Rudolf Virchow, and Carl Wunderlich. As we will see, each began publishing his own journal in the 1840s dedicated to creating a medical science based on this physiological approach to the study of disease. Henle's *Allgemeine Anatomie,* a book that was, according to the author, aimed at the "young, animated, and as yet independent," was an early step in this direction.[38]

Henle's hopes that his reform ideas would bring about a change in medical practice drew strength from a clinician he worked closely with in Zurich. Karl Pfeufer, who had studied under Johannes Schönlein in Würzburg and later worked as his assistant, was highly skilled in the modern clinical techniques of percussion, auscultation, and chemical analysis. Of particular importance for their joint work, moreover, was Pfeufer's fundamental belief in the value of physiology, and especially of pharmacology, for practical medicine. "I found in him," wrote Henle, "a man who is young and energetic enough to throw aside the old beaten track and accept my views. A man, as I need him to be."[39]

Karl Pfeufer (1806–1869)

Karl Pfeufer, a physician's son, had begun his university studies in Bamberg, unsure whether to follow in his father's footsteps or pursue his love for literature.[40] It was only after he transferred to Würzburg in 1825 that he decided in favor of medicine. From Pfeufer's letters to his father it is evident that Johannes Schönlein, then professor of special pathology and therapeutics, had inspired him to make this choice. Schönlein, whose name is associated with the natural historical school in German medicine, was responsible for introducing the new French diagnostic methods of auscultation, percussion, and pathological anatomy into the German clinics.[41] This methodological shift in clinical medicine would become a central issue in Pfeufer's later lectures and publications.

In 1828 Pfeufer became Schönlein's clinical assistant and began instructing students in the use of the stethoscope.[42] This instrument, invented by René Laennec in 1816, had changed medical diagnostics drastically, freeing physicians from their previous dependence on gross physical symptoms and patients' accounts of their own ailments. Like the microscope, which had exposed a previously unseen world to the scientist's gaze, the stethoscope permitted physicians to hear what still remained hidden from sight. It thus provided physicians with what seemed to be more objective information about the internal organic changes accompanying the diseased state (although the interpretation of this information often remained disputed).[43] What is interesting is that Pfeufer, not Schönlein, offered this instruction. As in the case of Henle and Müller, a generational difference existed in the pedagogical evaluation of scientific instruments. Pfeufer taught in Schönlein's clinic until he received the M.D. in 1831, passed the state medical examination, and moved to Munich to set up private practice. In the next twelve years Pfeufer tried repeatedly to get a position as *Privatdozent* at the university in Munich, but to no avail. Although both the philosopher Friedrich Wilhelm Schelling and the clinician Philipp von Walther supported these endeavors, Johann Ringseis, then professor in the medical faculty and government advisor, vetoed every application, with political and religious differences seeming to have been the determining factor. In 1840, when Zurich offered Pfeufer a professorship in clinical medicine, he asked once more about his chances of getting a position in Munich; obtaining a discouraging reply, he set off for Switzerland.

One month after arriving in Zurich Pfeufer held an inaugural address entitled "On the Present Condition of Medicine."[44] In this speech the young professor characterized German, French, and British medicine, discussing the advantages and disadvantages of each. The Germans, he claimed, placed a correct emphasis on careful observations, causal connections, and therapeutics but had too great a tendency to speculate. This trait he attributed to the absence of a clear methodology for investigating the disease process, and advised the Germans to learn from the French, who had already brought a high level of objectivity to diagnosis through the use of the stethoscope, pleximeter, uterine speculum, and vaccination. Pfeufer also credited his neighbors with having integrated pathological anatomy into the clinic, bringing it into closer contact with observations made at the bedside. Nonetheless he had a few words of criticism for the French, arguing that they confused goals and means. Diagnostic techniques and pathological anatomy, he explained, were not ends in themselves but merely methods for uncovering the nature of the disease process—the first step on the way to healing. In short, the Germans had the proper goal but overlooked the way to get there, whereas the French had the means but mistakenly believed it to be the goal.

Like Henle, Pfeufer focused his attention on the need for a method that would permit the scientific investigation of the disease process. To this end he placed great emphasis on diagnostic techniques and scientific research, arguing that a solid foundation in medicine would be acquired only when "the anatomical and physiological character of a disease are placed in a true light."[45] But the fight to reform medicine through the introduction of "objective" scientific methods had a significance over and above the increase in knowledge that would be gained. As Pfeufer pointed out in his speech:

> Since the first appearance of the *Traité de l'Auscultation,* in which Laennec— this Herschel of the human thorax—published his discovery, the doctrine of the diseases of the organs of respiration has made greater progress than in the previous thousand years. With this a new era in objective diagnostics begins, in which the less gifted can also diagnose such diseases whose diagnosis previously was a sort of private possession (although still very unsure) of a few brilliant men.[46]

The demand for "objective" methods in medicine was more than a fight for techniques that would allow the physician to distance himself from "subjective" patient accounts and collect information on his own. The new diagnostic methods would, presumably, also bring about a transformation in the definition of what it meant to be a physician—that is, in the qualifications expected of doctors. Knowledge of routine methods, such as microscopy, auscultation, and percussion, would replace talent and intuition as the basis for action. The shift from Tiedemann's focus on the "philosophical genius" needs emphasis; here the scientific method is presented as a tool that would allow "less gifted" scientific physicians to join the medical elite dominated at the time by only a few "brilliant" men. As we will see in the next chapter, Henle and Pfeufer developed their medical reform program with these democratizing principles in mind. It is not difficult to imagine the appeal this would have had for medical students and young physicians in the years of political turmoil leading up to the Revolution of 1848.

Henle, the anatomist qua pathologist, and Pfeufer, the clinician, formed a formidable team during the years they were together in Zurich. During this time Henle came to realize that the reform of medicine could be brought about only through the combined efforts of the theoretical and clinical sciences. He gave this conviction clear expression in 1842 when the University of Tübingen offered him a teaching position. During the negotiations Henle emphasized that his past success had come about because he had both learned and taught how to apply the methods of physiology to the study of diseased conditions. But, he added, in order to remain effective in this area

I am dependent more than others upon the cooperation and advice of the clinical teacher. Only with the approval of the latter could I teach with enthusiastic confidence. For my audience to find fruitful the things which I communicate to them . . . depends, because I do not practice, upon the extent to which the head of the clinical institute allows me to participate in his observations.[47]

As Henle was negotiating with Tübingen, Pfeufer received an offer from Heidelberg. The university had finally decided to hire a pathologist to replace Friedrich Christian Sebastian, who had died in 1840. Originally, the administration had hoped that Friedrich Puchelt could cover both his own and Sebastian's courses, but this had not worked out. In 1842 Friedrich Tiedemann wrote to Pfeufer to find out whether he would consider coming to Heidelberg.[48]

Pfeufer responded in early August. He showed an interest in the position, but made his acceptance conditional on a salary of 1800 gulden and the possession of his own polyclinic, independent of the clinics of Puchelt and the surgeon Maximilian Chelius.[49] The university did not at first agree to these conditions, presumably because of doubts voiced by the two older clinicians, but von Stengel succeeded in bringing them around. By that time, however, Pfeufer had reevaluated the situation. As he wrote in January to von Stengel, he had decided to decline the offer because of his fear that it would take years before a third clinic would flourish in Heidelberg. Moreover, he realized that a polyclinic could never be a substitute for the hospital he had in Zurich.[50]

Pfeufer may also have had a change of heart because Henle had decided, in December, to turn down Tübingen's offer and remain in Zurich.[51] Perhaps the two men had decided that the advantages of working together were too great to forego. Whether this was their intent or not, they soon had the opportunity to leave Zurich as a team. In October 1843 Heidelberg changed its strategy and offered positions to both men. Theodor Bischoff, associate professor of anatomy and physiology at Heidelberg, had recently left, and von Stengel decided to raise the position to a full professorship and offer it to Henle. In November Henle and Pfeufer both agreed to accept the offers if certain conditions were met. This time Pfeufer requested, in addition to his own polyclinic, sixteen beds in the stationary clinic and a yearly budget of 800 gulden. Henle demanded that he be granted the same rights as Tiedemann to the anatomical institute, and even part of the directorship. In December the university agreed to these demands, and later in the month both men expressed their interest in the new positions. On 17 January 1844 they were officially hired.[52]

During these negotiations Henle kept up a lively correspondence with his acquaintance Philipp Jolly, who was assistant professor of physics in Heidelberg. In his letters, Jolly mentioned several times that the government had great hopes that he and Pfeufer would breathe new life into the old and unpopular medical faculty. The Baden government was searching for teachers qualified in the new scientific methods who would be able to draw medical students to Heidelberg, and in these two men the state found the perfect team. Not only were they skilled in modern techniques, whether in the laboratory working with the microscope or at the bedside doing percussion and auscultation, but they both had outstanding reputations as teachers. Their wit, youth, liberal views, and the polemical tone of their writings made them immediate favorites among students and younger colleagues involved in the political and social unrest of the forties. As Jolly wrote to Henle,

> I only wish that you and your friend Pfeufer . . . could hear the tone that is dominating among the students since your appointment became known. I have already heard from many who were set on ending their studies at Easter that they want to remain on for at least one semester.[53]

Not only did many students remain, but many more came to Heidelberg specifically to study with Henle and Pfeufer. In the very first year after their appointment enrollment increased from 107 to 147. Among the forty additional students, only three were from Baden. The rest came from other German and European lands, and this at a time when every other German university was experiencing declining enrollments.[54] Heidelberg had made a good choice.

Notes

1. Ministry of interior to the state ministry, 21 November 1832, BGLA 235/3133.

2. Theodor Bischoff, *Gedächtnißrede auf Friedrich Tiedemann. Vorgetragen in der öffentlichen Sitzung der königlichen Akademie der Wissenschaften am 28 November 1861* (Munich, 1861), p. 17. See also the letter from Tiedemann to the state ministry, 23 December 1837, BGLA 205/524.

3. Ministry of interior to the state ministry, 21 November 1832, BGLA 235/3133. It should be mentioned that Puchelt had been very popular as a clinical teacher in the 1830s. He had even promoted the use of auscultation and percussion. See Werner Goth, *Zur Geschichte der Klinik in Heidelberg im 19. Jahrhundert* (Diss. Heidelberg, 1982), pp. 91, 93.

4. Statistics have been compiled from enrollment reports printed every year in *RB*, 1830–1843. For the introduction of the new techniques into the clinics, see Konrad Kläß, *Die Einführung besonderer Kurse für Mikroskopie und physikalische Diagnostik (Perkussion und Auskultation) in den medizinischen Unterricht an deutschen Universitäten im 19. Jahrhundert* (Diss. Göttingen, 1971). "Foreign" students are those who were not from the state of Baden.

5. Biographical information is from Friedrich Merkel, *Jacob Henle. Ein deutsches Gelehrtenleben* (Braunschweig, 1891); W. Waldeyer, "J. Henle. Nachruf," *Archiv für mikroscopische Anatomie*, 26 (1886): i–xxxii; Erich Hintzsche, "Friedrich Gustav Jacob Henle," *DSB*, 6 (1972): 268–270. Henle's father, a merchant and a Jew, converted to Protestantism in 1821, and Henle, whose school education focused on classical and modern languages, had considered strengthening this conversion by becoming a minister.

6. Cited in Hermann Hoepke, "Jakob Henles Briefe aus seiner Heidelberger Studentenzeit (26 April 1830–Januar 1831)," *Heidelberger Jahrbücher*, 11 (1967): 40–56, here p. 52.

7. Idem, "Der Bonner Student Jakob Henle in seinem Verhältnis zu Johannes Müller," *Sudhoffs Archiv*, 53 (1969): 193–261, here pp. 197–199.

8. Kläß, *Die Einführung besonderer Kurse für Mikroskopie*, pp. 53, 245. Also Merkel, *Jacob Henle*, pp. 154–155; Waldeyer, "J. Henle. Nachruf," p. iii. Henle claimed that he was the first to bring a microscope into the classroom. See Hermann Hoepke, "Jakob Henles Gutachten zur Besetzung des Lehrstuhls für Anatomie an der Universität Berlin 1883," *Anatomischer Anzeiger*, 102,8 (1967): 221–232.

9. For information on early microscopes, see E. Hintzsche, "Das Mikroskop," *Ciba Zeitschrift*, 115 (1949): 4238–4268; K. Fischer, "Die Utrechter Mikroskope," *Zeitschrift für Instrumentenkunde*, 55 (1935): 239–300; Viktor Patzelt, "Die Bedeutung des Wiener Optikers Simon Plössl für die Mikroskope," *Mikroskopie*, 2 (1946): 1–64; Josef Holzl et al., "Simon Plössl—Optiker und Mechaniker in Wien," *Blätter für Technikgeschichte (Wien)*, 31 (1969): 82; S. Bradbury, *The Evolution of the Microscope* (Oxford and New York, 1967), pp. 174, 200.

10. J. Henle, "Theodor Schwann. Nachruf," *Archiv für mikroscopische Anatomie*, 21 (1882): i–xlix, here p. ii.

11. From a report from the Dorpat prosector Friedrich Bidder, written after his visit to Berlin in 1834. Reprinted in "Vor hundert Jahren im Laboratorium Johannes Müllers," *Münchener medizinische Wochenschrift*, 82 (1934): 60–64.

12. Ibid., p. 63.

13. Ibid., p. 62.

14. Albert von Kölliker, *Erinnerungen aus meinem Leben* (Leipzig, 1899), p. 8.

15. Hermann Hoepke, "Jakob Henles Briefe aus Berlin 1834–1840," *Heidelberger Jahrbücher*, 8 (1964): 57–86, here p. 60; Merkel, *Jacob Henle*, p. 156; Max Lenz, *Geschichte der königlichen Friedrich-Wilhelms-Universität zu Berlin*, 4 vols. in 5 (Halle, 1910–1918), vol. 2, pt. 1, pp. 452–453.

16. Henle to A. Schöll, 30 April 1840, Personalakte Professor Henle, Universitätsarchiv Göttingen.

17. Henle to the state ministry, 31 August 1839, Darmstaedter collection, SPK 3c1844(4).

18. William Coleman, *Biology in the Nineteenth Century: Problems of Form, Function, and Transformation* (Cambridge, 1977), chap. 2.

19. Jacob Henle, "Ueber Schleim- und Eiterbildung und ihr Verhältnis zur Oberhaut," *Journal der practischen Arzneykunde und Wundarzneykunst (Hufelands Journal)*, 86,8 (1838): 3–62.

20. Jacob Henle, *Pathologische Untersuchungen* (Berlin, 1840), p. iv.

21. Jacob Henle, "Von den Miasmen und Contagien," in *Pathologische Untersuchungen*, pp. 1–82. Because of this article Henle is often seen as one of the earliest proponents of a germ theory of disease. (See George Rosen's English translation of this essay in his article, "Jacob Henle: On Miasmata and Contagia," *Bulletin of the Institute of the History of Medicine*, 6 (1938): 907–983. Rosen has added an introduction to his translation in which he discusses the significance of Henle's work in terms of the bacteriological revolution.) It must, however, be pointed out that although Henle believed that living organisms could stimulate the disease process, he never accepted an ontological definition of disease. In this regard his views

differed radically from those of Robert Koch and others who argued for discrete disease entities.

22. Owsei Temkin, "The Scientific Approach to Disease: Specific Entity and Individual Sickness," in *The Double Face of Janus* (Baltimore, 1977), pp. 441–454; idem, "Health and Disease," in *Dictionary of the History of Ideas,* ed. Philip Wiener, 4 vols. (New York, 1973–74), vol. 2, pp. 395–407; Guenter Risse, "Health and Disease: History of the Concepts," in *Encyclopedia of Bioethics,* ed. Warren T. Reich, 4 vols. (New York, 1978), vol. 2, pp. 579–585.

23. The deterministic implications of the demand in the 1840s for a physiological, rational, or scientific medicine are discussed by William Coleman in "Experimental Physiology and Statistical Inference: The Therapeutic Trial in Nineteenth-Century Germany," in *The Probabilistic Revolution,* ed. Lorenz Krüger et al., 2 vols. (Cambridge, Mass., 1987), vol. 2, pp. 201–226.

24. See Chapter 1 of this book, p. 21.

25. Jacob Henle, "Ueber Verlauf und Periodicität der Krankheit," in *Pathologische Untersuchungen,* pp. 166–205. Henle's discussion of the "type" is found on pp. 170–182.

26. Ibid., p. 183.

27. Ibid., p. 179.

28. Ibid., pp. 170–171.

29. Ibid., pp. 166, 184.

30. Idem, *Handbuch der rationellen Pathologie,* 2 vols. (Braunschweig, 1846–1853), vol. 1, p. 93.

31. Guido Gozzi, *Jakob Henles Zürcher Jahre, 1840–1844,* (Zürcher medizingeschichtliche Abhandlungen, Neue Reihe Nr. 103) (Zurich, 1974).

32. Henle to A. Schöll, 30 April 1840, Personalakte Professor Henle, Universitätsarchiv Göttingen.

33. Jacob Henle, *Allgemeine Anatomie* (Leipzig, 1841), here p. 131.

34. Cited in Merkel, *Jacob Henle,* pp. 192–193.

35. Henle, *Allgemeine Anatomie,* pp. 131–149.

36. Ibid., p. vii.

37. Erwin H. Ackerknecht, *Rudolf Virchow. Arzt, Politiker, Anthropologe* (Stuttgart, 1957), p. 42. Also John E. Lesch, *Science and Medicine in France. The Emergence of Experimental Physiology, 1790–1855* (Cambridge, Mass., 1984), chap. 8.

38. Cited in Merkel, *Jacob Henle,* p. 190.

39. Cited in ibid., p. 167.

40. Biographical information is from Josef Kerschensteiner, *Das Leben und Wirken des Dr. Carl von Pfeufer* (Augsburg, 1871).

41. Johanna Bleker, *Die Naturhistorische Schule, 1825–1845. Ein Beitrag zur Geschichte der klinischen Medizin in Deutschland* (Stuttgart, 1981).

42. Kerschensteiner, *Das Leben und Wirken des Dr. Carl von Pfeufer,* p. 9.

43. Stanley Joel Reiser, *Medicine and the Reign of Technology* (Cambridge, 1978), chap. 2; Michel Foucault, *The Birth of the Clinic* (New York, 1975).

44. Carl Pfeufer, "Ueber den gegenwärtigen Zustand der Medizin. Rede gehalten bei dem Antritt des klinischen Lehramts in Zürich den 7 November 1840," reprinted in *Annalen der städtischen allgemeinen Krankenhäuser in München,* 1 (1878): 395–406. The following paragraph is drawn from pp. 398–403.

45. Ibid., p. 400.

46. Ibid., p. 402. For a discussion of the change in pedagogy from "transmis-

sion and apprenticeship" to the "application of the so-called scientific method," see Hans H. Simmer, "Principles and Problems of Medical Undergraduate Education in Germany during the Nineteenth and Early Twentieth Centuries," in *The History of Medical Education*, ed. C. D. O'Mally (Berkeley, 1970), pp. 173–200.

47. Henle to the chancellor of Tübingen University, 21 November 1842, cited in Gozzi, *Jakob Henles Zürcher Jahre*, p. 55.

48. Although I have not found a copy of the original letter from Tiedemann to Pfeufer, Pfeufer addresses two letters to Tiedemann on the 2nd and 11th of August 1842, in BGLA 235/3133.

49. Ibid.

50. Von Stengel to Pfeufer, 15 December 1842; Pfeufer to von Stengel, 2 January 1843; von Stengel to Pfeufer, 11 January 1843; Pfeufer to von Stengel, 26 January 1843, all in BGLA 235/3133.

51. Henle to "Euer Hochwohlgeboren" (probably the university chancellor), 16 December 1842, cited in Gozzi, *Jakob Henles Zürcher Jahre*, pp. 60–62.

52. Ministry of interior to faculty senate, 31 October 1843; Henle to von Stengel, 9 November 1843; Report of meeting between von Stengel and medical faculty, 19 November 1843; Jolly to Henle, 29 November 1843; Ministry of interior to Pfeufer and Henle, 5 December 1843; Henle to von Stengel, 18 December 1843; Pfeufer to von Stengel, 20 December 1843, all in BGLA 235/3133.

53. Cited in Goth, *Zur Geschichte der Klinik*, p. 128. The link between Henle's and Pfeufer's medical reform program and the broader political and social developments of the 1840s is discussed in more detail in Chapter 4.

54. Reinhard Riese, *Die Hochschule auf dem Wege zum wissenschaftlichen Großbetrieb* (Stuttgart, 1977), pp. 23–24; Franz Eulenberg, *Die Frequenz der deutschen Universitäten von ihrer Gründung bis zur Gegenwart* (Leipzig, 1904), p. 255.

4

Scientific Medicine at the University of Heidelberg— the 1840s

Baden's decision to hire Jacob Henle and Karl Pfeufer signified more than a commitment to improving the medical faculty; it also reflected a change in the kind of education the state wanted to support. As we saw in Chapter 2, the Baden government had begun to place greater emphasis, backed by increased funding, on practical training in the sciences, seeing this as important both for modernizing the economy and refining the critical faculties of the mind. The reforms of the 1830s were originally confined to the secondary and technical schools, exerting only a minor influence on the universities. But by the 1840s the institutions of higher learning could no longer remain isolated from the broader social and economic developments transforming society; in this decade the government began to direct its attention to changing the content and structure of university education as well.

Historians of German science have tended to overlook the 1840s, focusing instead on the construction of impressive research and teaching institutes in the second half of the century. Yet the 1840s, I wish to argue, marked a significant "protophase" in the history of Germany's interest in, and support for, the medical sciences. Several states not only increased their university's budget during this period, earmarking most of this money for the improvement of existing scientific and medical collections, they also began to allocate specific discretionary funds for the remodeling and expansion of scientific institutes and clinical facilities.[1] These institutional and financial developments did not occur in an intellectual vacuum. Parliaments, university administrators, and professors continued to wrangle with each other and among themselves over the social function of the university. In the 1840s, moreover, academically trained physicians entered these debates in full force, joining together in a national movement for the reform of medicine that made one of its central goals the reform of university education. Henle and Pfeufer were among these physicians. Indeed, they were two of the movement's leaders, arguing from their positions of power within the university for the need to complement theoretical instruction with practical exercises in the laboratory and at the bedside.

This chapter explores the changes in medical education at the University of Heidelberg in the 1840s that laid the groundwork for the foundation of large-scale teaching and research institutes later in the century. These changes included the improvement of existing medical institutes and the construction of new ones; they involved curricula innovations designed to introduce students to scientific and clinical techniques; they were, in turn, accompanied by intellectual debates that focused on the reform of both medicine and the university. Such developments were not peculiar to Heidelberg, yet local events had an impact nonetheless. As we will see in the final section of this chapter, Henle and Pfeufer proved particularly skillful at exploiting the overwhelmingly liberal atmosphere at the university to carry out their reform plans in a swift and expedient fashion.

The Construction of New Medical and Scientific Facilities

As we have seen in Chapter 2, the government and medical faculty planned in 1835 to expand the clinical facilities after the psychiatric asylum moved out of the old Jesuit college.[2] When the move finally took place in 1843, renovation of the building began immediately. In the interim eight years, estimated costs for construction had increased from 5,000 to over 23,000 gulden, but the government supported the plan nonetheless.[3] By the end of the year construction was complete. The four-story building had space for an auditorium, administrative offices, a surgical assistant, and a dissection room on the first floor; a surgical clinic with forty beds on the second; and a medical clinic with seventy beds on the third and the possibility of another one hundred beds on the fourth floor. In 1844, the arrangement was modified when Pfeufer arrived; he received the west wing of the medical clinic with sixteen beds and several smaller rooms.[4]

Aside from the clinical facilities, other scientific institutes were also in need of improvement. Since 1818 chemistry, mineralogy, zoology, anatomy, and botany were all housed together in the old Dominican cloister, and by the mid-1840s the situation had become unbearable. In 1845 Leopold Gmelin, professor of chemistry, explained that lectures accompanied by experiments no longer provided an adequate education. As he wrote to the university curator, "The young chemists, in order to gain a practical education, want to use their own hands everyday."[5] Pfeufer, who began very early to demand more beds for his own section of the medical clinic, also argued along these lines. In a letter to the state ministry defending the young clinician's demands, the curator of the university, Josef Alexander Dahmen, emphasized Pfeufer's claim that the manner in which the clinical sciences were now carried out

> is no longer satisfied with scholarly argumentations of theory but rather applies itself totally to materials, demonstrations, independent observations and practice. [Consequently], the necessary material is lacking, and with ever increasing enrollment, will be lacking more and more.[6]

The two men, Pfeufer and Dahmen, sought to convince the government that with new institutes, particularly a new hospital, anatomy institute, museum for the natural historical collections, and chemical and physical laboratories, Heidelberg would rank among the best universities in Germany, would "soon attract over 1,000 students," and would probably be surpassed in enrollment only by Berlin.[7]

The government did not need much convincing. After Dahmen and the medical faculty met to discuss plans for a new anatomy institute that would include a room specifically for microscopical investigations, they sent the entire plan to Karlsruhe for approval.[8] At the budget meeting in April the ministry of interior presented these plans to the lower chamber of parliament, explaining that the old building lacked adequate space, had insufficient equipment, and could not meet the needs of physiology. By the ministry's estimate the new institute would cost 51,000 gulden, and it requested that these funds be allotted immediately.[9]

In addition to approving plans for a new anatomy institute, the ministry of interior also acknowledged the need to provide better facilities for zoology and chemistry. Specifically, it suggested that the old Dominican cloister be renovated for this purpose after anatomy moved out. Zoology, in desperate need of more room for its collections, could then take over the old anatomy gallery, and chemistry, which needed space where "students could perform chemical experiments themselves," could occupy the remaining rooms. Expected costs were 16,000 gulden for zoology and 10,000 for chemistry, bringing the total costs for the new science institutes to 77,000 gulden.[10]

The parliamentary representatives responded favorably to these plans, praising the government for its interest in improving "those institutes which have a particularly practical value."[11] On 3 September they approved 65,000 gulden for immediate use in construction.[12]

According to the new plans, anatomy would occupy the first floor with a large lecture hall (1254 sq. ft.), a room for the anatomical collection, a dissection room (1280 sq. ft.), a smaller lecture room for physiology and microscopical anatomy (600 sq. ft.), a small kitchen with running water, three rooms for equipment, and workrooms for the directors of anatomy, physiology, and surgery, and for the prosector and physiology assistant. On the second floor, zoology would have space for the zoological collection (680 sq. ft.), a lecture room (600 sq. ft.), and rooms for the conservator, director, microscopical observations, and materials. According to Hermann Hoepke, the institute, completed in 1849, was the first in Germany with its own auditorium and with all the necessary equipment for research and instruction.[13]

As a result of these arrangements, construction of a chemistry laboratory was made dependent on completion of the anatomy institute. In the interim, however, the plans broadened from a discussion of chemistry alone to the consideration of a complete natural science institute for chemistry, physics, mineralogy, technology, and archaeology. Improved laboratory space, more room for the presentation of scientific collections, larger auditoriums, and the possibility of live-in quarters for the professors played a central role in the discussions.[14] Furthermore, there was interest that this building serve the public good as well as the university. Members of the government's building and economics commission spoke out strongly in favor of opening the scientific collections to the public. It would be desirable, they wrote to the university curator, "if the building would be used not only for the lessons of the individual professors, but would be considered as a public institute as well, being open to the public at specified hours."[15]

The decision to construct new scientific institutes thus reflected a complex set of interests. As Joseph Ben-David, Avraham Zloczower, and R. Steven Turner have argued, faculty demands for adequate laboratory facilities, combined with government concern with enrollment and the prestige of the university, provided major incentives. Universities had come to symbolize the intellectual power of the state, and Germany's decentralized university system allowed professors to take advantage of this commitment to intellectual life to make demands that may have gone unheeded had the university system been centralized. (Indeed, such demands were being ignored in other countries that lacked a competitive university system.) But Baden's competition with other states for the best professors and the most students does not tell the entire story. Professors did not make demands that reflected their own needs alone; they presented arguments that appealed to the government by promising to teach students specific techniques and a method of problem-solving that many believed would best prepare future generations for the problems up ahead. But even more to the point, the government was not merely a passive participant in this process; indeed, pressure for new scientific and clinical institutes often came from individuals within the government ministries, as with Nebenius and Dahmen. And as we have seen, parliament's rapid approval of funds and its tendency to view the new institutes as public institutions, much like a museum or a library, suggests the extent to which the construction of new science and medical facilities reflected broader social, economic, and cultural changes occurring at the time.

The clinical facilities and anatomical institute were completed in 1847, but the grandiose plans for a natural science institute did not come immediately to fruition. As we will see in the following chapters, a number of events contributed to this delay, the most important being the social and political unrest of the late 1840s that directed the government's attention and funds to measures of a more immediate and pragmatic nature. Nevertheless, the interim period was by no means stagnant. The greater emphasis on scientific knowledge and instrumental techniques that informed educational reforms since the 1830s did not abate. It is true that large laboratories would not be built until the 1850s; nevertheless, by that time new chairs for the experimental sciences existed, the university owned large collections of instruments, and course instruction had been radically altered. Thus, the construction of large research institutes, which historians and sociologists of science have traditionally used as the primary measure of state commitment to the experimental sciences, marked the creation of an institutional home for a methodological approach to the study of nature that had long been in use.

Laboratory Instruction at the University of Heidelberg

In addition to improving the medical and clinical facilities, the University of Heidelberg expanded its medical staff, permitting the number of *Privatdozenten* to triple in size (from three to nine between 1840 and 1848).[16] It was primarily these young lecturers, along with a couple of younger professors, who introduced the new scientific methods into the curriculum. As early as 1841, for example, two courses were offered that permitted students to learn the new techniques of auscultation and percussion, one in connection with semiotics, taught by the *Privatdozent* Benno Puchelt, and the other in obstetrics, offered by the assistant professor Franz Josef Nägeli. One year later the semiotics course included instruction in chemical and microscopical investigations. By 1844 six practically oriented courses were available to the students, five taught by young lecturers and one by Nägeli. The techniques ranged from microscopical exercises to auscultation and percussion as aids in diagnosis. By the late 1840s between five and nine courses were offered every semester emphasizing "practical exercises," "microscopical exercises," "practical use," or simply "prakticum."

Heidelberg was by no means alone in making this transition. In the late 1830s and 1840s microscopical observations and demonstrations in anatomy and physiology courses became a part of the curriculum in every German medical faculty, and by 1850 fourteen of the nineteen universities were offering practical exercises in the use of the microscope. Of more importance, between 1845 and 1855 fifteen medical faculties also began including microscopical demonstrations in their courses on pathology, histology, semiotics, and diagnostics, and in ten of the universities practical microscopical exercises in these subjects had begun.[17]

This was a transition, as we have seen, for which Henle had fought, and beginning in 1846 he and his assistant Bruch offered a course every semester entitled "Exercises in the Use of the Microscope."[18] Of most importance to Henle was that each student have his own instrument with which to work. With only three microscopes initially at their disposal, Henle and Bruch decided to contribute their private instruments to the collection, raising the total to five. However, in the first semester over twenty students signed up for the course, and the two instructors had to divide the class into three groups to ensure that each student could work with his own microscope. Surprised at the large turnout, Henle wrote immediately to the curator requesting money for more instruments. At first he received only 175 gulden—probably just enough for one microscope—but repeated requests throughout the years permitted him to acquire eleven microscopes by the time of his departure in 1852.[19]

In 1850 Henle and Bruch expanded their course to include "physiological experiments." Unfortunately, little is known about the nature of these experiments, but it can be surmised from the list of instruments in the institute's collection that nothing more than the simplest vivisectional experiments could have been carried out. Other than the eleven microscopes just mentioned, the institute possessed one galvanometer (for measuring small electric currents), one balance, two thermometers, and a series of knives and instruments for cutting nerves and bones.[20]

Nevertheless it is clear that more than mere demonstration was going on, at least during the microscopical exercises. Given that each student had his own instrument, it may be assumed that he was being taught to work with the microscope, learning to see and identify the objects at the other end of the ocular. Moreover, these students did not comprise an elite group, selected by the professor because of demonstrated talent. They were self-selected: any interested person could sign up for the course. Presumably many of the students referred to by Pfeufer as "less gifted" were taking this class, learning the skills that would permit them to replace intuition and experience with routine scientific procedures and thus further the "objectification" of the practice of medicine.

Henle, who taught this course as part of a broader program for the reform of medicine, rapidly acquired a reputation as a leader in medical reform. This was a reputation he had helped to create. From the time of his and Pfeufer's arrival in Heidelberg in 1843, the two had been spokesmen for the importance of the natural sciences in medicine. They had communicated this in their lectures, their letters to the government, and most of all in a journal they began editing in 1843, the *Zeitschrift für rationelle Medizin*.

The Theoretical Foundations of Scientific Medicine

In the journal's introductory article, "Wissenschaft und Empirie," Henle consolidated ideas that he and Pfeufer had been entertaining for years into a polemic for a "rational" medicine. The program put forth, which could be found with some variation in Virchow's and Wunderlich's journals, focused criticism on the widespread empiricism flourishing in medicine.[21]

Although Henle shared in the empiricists' distrust of speculative systems, he harbored a similar distaste for a pure empiricism that collected facts without trying to understand them. Thus he campaigned for a balance between fact and theory whereby all hypotheses would be derived from, and tested by, a careful analysis of natural phenomena. He believed that recent developments in organic chemistry and microscopy would make this possible. But for a rational medicine to be successful, he told his readers over and over again, the notion of disease entities had to be replaced by a definition of disease as nothing more than a deviation from the normal physiological processes of life brought about by abnormal conditions.

Henle sought a method by which certainty could be brought to medicine, and he believed that this would be possible only by reintroducing theoretical considerations into the study of disease. It was on these grounds that he criticized the empiricists for consciously abandoning all investigations into the first cause and internal connection of symptoms, and for describing the form of the disease according to external phenomena alone. "The names which the empiric gives to diseases," wrote Henle, "are not definitions but only *Nomina propria.*"[22] They say nothing about the disease condition, but only represent complexes of material symptoms. In a similar fashion, Henle went on to complain, the empirics care little about the *modus operandi* of medicaments; instead, they rely on those remedies that have most frequently had a favorable effect. "Thus," he concluded, "the certainty of their different modes of cure is not determined by internal arguments, but only by a number of medical observations."[23]

Henle believed Louis' numerical method to be the logical consequence of the empirical approach—in fact the only method from which empirical medicine could really benefit—and he praised the Frenchman's caution and distrust of treatments based on a limited number of cases. Nevertheless, the numerical method could provide only probable knowledge, and Henle questioned the practical value of such results. Knowing that a certain medicament had a positive effect in the majority of cases could not, for example, tell the physician how to treat the exceptions to the rule. "Shall we therefore adopt it [the treatment] for all cases," questioned Henle, "and therein resign ourselves for the future to sacrifice a certain number of patients? . . . Do we console ourselves, like gamblers, with the prospect that in the end the gain will surmount the loss?"[24] Henle believed the only possibility for achieving the certainty he wanted was through analysis of the internal connections of the symptoms, and this demanded going beyond the mere collection of data to the construction of theories.

The use of theory had, according to Henle, been carried to an extreme by the nature philosophers at the beginning of the century, and he realized that the empiricists were reacting against this excess. Nevertheless, he defended the former's conception of organic nature, their recognition that matter and force are not separable, and their emphasis on the development of organic beings, and thus on comparative anatomy and embryology. He praised highly the search for relations between phenomena and for causal explanations, but he did not hesitate to point out that however fruitful nature philosophy may have been for embryology and comparative anatomy, its influence on pathology and practical medicine had been a disaster, in part because of the false application of theories to the explanation of empirical data, and in part because of the a priori construction of empirical knowledge.[25] His alternative approach, which "stood to a certain extent in the middle of these two [the empirical and philosophical systems]," sought on the one hand to retain the philosophical interest in causal connections while, on the other hand, abandoning a priori theories and adopting the empirical method of the natural sciences. "I want to name this method rational," he wrote,

> because it aims to give an account of the causes of phenomena as well as of the manner of operation of remedies. It strives to understand the symptoms in their dependence upon one another and in their connection to internal organic changes, and it considers these changes as the result of the interaction of abnormal external influences on organic matter endowed with specific forces.[26]

The means for acquiring this information would be pathological anatomy, microscopy, chemistry, clinical observation, and experiment. Theories would not be constructed a priori; rather, hypotheses would be derived from an analysis of the data and then tested.

Henle's rational medicine thus permitted and supported an eclectic approach to the study of the physiological processes of the organism. In a letter to his publisher Vieweg in 1864, Henle referred back to this decade as a time "when anatomy, physiology, and even practical medicine believed they could progress united for all times."[27] In the 1850s this approach would begin to break down into scientific specialties, but in the 1840s the argument that medicine must be based on physiology did not connote a particular methodological approach tied to specific experimental techniques. This is evident not only in Henle's *Zeitschrift*, but in Wunderlich's and Virchow's journals as well. All three published articles in pathology, histology, therapeutics, physiology, microscopy, pharmaceutics, nosology, and practical medicine. A "physiological" approach to the study of disease had the much broader meaning of a search for the laws governing organic function and dis-function. It meant that one was going beyond the mere collection of facts to an investigation of the causes of disease and the laws governing the pathological process. This search for laws must not be confused with the derivation of statistical norms; as we have seen, Henle remained skeptical of the value of probable knowledge. The laws he and the other "physiological pathologists" sought to uncover were deterministic in nature. Wunderlich expressed this most succinctly in his comment that "a law of nature cannot tolerate any exceptions."[28]

In their attempt to create a medical science based on physiology, Henle, Wunderlich, and Virchow were also involved in a redefinition of physiology itself. In the past it had often carried connotations of philo-

sophical speculation and a priori hypothesizing. "The medicine," wrote
Henle, "of Hippocrates, Paracelsus, Stahl, even the one-sided pathology of
Brown, and every philosophical pathology is based on physiology."[29] A
foundation in physiology could not, therefore, be sufficient for guarding
against use of a priori principles in medicine. Thus Henle was extremely
cautious in establishing the relation between rational medicine and physiology. While he was prepared to argue that "physiology and pathology are
one" in order to support his physiological notion of disease, he showed
more caution when it came to defining his particular methodological approach: "One is justified in demanding that the rational method be
founded upon physiology. This trend is called physiological. But this is not
what characterizes it."[30] How the information was acquired and how it
was applied were also of extreme importance, and here, similar to Virchow
and Wunderlich, Henle insisted that theories be based solidly on an investigation of the material basis of disease.

Henle had another reason for cautioning against a total identification
of rational medicine with physiology, and here he distinguished himself
very clearly from Wunderlich. He did not believe pathology could simply
be reduced to physiology. The laws governing organic function may be the
same under healthy and diseased conditions, he explained, but the phenomena being investigated were not identical. The pathologist began with
bedside observations and attempted to identify the organic functions responsible for the disease symptoms, while the physiologist took the oppo-
site route, working from the organs to the symptoms. These two reasons—
the speculative connotation attached to the word physiology, and the need
to defend the autonomy of pathological research—led Henle to insist that
the rational method was not characterized by physiology, but rather by the
fact that it

> proceeds from individual facts for which it attempts to find an explanation,
> and in this task physiological and pathological facts are equally valid. The final
> goal is, as far as it is possible, to trace both back to physical and chemical
> processes, and in this way to bring these facts under common viewpoints with
> the phenomena of inorganic nature.[31]

This statement demonstrates the extent to which the rational method
represented a bridge between scientific research and clinical medicine, and
why, consequently, Henle found it so important to work closely with a
clinician. Physiology and pathology were complementary, dealing with
different phenomena but guided by the same goal and applying similar
methods. For both Henle and Pfeufer the classical proof of this bond was
Charles Bell's experimental work of 1811 in which the British physiologist
had demonstrated the functional specificity of the peripheral nerves of the
brain. Pfeufer placed particular weight on the fact that Bell had "derived
his brilliant idea from exact observations at the bedside." Here was proof
that physiology was indebted to pathology for one of its most important
discoveries. "And it may easily happen," he added, "that more light will

come to the theory of the movement of the heart through pathological observations by means of the stethoscope than through all the physiological experiments done to date."[32]

Bell had demonstrated that the study of disease could provide an invaluable source for learning about the normal physiological functions of the body, but the reverse was also true. "If," Henle explained, "diseases can be considered as physiological experiments which originate accidentally, then on the other hand the effects of physiological experiments are nothing else than arbitrarily produced diseases."[33] The physiologist who cut through nerves, tied ligatures, or severed glands was doing nothing more than creating a diseased state under controlled conditions. Experiment had made pathology physiological, "and more . . . physiology, pathological."[34]

In 1846 Henle published his *Handbuch der rationellen Pathologie,* a book that represented the culmination of eight years of work and the fulfillment of the program he had laid out in his journal article "Wissenschaft und Empirie." In the introduction Henle repeated the polemic that had characterized that article, this time concentrating more specifically on the distinctions between the empirical and the philosophical methods. He wanted, he explained, to separate them from one another "more rigidly than has ever been possible in practice," in order to clarify the role of his rational method as a synthesizer of these two approaches to the study of disease.[35]

The text consisted of two parts divided into three volumes. The first volume, published in 1846, focused on general pathology and provided a discussion of the physiological notion of disease, etiology, and the spatial and temporal characteristics of disease. The second part, consisting of two volumes, published in 1847 and 1853 respectively, dealt in greater detail with the specific areas of pathogenesis, symptomology, and, once again, etiology. It was a massive work, attempting to bring together the newest discoveries in chemistry, physiology, pathological anatomy, and microscopy, and to evaluate their significance for pathology. The text was an immediate success—the first volume barely leaving the press before a second printing was already in demand—but less so for its specific interpretations than for its methodological intentions. The young experimental physiologist, Carl Ludwig, then assistant professor for anatomy and physiology at the University of Marburg, wrote to Henle immediately after reading the *Handbuch,* expressing his belief that the book "will be particularly fruitful for teaching the correct method of study to the young." He even went so far as to speak of Henle's "microscopical school."[36] And Rudolph Virchow, in an attempt to convince the Prussian ministry to build an institute for pathological anatomy, described his own work as being "in Henle's spirit."[37] By this he was referring to a methodological approach to the study of disease that used microscopy, chemistry, and experiment to investigate the conditions under which disease occurred and the laws governing this process.

There is little doubt that Henle enjoyed this reputation as a reformer; in fact, he actively sought to promote it. In 1845, just before completing his *Handbuch,* he had written to his publisher that he "wanted to pave the way for a new direction" in medicine; and on the day he finished the book he expressed his hope and belief that it would "cause a revolution in medicine, making me an enemy of the old, and binding me to the young."[38] Henle was not disappointed. As the statistics in Table 4.1 show, the "young" certainly were attracted to him and his colleague Pfeufer. Enrollment, falling in every other German medical department, did not cease to increase at the University of Heidelberg until the troublesome times just before the Revolution of 1848.

Table 4.1   Medical Department Enrollment at
the University of Heidelberg[39]

Year	Baden Students	Foreign Students
1842/43	29	84
1843/44	30	87
1844/45	33	114
1846/47	36	129
1847/48	39	89

"Rational" medicine was a reform program aimed at the younger generation, and those students coming to Heidelberg could expect to be introduced to its principles and methods. In the eight years Henle and Pfeufer spent at the university (1844–1852) they offered courses in, among others, general and special pathology, general and special therapeutics, general anatomy, physiology, and rational pathology. Henle's lectures, drawn primarily from his textbooks on general anatomy and rational pathology, provided students with the theoretical principles of the new scientific medicine, and in the clinic and anatomical institute, as we have already seen, these same students began to work with the tools of the trade.

The popularity of this program rested to some extent on the dynamic personalities of its leaders. Indeed, in a torchlight parade held in Henle's honor one year after his arrival in Heidelberg, the students hailed him

> as a thinker and scientist who campaigns unremittingly and without stop at the head of those who are struggling and fighting against a desolate empiricism in our science. . . . In the same way that Kepler led us to the unmeasurable breadth of the firmament through the depth of his spirit and through telescopic research, so has Henle revealed to us the infinite nearness of organic life through microscopical research. We admire him, I say, as teacher, because he is able to represent the truth, simply, convincingly, and free from all auras of affected scholarship. . . . We love him as a human being, as a man, because feelings for the good of mankind and for the fatherland have not died in his heart through science.[40]

This speech attests to the students' admiration for Henle as a trail-blazer; but perhaps more interestingly it reveals the symbolic importance of the microscope to these young students. Similar to Ludwig, they too perceived Henle's greatest contribution to be his exhaustive use of this instrument in his teaching and research. One has only to think of the inaugural address Pfeufer gave in 1840 in Zurich to understand why the microscope carried so much meaning. It, like the stethoscope, signified a "new era in objective diagnostics," in which the success of a physician no longer depended, presumably, on the possession of obscure qualities, such as talent and intuition, but rather on routine scientific procedures. During the highly political years of the 1840s, many saw the scientific method as a tool for the democratization of medicine. As in political circles, here, too, the target was an elite that had come to power either through family connections or through an immeasurable quality referred to as "talent." It was the apparent subjectivity surrounding the definition of talent that most disturbed the medical reformers.[41] Nevertheless, they were not seeking total democratization. Parallel to the liberals' wish to keep their distance from the "masses," medical reformers sought a means by which to distinguish themselves from "quacks" (their term for nonlicensed medical practitioners). At the same time, they wished to gain access to the select community of the medical elite. The scientific method provided the tool by which to accomplish both goals. By standardizing requirements for entry into the medical community, the medical reformers hoped both to disqualify non-licensed practitioners, and to provide a tool for replacing talent and intuition by routine methods. In the future young medical students would merely have to learn the techniques of auscultation, percussion, microscopy, and chemical analysis to become successful physicians. To accomplish this no particular aptitude or insight was necessary: the scientific method was something that could be taught even to the "less gifted."

Henle had achieved much of what he had set out to do. Young medical students were coming to Heidelberg to learn from him and join him in his reform of medical theory and practice. But he soon decided more was needed—he also desired changes in the medical faculty at the university. Although all his conditions had been met when he was hired, he soon decided that the arrangements were not to his satisfaction. In particular, he regretted having agreed to joint control of the anatomical institute. In Henle's battle to oust Tiedemann and assume sole directorship of the institute, he relied on student support to bring about the change.

Local Contingencies: Politics and the Battle over the New Anatomical Institute

Reform of the university and reform of medicine were a single issue for Henle in the 1840s, and the specific target of his criticisms was the aged medical faculty and particularly his senior colleague, Friedrich Tiedemann. Problems between the two men had already begun in 1843 during negotiations over Henle's appointment. Although Tiedemann had played a central role in bringing Henle to Heidelberg, it was evident that he had expected his younger colleague to accept a subordinate position in the faculty.[42] Knowledge of this had almost led Henle to turn down the offer, but further negotiations had resulted in a compromise. Tiedemann would retain the anatomy lectures, dissection exercises, and directorship of the institute, while Henle would be given responsibility for physiology, general pathology, comparative anatomy, pathological anatomy, and the promise that the institute would pass into his hands upon Tiedemann's retirement.

Henle, although initially in agreement with these terms, expressed dissatisfaction with the arrangement almost from the start. In the following letter, written shortly after his arrival, he showed his awareness of how student support might assist him in his plans to make changes.

> Nothing is left here but to let that which is old wither and to ground a new colony. The government and students seem to want to help that come to power. The government, whose eyes are now opened, is astonished at how the faculty has used Heidelberg's reputation and beautiful setting in order to grow fat in luxurious tranquility and to seclude themselves from intruders. . . . The students, however, already notice quite well that something new and capable of developing is being offered them now. They are full of enthusiasm for our rational medicine and subsequently furious at the boredom in which they have been educated.[43]

The polemic that Henle carried on in his early years in Heidelberg soon took a concrete form over the construction of the new anatomy building. In 1847, without first consulting Tiedemann, he wrote directly to the curator of the university with suggestions for improving the building.[44] This attempt to carry on negotiations without his participation troubled Tiedemann. It brought to the surface the question of who had primary responsibility and control of the institute—a question that had been latent since Henle's arrival in 1843. However, not until January 1849 did tensions reach a peak. The problem, on the surface, was Henle's claim that both Tiedemann and the construction commission had repeatedly ignored his suggestions, and that the auditorium had thus been poorly built. In an attempt to settle matters the director of the commission called a meeting of all parties involved, but the interchange that followed only aggravated the situation. Tiedemann claimed the suggestions made by Henle were in fact his own, and even held his younger colleague responsible for the faulty construction of the auditorium. A heated debate followed that very soon took a personal tone, and in his anger Tiedemann resorted to anti-semitic remarks, attributing Henle's impertinence to his Jewish heritage. At this point the meeting broke up.

Responsibility for this final eruption cannot, however, be placed solely with Tiedemann. Henle had done little in previous years to establish good working relations with him. On the contrary, as a letter from Pfeufer to Henle demonstrates, the two younger colleagues were intent on improving their positions in the university at the expense of Tiedemann and Puchelt. Explaining that under the present circumstances an improvement of the clinic could not be considered, Pfeufer added that "these circumstances could only be changed if I go after Puchelt's ruin, whereby I must do the greatest violence to my nature, as you know that I am more humane than you."[45] That the two men may have created tensions deliberately in order to encourage the early retirement of their older colleagues finds further support in a letter written three months before the final break between Henle and Tiedemann, in which Pfeufer advised his friend: "If you want him [Tiedemann] absolutely cleared out, then procure a threatening letter through one of your old friends . . . I, meanwhile, am doing my part."[46]

In the early months of 1849 the university tried to make peace between the two men, but in mid-February matters grew serious as the rumor reached the government that not only Henle, but Pfeufer and Karl Adolf von Vangerow, the most popular and highest paid professor at the university, would leave Heidelberg if Tiedemann did not retire.[47] The curator wrote immediately to the prorector of the university, Karl Heinrich Rau, requesting his advice and asking specifically whether it would be possible to encourage Tiedemann to submit an application for his pension. Rau's response was clear:

> Henle is an exceedingly stimulating and popular teacher. . . . Tiedemann no longer lectures but only looks after the preparation exercises of the students, and it is not to be expected that he would achieve great effectiveness again even if he would try. Were he to be considered the cause of Henle's departure, his position would be completely untenable. Therefore it seems to me as well that there is no other way out, as the one you have implied.[48]

In the next couple of weeks the government received increasing pressure to follow through with this decision. Henle had received an offer from Zurich and was threatening to accept if Tiedemann did not leave.[49] Furthermore, on 13 March von Vangerow sent a letter to Rau in which he fully defended Henle's ultimatum and stated quite clearly what the consequences would be were the government not to act quickly:

> Finally, consideration of the long-term well-being and flourishing of our university is decisive for my view. Already if Henle were to depart, it would be very difficult to replace him. But it is not at all a matter of that alone, nor is it merely a matter of Henle's and Pfeufer's departure, but I believe I may guarantee that a no small number of other talented teachers would thereby become so estranged from the university that quite soon consequences would be seen as well outside of the medical faculty.[50]

Although von Vangerow mentioned no names, the "small number of other talented teachers" were most likely the members of Henle's, Pfeufer's, and von Vangerow's circle of liberal-minded professors and friends, men such as Ludwig Häusser, Philipp Jolly, and Georg Gervinus. This group enjoyed great popularity with students; it had, moreover, close ties to like-minded government officials, particularly von Stengel. Yet the government did not respond immediately to von Vangerow's threat. The faculty senate, composed solely of senior professors, believed forced retirement to be too harsh a punishment for Tiedemann and put pressure on the government to find a milder solution than that which Henle had proposed. In addition, the government wanted to do everything possible to prevent a scandal. Henle, realizing that his terms might not be met, presented an alternative: Tiedemann remain director but he, Henle, be given responsibility for the cadavers and dissection exercises. As Rau pointed out, the consequence of this arrangement was expected: Tiedemann submitted to voluntary retirement. Remaining director of an anatomical institute, he explained, when one cannot conduct the dissection classes is like heading a clinic without being able to treat the patients. On 1 October Henle took over directorship of the institute.[51]

Henle had demonstrated an acute awareness of the power of student and collegial support in accomplishing his goals, using them to manipulate Tiedemann's early retirement so that he could take over directorship of the new anatomy institute. But other concerns had motivated Henle's actions as well: he desperately needed someone who could take over some of his classes. Since 1838 Tiedemann had been teaching only general anatomy, the anatomical examinatorium, repititorium, and dissection exercises, offering these courses semester after semester, whereas Henle held lectures in physiology, general pathology, splanchnology, neurology, myology, comparative anatomy, anthropology, pathological anatomy, and microscopical exercises.[52] Although Henle had agreed to these terms in 1843, that had been at a time when the study of function and the study of form were still intimately connected. In fact, he had derived his lectures on physiology from the content of his textbook on general anatomy. Physiology may have been "the science of the forces, functions, and activities of the organic body," but the study of these phenomena depended as much on anatomical investigations and comparative anatomy as it did on physiological observations and experimentation.[53] Moreover, the common use of the microscope had strengthened the bond between these two sciences. Only in this way can one explain why Henle, as second professor for physiology, spent his yearly budget of 200 gulden almost exclusively on microscopes.[54]

In the early 1840s the difference between a morphological and an experimental approach to the study of function did not yet exist, or it was at best in incipient form. Henle, Johannes Müller, Jan Evangelista Purkyne, Gabriel Gustav Valentin, and Rudolph Wagner—to name only a few—were all involved in what Karl Rothschuh has termed "histophysiology": microscopical investigations of the fine structure of tissues as a means of studying physiological function.[55] This was not functional anatomy—function was not merely derived from form—rather the microscope was used to observe physiological behavior directly (when one had luck), or, more often, to study structure with the hope of raising and perhaps answering questions of physiological importance.

Physiology had been thus little more than microscopical anatomy accompanied by occasional chemical tests and investigations. But this began to change around mid-century as a methodological approach to the study of function slowly took form which was based on sophisticated instrumental techniques. The leading advocates of this new research style— Emil du Bois-Reymond, Hermann Helmholtz, Ernst Brücke, and Carl Ludwig—hoped to transform physiology into an "organic physics" based exclusively on mathematical, chemical, and physical laws.[56] Accurate measurement of biological function had priority for them, and the instruments used for accomplishing this end—galvanometers, multiplicators, kymographs, induction apparatuses, and vacuum pumps—demanded new skills, mathematical knowledge, and a certain technical dexterity. Henle, a man of the microscope, recognized his inability to keep pace with these new developments, and by mid-century was pressuring the Baden government to hire a physiologist.

The details surrounding Henle's fight to bring a physiologist to Heidelberg will be discussed in detail in Chapter 6. During this battle Henle began to define himself more and more as an "anatomist," finally leaving Heidelberg in 1852 to accept a position as professor of anatomy at the University of Göttingen. As we will see, the establishment of an autonomous physiological discipline thus involved not only the concerted efforts of physiologists to distinguish their research interests from those of anatomists, but a decision on the part of anatomists to abandon physiology as well. Before, however, turning to the specific circumstances surrounding Henle's "retreat into anatomy," his departure from Heidelberg, and the university's subsequent search for his replacement, it is essential to return to the political climate in Baden. In the 1850s, as a response to changing social and economic conditions, the government greatly increased its financial support of the experimental sciences. This reflected in part a continuation of its ideological commitment to science education that dated back to the 1830s. But the political and social events surrounding the Revolution of 1848, particularly the unparalleled agricultural crises, deepened this commitment and added an urgency to the situation. It is because of these broader issues that Baden invested exorbitant sums to support the production of scientific knowledge. Decisions to create new positions and construct new institutes for the experimental sciences reflected the perception that the methods taught in these laboratories would help solve essential problems in the economic and social life of the state.

Notes

1. Between 1840 and 1850, for example, the University of Heidelberg's budget jumped from 85,000 to 101,000 gulden; the University of Berlin's from 100,000 to 170,000 taler. For the University of Heidelberg, see "Vergleichung der Budgets-Sätze mit den Rechnungs-Resultaten für die Etats-Jahre 1840 bis 1850," in *Verhandlungen,* usually, but not always, in Beilagenheft 2. For the University of

Berlin, see Charles E. McClelland, *State, Society and University in Germany, 1700–1914* (Cambridge, 1980), pp. 211–212.

According to Horst Werner Kupka, who analyzed the money spent by southern German universities on science and medical institutes, the following new institutes were built in the 1840s: at the University of Erlangen, a physics institute and a zoology institute (1840 and 1848 respectively); at the University of Munich, an institute for physics, zoology, mineralogy, and pharmacology (1840); at the University of Tübingen, an institute for physics and chemistry (1846), and at the University of Heidelberg, an anatomy institute (1849). This is probably a low estimate and only reflects brand new institutes. See Horst Werner Kupka, *Die Ausgaben der süddeutschen Länder für die medizinischen und naturwissenschaftlichen Hochschul-Einrichtungen 1848–1914* (Diss. Bonn, 1970).

2. See Chapter 2, p. 43.

3. Parliament contributed 10,000 gulden toward the new buildings. The rest of the funds came from the university's own budget and the sale of some old property. See von Stengel to the state minister, 30 March 1842, BGLA 235/676.

4. Eberhard Stübler, *Geschichte der medizinischen Fakultät der Universität Heidelberg, 1326–1925* (Heidelberg, 1926), pp. 289–294.

5. Gmelin to the curator, 25 March 1845, BGLA 235/571. The generally poor state of the clinical facilities is discussed in Stübler, *Geschichte der medizinischen Fakultät*, pp. 225–227.

6. Dahmen to the state ministry, 9 March 1845, cited in Werner Goth, *Zur Geschichte der Klinik in Heidelberg im 19. Jahrhundert* (Diss. Heidelberg, 1982), pp. 171–174. For Pfeufer's complaints about inadequate clinical space, see his letters to the building and economics commission on 26 September 1844, and to Dahmen on 18 March 1845, both in ibid., p. 160 and pp. 167–170 respectively. Pfeufer, who received an offer from Tübingen in 1845 to head a brand new clinic, succeeded in negotiating an additional eight beds for his clinic. See BGLA 235/607, esp. ministry of interior to Dahmen, 12 April 1845.

7. Dahmen to the state ministry, 15 March 1845, in Goth, *Zur Geschichte der Klinik*, pp. 171–174; Pfeufer to the state ministry, 19 March 1845, in ibid., pp. 165–166.

8. Minutes of the medical faculty meetings from 8 January 1846, in *Acten*, III, 4a, 89, Universitätsarchiv Heidelberg. The first discussions on the improvement of the natural science institutes actually took place in 1844, but no action was taken until two years later. This is mentioned in a report from the medical faculty, 11 November 1846, BGLA 235/571.

9. *Verhandlungen*, 2. Kammer, 1846, Beilagenheft 4, pp. 292–294.

10. Ibid. The history of Baden's interest in promoting chemical research is dealt with in great detail in Peter Borscheid, *Naturwissenschaft, Staat und Industrie in Baden, 1848–1914* (Stuttgart, 1976).

11. Bissing in *Verhandlungen*, 2. Kammer, 33. Sitzung, 13 July 1846, Protokollheft 5, p. 227.

12. *Verhandlungen*, 2. Kammer, 1846, Beilagenheft 8, pp. xxxiv–xxxvii. See also Dahmen to the ministry of interior, 4 September 1846, BGLA 235/571.

13. Hermann Hoepke, "Zur Geschichte der Anatomie in Heidelberg," *Sonderdruck aus Ruperto Carola*, 67/68 (1982): 115–122. The architectural plans are included in a report from the medical faculty on 14 November 1846, BGLA 235/571.

14. Dahmen to the ministry of interior, 15 February 1847, BGLA 235/352.

15. Building and economics commission to Dahmen, 4 August 1847, in ibid.

16. Compiled from the lists of courses and teachers in *Anzeige,* 1840–1850. The following information is taken from this source.

17. See Konrad Kläß, *Die Einführung besonderer Kurse für Mikroskopie und physikalische Diagnostik (Perkussion und Auskultation) in den medizinischen Unterricht an deutschen Universitäten im 19. Jahrhundert* (Diss. Göttingen, 1971), p. 14.

18. *Anzeige,* 1846–1852.

19. Henle to "Geheimen Rath" (who was either the curator or the minister of interior), 11 April 1847, BGLA 235/604. Henle's repeated requests for more microscopes can be found both in this file and in BGLA 235/559.

20. A description of the instruments found in Henle's institute in 1852 is offered in Friedrich Arnold, *Die physiologische Anstalt der Universität Heidelberg von 1853 bis 1858* (Heidelberg, 1858). See also Chapter 6 of this book.

21. Jacob Henle, "Medizinische Wissenschaft und Empirie," *Zeitschrift für rationelle Medizin,* 1 (1844): 1–35; Carl Wunderlich, ed., *Archiv für physiologische Heilkunde* (first volume in 1842); Rudolf Virchow, ed., *Archiv für pathologische Anatomie und Physiologie und klinische Medizin* (first volume in 1846).

22. Henle, "Medizinische Wissenschaft und Empirie," pp. 15, 18.

23. Ibid., pp. 18–19.

24. Ibid., pp. 18, 34.

25. Ibid., p. 4.

25. Ibid., p. 23.

27. Henle to Vieweg on 30 May 1864, private papers of Prof. Dr. Hermann Hoepke. I am grateful to Prof. Hoepke for letting me see this correspondence.

28. Wunderlich, "Einleitung," *Archiv für physiologische Heilkunde,* 1 (1842): xvi.

29. Henle, "Medizinische Wissenschaft und Empirie," p. 31.

30. Ibid.

31. Ibid.

32. Carl Pfeufer, "Ueber den gegenwärtigen Zustand der Medizin. Rede gehalten bei dem Antritt des klinischen Lehramts in Zürich den 7 November 1840," reprinted in *Annalen der städtischen allgemeinen Krankenhäuser in München,* 1 (1878): 395–406, here pp. 404–405.

33. Henle, "Medizinische Wissenschaft und Empirie," p. 30.

34. Ibid.

35. Jacob Henle, *Handbuch der rationellen Pathologie,* 2 vols. (Braunschweig, 1846–53).

36. Carl Ludwig to Jacob Henle on 19 July 1846 and on 22 November 1848, in Astrid Dreher, *Briefe von Carl Ludwig an Jacob Henle aus den Jahren 1846–1872* (Diss. Heidelberg, 1980), pp. 43–45, 57.

37. Rudolf Virchow, "Ein alter Bericht über die Gestaltung der pathologischen Anatomie in Deutschland, wie sie ist und wie sie werden muss," *Archiv für pathologische Anatomie und Physiologie und klinische Medizin,* 159 (1900): 31.

38. Cited in Walter Artelt, "Jacob Henle," in *Geschichte der Mikroskope. Lehren und Werk grosser Forscher,* ed. Hugo Freund, Alexander Berg, 3 vols. (Frankfurt a.M., 1963–1966), vol. 2 (1964): Medizin, pp. 147–159, here p. 155.

39. Statistics are compiled from enrollment reports printed in the *RB,* 1842–1848.

40. Cited in Friedrich Merkel, *Jacob Henle. Ein deutsches Gelehrtenleben* (Braunschweig, 1891), pp. 227–228.

41. The specific demands of the medical reform movement in Baden will be discussed in Chapter 6.

42. Mentioned in Goth, *Zur Geschichte der Klinik in Heidelberg,* pp. 127–128.

43. Cited in Merkel, *Jacob Henle,* p. 214.

44. The following events are from BGLA 235/576. See also Hermann Hoepke, "Der Streit der Professoren Tiedemann und Henle um den Neubau des anatomischen Institutes in Heidelberg (1844–1849)," *Heidelberger Jahrbücher,* 5 (1961): 114–127.

45. Pfeufer to Henle on 7 April 1844, in Hermann Hoepke, *Der Briefwechsel zwischen Jakob Henle und Karl Pfeufer, 1843–1859* (Sudhoffs Archiv. Beihefte 11.) (Wiesbaden, 1970), p. 3.

46. Pfeufer to Henle, 15 October 1848, in ibid., p. 6.

47. Ministry of interior to Rau, 14 February 1849, BGLA 235/576.

48. Rau to Dahmen, 15 February 1849, in ibid.

49. Rau to Dahmen, 24 February 1849, in ibid.

50. Von Vangerow to Rau, 13 March 1849, in ibid.

51. Henle to Dahmen, 9 July 1849, in ibid.; Rau to Dahmen, 23 July 1849, in ibid.; Ministry of interior to the faculty senate, 10 October 1849, BGLA 235/3133.

52. *Anzeige,* 1838–1849.

53. Jacob Henle, unpublished lecture notes for his course, "Physiologie der Menschen," Summer Semester 1846, pp. 1–4. These notes were taken by the student C. Rauschenbusch. I am grateful to Prof. Dr. Johanna Bleker for lending me this source.

54. Henle's budget is mentioned in a letter from the ministry of interior to Henle, 5 December 1843, BGLA 235/3133.

55. Karl Rothschuh, "Von der Histomorphologie zur Histophysiologie unter besonderer Berücksichtigung von Purkinjes Arbeiten," in *J. E. Purkyne 1787– 1869. Centenary Symposium, Prague, 8–10 September 1969,* ed. Vl. Kruta (Brno, 1971), pp. 197–212. See also Mikulás Teich, "Purkyne and Valentin on Ciliary Motion: An Early Investigation in Morphological Physiology," *British Journal for the History of Science,* 5 (1970/71): 168–177.

56. I discuss this in more detail in Chapter 7.

5

Revolution, Reaction, and the Politics of Education

In the first decade following the Revolution of 1848 Baden spent a larger percentage of its budget (1.9%) in support of the natural sciences than any other German land, with the exception of Bavaria (2.2%). It invested more than twice as much as Prussia (0.8%) and one and a half times as much as Saxony (1.2%). When looked at in terms of money spent per individual in the population, the statistics are even more remarkable. Here Baden far exceeded all others, spending the equivalent of .42DM per person in comparison with .26DM in Bavaria, .18DM in Saxony, and only .15DM in Prussia.[1]

Why did Baden invest, relatively speaking, more heavily in the production of scientific knowledge than any other German state? The best explanation to date is Peter Borscheid's thesis that interest in the experimental sciences was linked to the severity of the agricultural crises experienced by the various states in the 1840s.[2] Much of this chapter will draw on this thesis in order to bolster my claim that the institutionalization of the experimental sciences did not, as Ben-David has argued, reflect a process of unintentional social evolution. But there is, as I have been arguing, more to the story than Borscheid suggests. Baden stood out in the 1850s not only for its support of the experimental sciences; this is the period when it also acquired its peculiar "German mission (*deutsche Sendung*)"[3] as a bulwark of political liberalism. The two were intimately linked, for at a time when most German states entered a period of severe reaction, viewing the schools and universities as seats of radical ideas, Baden turned to its educational institutions for help in alleviating problems it believed had led to the

Revolution. Thus while a state as powerful as Prussia bowed in 1856 to the pressure of philologists and reduced the number of hours spent on the natural sciences in the classical *Gymnasia* from sixteen to six hours per week, Baden continued its program of integrating the natural sciences into the traditional humanist curriculum.[4] This is not to say that reactionary and conservative forces were absent from the Baden government; quite the contrary, conservatives and liberals jockeyed for power here as in other lands during the first half of the decade. As we will see in Chapter 6, the former succeeded in blocking the appointment of an experimental physiologist at the University of Heidelberg for several years. But, in comparison to other states, the conservatives' base of power in Baden was never secure and their period of influence was short-lived. This chapter begins with a brief discussion of the political events just before, during, and immediately after the Revolution of 1848; it then turns to an analysis of the particular path Baden pursued in the 1850s when, following a brief period of reaction, the government returned to its liberal program, preferring education over repressive measures for carrying out its social and economic plans.

The Political Climate in Baden, 1840–1852

By 1840 the mood of cooperation that had characterized Baden's earlier parliamentary sessions had begun to wane. Ironically, this was a partial consequence of reform measures, enacted by a parliament composed predominantly of liberal civil servants, that had worked to stimulate civic interest in the affairs of the government and to encourage social and political equality. Enlightened citizens, elected to parliament and taking the constitutional rhetoric of the early 1830s seriously, began now to challenge the power of the government and to fight to defend their own interests.[5] Differences of opinion, which had always existed in parliament without necessarily leading to distinct factions, were slowly translated into party lines. While one cannot yet speak of "party politics," parliament did begin to divide into general groups that we would identify as democrats, liberals, and conservatives. The death in 1839 of Ludwig Winter further aggravated this divisive tendency. As one of the strongest defenders of liberal principles in the government and extremely competent in assuaging parliamentary opposition, he had contributed significantly to maintaining harmony between the government and parliament throughout the decade. His replacement, none other than Carl Nebenius, held similar political views and convictions, but he lacked the strength to keep the reactionary forces in check. The greatest challenge came from Friedrich von Blittorsdorff, minister of foreign affairs since 1835 and a man who favored a conservative revision if not abrogation of the constitution. No two men could have differed more in their political views, and by 1839 von Blittersdorff had already made it clear that it would be "him or me." On 2 October Nebenius was asked to resign his post in the interest of unity and harmony in the ministry; his replacement, Rüdt von Collenberg, shared the views of his reactionary colleague.[6]

In the following years tensions escalated between parliament and the government, and each new election made matters worse as the number of representatives opposed to the conservative ministry increased. Parliament also began to take a more radical turn, with men such as Friedrich Hecker, later to become one of the leaders of the Revolution of 1848, appearing for the first time. Grand Duke Leopold bowed to pressure in 1843 and appointed a more liberal ministry, led by Alexander von Dusch, but relations with parliament remained strained. The ministry, while liberal, favored a path of moderate reform and had nothing but hostility for the democratic tendencies of the dissenting representatives. But by the mid-1840s a moderate solution no longer appealed to many of Baden's citizens. In the following years the opposition continued to increase its representation in parliament. Although Leopold made a final attempt to stop this trend by dissolving parliament and calling for new elections, the opposition continued to grow. The Grand Duke had no choice but to appoint the liberal Johann Bekk to the presidency of the ministry of interior. For the moment this move seemed to appease the voting public. After the fall election of 1847 the majority of representatives sitting in parliament's lower chamber sympathized with the government.[7]

The tensions threatening to split parliament during the 1840s reflected similar strains pulling at the social and economic web of the state. Abolition of manorial obligations, restrictions on the guild system, and membership in the *Zollverein*, among other reform measures, had begun to dissolve the old aristocratic structure. However, a new order had not yet materialized. The result was an unfortunate no man's land. Peasants, for example, may have won their "freedom," but only at a price: service obligations had merely turned into rents, and to free themselves of these new "capitalistic obligations" and gain ownership of the property they had been tilling for their manorial lords, they had to pay between eighteen and twenty times the annual value of these rents.[8]

The difficulty of the peasants' plight was aggravated by the richness of their fertility compared with that of the soil. Between 1815 and 1849 the population of Baden increased by 38 percent from 989,000 to 1,361,000, making Baden, after Saxony, Hessen, and Nassau, the most densely populated of all German lands.[9] Furthermore, the vast majority of these people (77%) lived in small villages or in the country, constantly dividing their property into ever smaller parcels to distribute among the ever increasing number of children. With the crop failures in the late 1840s, the seriousness of this situation became painfully evident. Food grew scarce, prices rose catastrophically, starvation became widespread, and the peasant came to the brutal realization that freedom in a society striving toward a free market economy meant the "freedom" to go under in times of hardship as well—the government did not assume the same social responsibilities that the manorial lord had once shown toward his serfs.[10]

The 1840s did not mean disaster for the peasants alone; the villages, inhabited predominantly by small farmholders and artisans, had already had to deal with increased poverty in the previous decade, and further crop failures proved calamitous. In addition, an economic crash in Great Britain in 1845 triggered a depression on the continent that brought many businesses near the point of bankruptcy, adding the plight of the city factory worker to those of the peasants and artisans. Most serious in Baden was the near ruination in December 1847 of the three largest factories in the state—the Kessler machine factory in Karlsruhe, the spinning and weaving mill in Ettlingen (about ten kilometers outside of Karlsruhe), and the society for sugar production in Waghäusel, a town also not far from Karlsruhe. Closure of these factories would have meant the immediate loss of 3500 jobs, not to mention countless repercussions in other branches of industry. The government's decision to grant a loan of 1.5 million gulden prevented what would certainly have proved a disaster for owners and workers alike, but it also drew attention to the ambiguous relationship that had developed between self-regulation and state intervention in the newly emerging economy.[11]

By no means did a single opinion reign in Baden as to how the government should handle the economic and social problems threatening the state. In 1846 an article appeared in the pro-government newspaper, the *Karlsruher Zeitung,* warning citizens of the dangers of the present crisis and emphasizing that a failure to improve the plight of the lower classes would prepare the path for the triumph of communism.[12] The solutions suggested here reflected the thoughts of the conservative forces in the government. To help the depressed agricultural situation, the author favored both the repeal of many of the agrarian reforms and forced emigration; to alleviate the financial difficulties of the artisans, he advocated the establishment of credit banks. The liberals, on the other hand, saw further modernization as the necessary solution. In their eyes the present crisis resulted less from the evils of capitalism than from the failure to complete the transition to a modern constitutional state. Karl Mathy, a parliamentary representative who, in 1864, became the Baden minister of trade, argued, for example, that the absence of a banking and credit system greatly hindered the economic development of the state. Moreover, in a classic mixture of enlightenment and liberal ideologies, he emphasized the need to interest and engage citizens in the affairs of the state, recommending universal suffrage, greater autonomy for community governments, and, most important for my argument, improvements in education.[13]

Liberals in the ministry hoped to win support for the government through a program of moderate reforms, but they moved too slowly. In February 1848 the Paris uprisings took place, and Hecker, joined by Gustav von Struve and other democrats, began campaigning for the abolition of the monarchy and the establishment of a republic. By the second week of March the first peasant revolts had begun (although these were unorganized and rapidly subdued by government troops); in September a second revolt occurred; and in May 1849, following the failure of the National Assembly in Frankfurt, the revolution succeeded in Baden. On the 13th of the month, the Grand Duke fled from Karlsruhe, and a provisional government was established. It survived, however, only one month. By mid-June Prussian troops had entered Baden, and by the 25th of the month they had occupied Karlsruhe. Leopold's ministers, a newly appointed conservative-minded group, returned shortly thereafter, and the Grand Duke followed suit in August. The reaction had begun.[14]

The new ministry, organized under Friedrich Klüber, began to revoke some of the liberal reforms of the previous years. Working closely with Prussian emissaries—often, in fact, being forced to take orders—the government declared Baden to be in a state of war, fired all civil servants who had taken an oath to the provisional government, and sought out, sentenced, and in severe cases executed those who had participated actively in the revolution. Nevertheless, a severe period of reaction was short-lived—a phenomenon that troubled both Prussia and Austria—and had no effect at all on many facets of government and public life.[15] The constitution, for example, remained principally intact, and although the government actively persecuted the radical left, well over one-half of the moderate liberals who had sat in the lower chamber in 1847 returned to parliament after the 1850 election.[16] These men had fully opposed Hecker's and von Struve's attempt to establish a democracy, and in the early 1850s they adopted a moderate *"Realpolitik,"* working together with the government to reestablish order in the state. Thus the political measures of this decade continued to be drawn from a liberal tradition—one that had its roots in the *Vormärz* parliament, in political leaders such as Winter and Nebenius, and, most significantly, in the history, economic, and constitutional law courses attended by ministers and parliamentary representatives alike at the state universities in Heidelberg and Freiburg. This common intellectual history, grounded in the lectures of such liberal professors as Karl von Rotteck, Karl Theodor Welcker, Georg Gottfried Gervinus and Ludwig Häusser, played an extremely important role in preventing the reaction from taking root in Baden as it did in Prussia, Hessen, or Austria. Of equally great significance was the death of Grand Duke Leopold in 1852 and the appointment of his youngest son Friedrich as prince regent.[17]

Born in 1826, Friedrich had received a modern education at the hands of his tutor Karl Friedrich Rinck, a man who held firmly to the conviction that the days of absolutism were gone when royal families could live in intellectual and social isolation.[18] The young prince was schooled in history, modern language, art, and the sciences, continuing his education in the mid-1840s at the University of Heidelberg. Here he came into close contact with the young, liberal-minded *Privatdozent* Ludwig Häusser and his circle of friends, men such as Franz von Roggenbach, August Lamey, and Julius Jolly who would later serve the prince as leading ministers in his government. Like them, Friedrich became inspired by the idea of national unification, and came to believe that education and political constitutionalism provided the best tools for accomplishing this end. Later in life he even developed a plan to try and bring about the unification of Germany through education. Skeptical of Prussian political life, yet convinced that unification under Prussian hegemony would benefit Baden economically and protect it from the territorial aspirations of France, Friedrich favored the establishment of a school for German princes where, through a modern education, traditions of particularism would be broken and feelings of German nationalism awakened. Thus in contrast to Prussia and Austria, Baden was ruled after the revolution by a man sympathetic to liberal ideals. Although he did not surround himself with strong-minded liberal ministers until he became Grand Duke in 1856, he immediately lifted the state of emergency after assuming the prince regency in 1852, making it known that he would not tolerate any attempts to abolish the constitution or limit the rights of parliament.[19]

These factors—a strong liberal tradition, the return to parliament of many of the *Vormärz* liberals, and the enlightened education of the monarch—worked together, as has already been mentioned, to prevent the occurrence of a long severe period of reaction. Not that the government took lightly the events of the preceding years—on the contrary, most of the measures it adopted in the early 1850s were directed specifically toward prevention of further revolutionary outbreaks—but it favored reform over force as the best way of restoring law and order to the land and encouraging improvements in the material conditions of life. Among these reforms, changes in the educational system played an absolutely central role.

Baden's Commitment to Science Education

In the years following the Revolution of 1848, the Baden government showed a particular concern with educational reforms that would provide students with "knowledge of those basics desirable and necessary for home and life."[20] These "basics" were, for one, religion and discipline, but they also included skills in business, trade, and agriculture needed by the state for improving the economy. As Karl Mathy explained, the future of the state depended on increasing "the productivity of the national economy (*Volkswirthschaft*) through the productive employment of the lower classes"; and this required improvements in education.[21] As a feature article in the *Karlsruher Zeitung* pointed out, reform measures aimed at introducing new skills often necessitated a different way of conceiving and solving problems. Dealing specifically with farmers' resistance to new agricultural techniques, the author argued that the best way to create a "modern" mentality was to begin with the youth:

> A main cause of the difficulty that is preventing the rational method of education and upbringing from having an influence on the farmer has been pointed out often enough. It rests in the conventional use of the traditional, in the laziness and disinclination to adopt something new, even when it is the best, in the aversion toward any exertion or expenses that could prove necessary. One

is dealing with men who are mostly without any internal desire to make advancements in the area of their life's occupation. Thus they cannot easily be weaned away from those things that they have acquired from father and grandfather, which they have practiced since their childhood, and which others around them practice. [They are] rusted in the views, opinions, and prejudices with which they have grown up and which, consequently, are not easily cast aside.

We believe that if improvements are to occur here among the bulk of the population living on the land, then it is necessary to turn to another part of this population. It should be tried for once with the youth. The beginning of the agricultural reform should be placed in the elementary schools and one can see whether the education of the masses does not make better progress. It seems that the youth, receptive as they are and without generation-old prejudices, should be capable of being educated in regard to agriculture as well. The seeds which can be sowed in the youthful temperament take root more easily than at a mature age; first impressions leave their mark easily and remain the entire life. The elementary schools, we believe, should try at any event to educate their pupils to be efficient in general, but certainly particularly in regard to the occupations they will have later in life, and for the vast majority of pupils in the country schools this consists of agriculture.[22]

The politics of education in the 1850s focused on introducing a practical orientation into the school system with the goal of acquainting pupils with modern techniques and conceptions. From this quotation it is clear that reformers were concerned with teaching more than new skills to the members of the younger generation. Schools, in their eyes, had also to combat laziness, teach efficiency, and encourage ambition and the taking of risks. In short, traditions and habits held responsible for the underdeveloped state of the economy had to be overcome by "sowing the seeds" of modernity in the younger generation. And the natural place for doing this, added the author of this article, was during lessons in the natural sciences.

If the younger generation were to learn new skills teachers had to be trained in the new techniques. In the summer of 1850 the Heidelberg professor Wilhelm Dellfs began offering a lecture series on agricultural chemistry primarily for teachers employed in country schools. They were expected to bring this information back to their pupils—children of peasant farmers, for the most part—and educate them in the modern techniques of farming. In addition, to encourage young entrepreneurs to branch out into new areas, it was also necessary to offer them scientific training. Consequently, in the fall of 1851/52 Heidelberg began a second lecture series for industrialists and farmers that emphasized the importance of chemistry for the different branches of the economy, and which included practical work in the laboratory.[23]

Baden's particular interest in improving the agricultural situation led as well to a decision to move the state's agricultural school from Weinheim, a town roughly fifteen kilometers north of Heidelberg, to Karlsruhe. The government's intent was to give students the opportunity to attend classes in the natural sciences at the polytechnic school.[24] This move represented a shift in the content of the program and the kind of student the school wanted to attract, as well as an attempt to raise the standards and status of agricultural education. In the 1840s the Weinheim school had focused primarily on practical instruction, and students were predominantly sons of small landholders and tenant farmers. This was consistent with the view, voiced in the 1830s, that instruction in these technical schools should differ from that of the universities where theory had overwhelming precedence over practical training. In the 1850s, with the growing conviction that the quality of the land could only be improved through the development of a "rational" system of agriculture, the state altered its strategy and decided that at the very least courses in geometry, botany, and agricultural chemistry must accompany practical instruction. This alone may not have warranted the move from Weinheim to Karlsruhe, but the state had higher intentions: it wished to make the study of agriculture more attractive by placing it on a par with other technical sciences. Thus for those students interested in "agricultural science" the opportunity now existed to spend two years at the polytechnic school acquiring a comprehensive background in "zoology, botany, physiology, chemistry, mineralogy, geology, physics, and mathematics" before transferring to the school of agriculture for more specialized training. But even the latter offered subjects such as modern languages, general history, and popular law, "in short, all those subjects with which a well-rounded cultivated farmer must be acquainted."[25] The students intended for this more scientific course of study were not, of course, the sons of tenant farmers, but those of wealthy landowners—the only ones who could finance such an education and afford the materials and machinery for implementing a rational system of agriculture.[26]

Changes and improvements occurred at the polytechnic institute as well. It received a higher yearly budget, and chemistry education was totally reformed. Already in December 1849 the rector of the polytechnic school in Karlsruhe, the forester Johann Ludwig Klauprecht, had advised the ministry of interior to replace the current professor of chemistry, Friedrich August Walchner, with C. Weltzien, an assistant professor who taught agricultural chemistry at the forestry school.[27] This request reflected an interest in supporting not simply a younger man, but one who represented a different style of scientific research as well. Walchner, whose interests were primarily in mineralogy and geology, viewed chemistry as a subsidiary science and saw no reason to invest in a sophisticated laboratory for this subject. Weltzien, on the other hand, had petitioned the government numerous times to give more support to the chemical sciences. In January 1850 the minister of interior showed the first signs of a willingness to listen, and by November, with the help of Klauprecht, the polytechnic school offered Weltzien the chair of chemistry. Plans began simultaneously for the construction of a new research laboratory. The Grand Duke donated the building site, and parliament contributed 9000 gulden. The rest of the money—total costs came to 59,693 gulden—came from the school's own funds (student fees and taxes). The building was completed at an outstanding rate. By the beginning of the academic year 1851/52 the polytechnic school was offering classes in experimental chemistry.

Clearly Baden had a particular interest in supporting an education in chemistry after the revolution. Peter Borscheid has studied the reasons for Baden's commitment to this science, demonstrating a direct link between the degree to which a German state invested in chemistry in the early years of the reaction and the severity of the agricultural crises of the 1840s. He argues that the more serious the crisis (meaning the more it contributed to the unrest and violence in 1848/49), the more anxious a government was to improve the quality of the soil and thereby the economic position of the small farmholders and peasants.[28] Baden, with an exceptionally rapid population growth and a tradition among farmers of continually dividing their property, however small, among their many sons, was one of the hardest hit of all European lands.

Borscheid shows that the government had not been unaware of the seriousness of the agricultural situation in the *Vormärz* period, but without the scare of the revolution the incentive to employ unconventional techniques was lacking. Instead, recourse was taken to the traditional methods of the Thaer school, attempting to increase agricultural output through crop rotation, fertilization with manure and humus, and intensive tillage of the soil. However, these methods had major drawbacks: manure lacked many crucial nutrients, and the mineral content of the humus depended directly on the richness of the crop. A vicious cycle thus set in, and with the constant use of the land under crop rotation the soil became more and more depleted of minerals every year.[29]

Since the 1840s the chemist Justus Liebig had been fighting to convince government ministries of the need to approach agricultural problems from a different perspective. He insisted that the land be viewed not as something with an endless source of fertility but rather as a substance that had to be—and could be—treated artificially by science and technology. Liebig meant, for the most part, by chemistry. In his fight to establish disciplinary autonomy for his subject, he was not shy about proclaiming the centrality of this science not only for agriculture, but for industry and medicine as well. Still, the scientific program for which he fought, and the scientific research that he himself conducted, were both based on collaborative work between all the natural sciences. As with Henle's ideas for the reform of medicine, Liebig's program aimed at developing a rational method of procedure for attacking and solving complex problems in various branches of the economy.[30]

Like Henle, moreover, Liebig was interested in teaching these methods to his students. Since the 1820s he had been doing this at the University of Giessen, introducing his industrious students to standard analytic techniques. His wish to increase government support of laboratory instruction, particularly in Prussia, led him to write a polemical piece in 1840 in which he extolled the virtues of large institutes and laboratories, while chastising the government for its neglect of chemistry. The debate that arose, which R. Steven Turner has analyzed in great detail, centered around different understandings of the social function of the university.[31] The majority of older chemists believed that the large-scale laboratories demanded by Liebig served utilitarian ends alone and thus did not belong in the universities. In a fashion reminiscent of the debates over university reform carried out in Baden a decade earlier, they argued that practical exercises should remain where they belong—in the technical institutes, where students were preparing themselves for later work in industry and manufacturing. Liebig, however, adopted two strategies to challenge this position. For one, he praised, rather than scorned, the material advances that occasionally resulted from scientific research. For him this was a virtue, not a vice, providing justification for, not against, increased support of the experimental sciences. But he also insisted that laboratory work entailed much more than routine mechanical exercises. In other words, at the same time that he praised the link between science and industry he also sought to dissociate laboratory work from its strict identification with industrial training and recast it within the humanist tradition. Scientific research, he argued (and believed, I would contend), developed the student's moral and intellectual character just as well, if not better, than the study of dead languages and classical texts.

Liebig's two-pronged attack on philologists and old-styled humanists remained the strategy of experimentalist scientists fighting for disciplinary autonomy for years to come. Indeed, over twenty years later Hermann Helmholtz, then professor of experimental physiology at the University of Heidelberg, drew attention in a similar fashion to the virtues of the experimental sciences.[32] Although speaking from a different vantage point—a brand new laboratory with work space for about sixty students was well under construction—he, too, emphasized the link between scientific knowledge and material interests while extolling the pedagogical virtues of experimental research. The advantages of this tactic are perhaps obvious to us today—scientists could argue for the usefulness of the knowledge they were producing while still defending the freedom of scientific research (*Wissenschaft um ihrer selbst willen*)—yet the success this strategy would later enjoy was not evident at the time. As Turner's article so clearly shows, ideas about the theoretical nature of university education were still so deeply entrenched that any hint of an association between university and industry challenged the very definition of the former's social function.

Liebig's views on science education, particularly his ideas on how to improve agricultural output, had a few advocates in Baden in the 1840s, but they did not find ready and willing ears until the years following the revolution. The change at that point was, as we have already seen, extensive, beginning with the elementary schools and extending to the polytechnic institute. But the greatest investment made by Baden for the promotion of chemistry was the hiring of an experimental chemist and the construction of a new research laboratory at the University of Heidelberg.

Leopold Gmelin, professor of chemistry in the medical faculty since 1814, was sixty-three years old in 1851 when he requested his retirement. In his own words, he wished to make room for someone who would contribute both to the success and reputation of the university through teaching and research, as well as to the promotion of science and to improvements in public welfare.[33] The medical and philosophical faculties and the ministry of interior all agreed that Liebig himself should be given first choice, and negotiations began in the spring.[34] Liebig, then at Giessen and frustrated with the lack of government support for the natural sciences, showed a definite interest in Heidelberg's offer, expecially since he recognized Baden's intent to make this university town "a midpoint for the study of the natural sciences and medicine in Germany."[35] But he made his acceptance contingent on the hiring of two colleagues of his in technical and physical chemistry, the construction of a laboratory according to his plans, and a yearly budget of 2000 gulden for laboratory costs. The ministry had no problem with the latter two requests. It had, in fact, already decided that a laboratory "had become, independent of Liebig's call, a necessity for the university," but it held the hiring of two additional chemists to be unwarranted. Heidelberg already had a number of young lecturers in chemistry, and the government was not interested in building up this science at the expense of all other subjects.[36]

In August 1852 Liebig decided to accept an offer from Munich, primarily because the appointment involved no teaching responsibilities and allowed him to dedicate his time to research.[37] Baden, long aware of Liebig's lack of interest in teaching and frustrated that negotiations had been taking so long, had contacted Robert Bunsen before receiving this final rejection. Bunsen, professor of chemistry in Breslau and an equally talented experimentalist, accepted Heidelberg's offer in August.[38]

A student of Friedrich Stromeyer, Bunsen had begun his career in 1833 as a young lecturer at the University of Göttingen. Before moving on to an associate professorship at the University of Marburg in 1838, he spent a couple of years at a trade school in Kassel, teaching chemistry to artisans and industrialists. Throughout his career Bunsen showed an interest in the application of experimental techniques to industry—perhaps a result of the early contact with young entrepreneurs. By 1838 he was investigating the industrial production of cast iron, developing methods for the analysis of gases released in the process. As a result of this work, carried out together with the Englishman Lyon Playfair, he demonstrated the great amount of heat lost through traditional charcoal-burning methods. Their suggestions on how to develop more efficient procedures for the production of metals resulted in major financial gains for founding industries.[39]

In 1838 Bunsen accepted an associate professorship in Marburg where he remained thirteen years. Here, in 1841, he developed the "Bunsen battery," which permitted the inexpensive production of strong electric currents. This invention allowed him in the 1850s to use electrochemical techniques to isolate pure metals such as chromium, magnesium, and aluminum, work that resulted once again in improved industrial techniques.[40]

When Bunsen came to Heidelberg in 1852 (he spent a brief period at the University of Breslau just prior to this move) he had already made a name for himself as a master of analytic methods. This reputation applied not only to his research but to his teaching as well, and Baden was clearly interested in both. Parallel to the negotiations with Liebig and Bunsen, parliament had granted the first 15,000 gulden for the construction of a chemistry laboratory that would serve both teaching and research purposes.[41] As we will see, the government actually hoped to return to its earlier plans to build a large institute for all the natural sciences, but Bunsen insisted on his own laboratory.[42] The new professor argued that the fumes and emanations resulting from chemical experiments would damage the equipment and instruments of the other sciences. Moreover, he insisted on having enough space for an apartment within the institute in order to guarantee his proximity to the laboratory. Although estimated expenses for this institute totaled 65,000 gulden, and those for an entire natural science institute 80,000 gulden, Bunsen got his way. His laboratory, built at an expense of almost 70,000 gulden, was completed in 1855.[43] Chemistry, previously a subsidiary science subordinate to medicine and pharmacy, had become the first science at the University of Heidelberg to be granted an experimental laboratory.

Chemistry's success story in Baden is dealt with in great detail by Borscheid. Using a host of different source materials—letter correspondence, ministerial reports, parliamentary proceedings, and newspaper articles—he provides a sophisticated analysis of the emergence of a scientific discipline. Of great importance, he demonstrates that knowledge of chemistry, however advanced, was not sufficient to free this discipline from its subordinate position to pharmacy and medicine. This was something Liebig himself had realized and which had led him to campaign actively for the emancipation of his science, laying particular emphasis on the potential benefits for agriculture, medicine, and industry.[44] These promises, however, had not been sufficient to bring immediate success. What Liebig wanted had gone against established traditions in agricultural methods, not to mention the lack of precedence for the construction of expensive laboratories in the universities. Borscheid thus illustrates the intimate relationship between the establishment of a scientific program and the perception that what it has to offer is needed—in this case Baden's belief that experimental chemistry would help alleviate the agricultural depression and prevent a second revolutionary uprising.

Although Borscheid does not develop the consequences of his study for Ben-David's thesis, it is clear that his work forces a reassessment of the claim that the institutionalization of the sciences occurred solely because of the decentralized German university system. In the decision to build a research laboratory for chemistry, Baden was not merely responding to the demands of Liebig and Bunsen. Nor was it motivated primarily by the desire to attract students and maintain the intellectual prestige of the university. These factors definitely played an important role, but the hiring of an experimental chemist and the construction of a new research laboratory occurred because of more immediate economic and political concerns as well. To be sure, the government would not have granted Bunsen his own laboratory had he not insisted on it. To this extent the competitive atmosphere of the German university system allowed the young chemist to determine the form of his own institute. But the government, intent upon improving the agricultural situation, had already acknowledged the need for a chemistry laboratory in 1851, and parliament had even included funds in the budget for 1851/52 for its construction. The laboratory did not come about because of unintentional social evolution; instead young scientists promised, and state officials believed, that experimental techniques would be able to solve important problems in the economy.

If Borscheid's work needs any qualification, it is to point out that Baden's support for science education neither began in 1848 nor did it focus on agriculture alone. Because his study begins with the revolution, he does not explore the extent to which the important ideological groundwork for the transition to the research university had already been laid in the *Vormärz* period. There is no doubt that investments in the 1850s far outshadowed money spent in previous decades, but the utilitarian concerns of the government in the early years of the reaction did not lead to a new conception of science education; they merely added fuel to a fire that had long been burning.[45] In the *Vormärz* period parliament already showed a growth of interest in practical education and scientific institutes, spending over 78,000 gulden on a new anatomy building, allotting 10,000 gulden for the erection of a chemistry laboratory, and showing definite interest in the construction of an institute for the natural sciences.[46] Furthermore, in the years just after the revolution the government's immediate concern had not been with the construction of a chemistry laboratory alone, but with the revival of the earlier plan for a natural science institute.

In 1850 temporary arrangements had to be made quickly for the scientific collections when the government set up quarters for Prussian troops in the old Dominican cloister where many of the sciences were still housed. The zoology cabinet was thus moved to the new anatomy building, and physics, technology, and mineralogy took up temporary residence in a building rented for this purpose (*"im Haus zum Riesen"*). In 1851, when the troops moved out of Heidelberg and over to Mannheim, the ministry of interior considered the advisability of renovating the cloister for rehabitation by the natural science collections. The government building and economics commission advised strongly against such a move, arguing that "the restoration of this old building, which is multiply deficient and unsuitably designed, would require too great an expenditure without anything purposeful being thereby attained."[47] And Philipp Jolly, professor of physics, saw no reason for this expense when the government had already decided in 1846 to build a new institute. He expected it to happen soon, and he was willing to wait.[48]

The argument that what we see in Baden is a continuum and not a sudden interest in the sciences is further strengthened when one looks at total state expenditures for education between the years 1831 and 1871. As Table 5.1 and Figure 5.1 demonstrate, contributions to science, technology, and agriculture, although increased greatly in the decades after the revolution, received their initial boost in the late 1830s and 1840s.

My qualification of Borscheid's work should not be taken as criticism of his main thesis. Only the scare of the revolution can explain the willingness of parliament to spend tens of thousands of gulden in the 1850s to build experimental laboratories. Moreover, it alone can explain the priority given to chemistry over all other sciences, and the rapid ascent of this science to a fully autonomous discipline within such a short period of time. Nevertheless, the role played by the revolution was one of catalyst in a

Table 5.1   State Expenditure for Science Education

Year	I	II	III	IV	V	VI	VIa	VII	VIIa
1831/32	41,240					41,240	1.0	498,438	1.0
1833/34	41,600	12,000			4,950	58,550	1.4	536,488	1.1
1835/36	59,727	14,400				74,127	1.8	551,694	1.1
1837/38	58,700	14,000		10,725	6,000	89,425	2.2	634,067	1.3
1839/40	51,700	14,221		21,592		87,513	2.1	629,553	1.3
1842/43	60,213	16,087		23,750	14,010	114,060	2.8	683,711	1.4
1844/45	66,254	16,784		29,332	4,773	117,143	2.8	702,579	1.4
1846/47	67,784	18,709	17,522	34,250	60,621	198,886	4.8	880,393	1.8
1848/49	67,784	19,025	21,162	37,153	34,935	180,059	4.4	807,425	1.6
1850/51	76,784	19,698	20,408	36,018	—	152,908	3.7	739,718	1.5
1852/53	76,064	20,500	19,793	35,486	—	151,843	3.7	752,416	1.6
1854/55	71,184	22,997	21,600	33,851	69,507	269,139	6.5	869,532	1.7
1856/57	71,184	22,974	21,600	33,975	—	199,733	4.8	829,710	1.7
1858/59	139,184	27,268	21,600	39,930	2,600	280,582	6.8	956,590	1.9
1860/61	91,184	27,755	21,600	40,139	43,900	274,578	6.7	971,031	1.9
1862/63	201,184	37,453	26,341	57,556	149,500	522,134	12.7	1,389,126	2.8
1864/65	91,184	37,423	20,918	69,999	18,200	237,724	5.8	1,188,938	2.4
1866/67	143,436	42,848	42,633	70,388	167,563	466,818	11.3	1,487,607	3.0
1868/69	147,268	41,944	59,999	79,956	80,888	410,055	9.9	1,810,289	3.6
1870/71	148,600	54,355	52,313	84,908	75,500	415,676	10.1	2,102,185	4.2

I	= Polytechnic school	V	= University science institutes
II	= Trade schools	VI	= Total (columns I–V)
III	= Agricultural education	VIa	= Rate of growth (column VI)
IV	= Non-classical secondary schools	VII	= Total budget for education
	(*höhere Bürgerschulen*)	VIIa	= Rate of growth (column VII)

Source: "Vergleichung der Budgets-Sätze mit den Rechnungs-Resultaten für die Etats-Jahre 1831 bis 1870," in *Verhandlungen*, 2. Kammer (usually, but not always, in Beilagenheft 2).

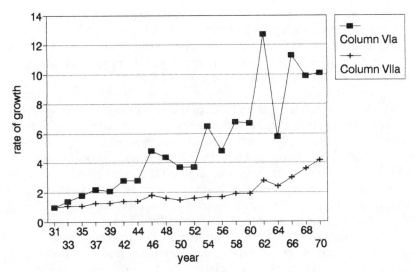

Figure 5.1 Graphical Representation of Columns VIa and VIIa

process that was already underway. It did this by giving utilitarian value, both economically and politically, to what was already a general shift in ideology tied to broader changes in the social and economic structure of the state.

The Ideology of Material Interests

This ideological shift can best be described as a greater concern with "material interests"—a term used by contemporaries of the time. It was popular enough to warrant articles in both Rotteck's and Welcker's *Staatslexikon* and Brockhaus's *Conversations-Lexikon der Gegenwart,* two encyclopedias that represented and promoted an ideology of moderate liberalism. According to these encyclopedias, material interests was a "catchword of the day" referring to those interests aimed at improving the material conditions of life.[49] Because the term "interest" had as negative a connotation in the nineteenth century as it does today, the authors took care to distinguish it sharply from "egoism" or "materialism." For them, the latter gave priority to individual or particular matters, whereas the pursuit of material interests was highly social and directed toward the betterment of life in general. Nothing, they believed, demonstrated this better than the construction of railroads and the *Zollverein.* Both improved economic conditions, raising the standard of life throughout the nation, while also feeding the spirit of the land, for the speed and ease with which people could now travel fostered intellectual communication as well. Thus the goal of these authors was to convince their readers that the pursuit of material interests did not represent a less valuable intellectual exercise than the study of traditional humanist subjects. In a fashion similar to Liebig's polemic on behalf of science education, one author argued that the promotion of material interests was nothing more than "the exercise and strengthening of these intellectual powers in a varied form."[50]

Although in the years following the revolution individuals from across the political spectrum began to speak of the importance of developing the nation's material interests, its loudest advocates remained those with more liberal views. As is well known, many liberals responded to the Frankfurt parliament's failure to bring about the political unification of Germany by shifting their attention to economic affairs. Their hope was that stronger economic ties between the various states would succeed where political struggles had failed—that is, in bringing about the desired unification of the nation. On the front page of the *Karlsruher Zeitung,* for example, the author of a feature article entitled "Die materiellen Interessen" argued that the development of transportation, trade, industry, and agriculture satisfied political, intellectual, and social needs. Indeed, a trade policy had become a surrogate constitution:

> Unification through a trade policy is a substitute, a necessity, and a condition: a substitute for the political constitution, recognized by all to be inadequate; necessary for a sense of national unity without which Germany would be destroyed; necessary for the existence of individual states and individual families; a condition and a foundation for every advancement in the development of a better constitution for the German Union.[51]

The phrase "material interests" thus symbolized many things. It offered promises of economic improvement; it suggested an alternative to communism (a welcome message to liberals and conservatives alike) for alleviating the problems that had given rise to so much dissatisfaction and frustration; it fed the liberals' dream of a modern Germany united by economic necessity and bound by a constitution. But for any of this to become a reality, certain social and economic traditions had to be broken, and one place to begin, liberals argued, was in the schools. Changes in this direction had already begun in the *Vormärz* period. The creation of trade schools and non-classical secondary schools, greater support for the polytechnic school, and the reform of the classical *Gymnasia* had all reflected these interests. In the 1850s this trend continued. As Figure 5.1 showed, Baden's support of the *Realwissenschaften* increased substantially during this decade. Although the greatest investments were initially in agricultural instruction—obviously an attempt to make up rapidly for time lost—expenditures for the other schools soon caught up and eventually reversed this relationship. The non-classical secondary schools, for example, received substantial financial increases after a somewhat slow start, and the polytechnic school, in addition to receiving funds specifically for the construction of experimental laboratories, was granted a higher yearly budget that continued to grow during the 1850s.

This was the environment in which the experimental sciences took form and eventually found a home in the university system. It was characterized by a higher estimation of knowledge and skills that could translate into improving the material interests of the state. In the universities, of course, discussion of the utilitarian value of laboratory exercises remained subdued. Professors continued, instead, to define the universities as educational institutions dedicated to the cultivation of the student's intellect, but the content of this education had begun to change. Although the universities still had advocates of a more theoretical and (in their eyes) scholarly education, the number of professors and ministers who promoted the combination of theory and practice continued to grow. Not ignoring the possible material benefits to be gained from such a union, they preferred to emphasize, in true liberal fashion, the value of practical exercises as a tool for teaching students to think "exactly," critically, and, of great importance, independently of any authority.[52]

The teaching laboratory became the symbol of this educational ideology, and for a brief period the University of Heidelberg was one of its most important champions. Impelling agricultural concerns had played a major role in Baden's decision in the 1850s to invest heavily in the experimental sciences, but the persistence of a liberal tradition that linked material improvements, educational reforms, political constitutionalism, and national unification contributed as well. This becomes clear when one considers the situation at other universities. At a time when Baden allocated funds for Bunsen's institute and began to draw up and then execute plans for a new natural science laboratory, Prussia entered a period of reaction, placing educational affairs in the hands of Karl von Raumer, a conservative-minded minister whose indifference toward the natural sciences (his passion was the church) led to a decade of stagnation. Not only did he concede to the wishes of philologists in 1856 and reduce the number of hours spent on the natural sciences in the classical *Gymnasia* from sixteen to six per week,[53] he repeatedly ignored the requests of university professors for laboratories where students could engage in practical exercises. This was most evident at the University of Berlin, where Gustav Magnus, professor of physics, fought in vain for a laboratory modeled after the ones in Heidelberg and Göttingen. As late as 1867 he was still offering practical instruction in his own home. A similar fate befell Emil du Bois-Reymond, whose physiology "laboratory" consisted of a long, relatively dark and narrow room on the second floor of the anatomy museum; construction of a new institute did not begin until the early 1870s. Nor did Eilhardt Mitscherlich have any better luck trying to persuade the government to build a new chemistry laboratory. Not until the beginning of the new era, when Prince William succeeded his father and surrounded himself by more liberal-minded ministers, did Prussia even begin to pursue a more active science policy in regard to the universities.[54]

A similar dynamic occurred at the University of Leipzig. There, too, the construction of major teaching and research laboratories occurred after the onset of the new era, when Johann Paul Freiherr von Falkenstein, head of the ministry of culture, worked together with parliament to upgrade science education.[55] A long-term liberal, Falkenstein had served the government in various capacities in the 1830s, during which time he convinced the government to finance a state-owned railroad, advocated the creation of a customs union, fought for freedom of the press, and arranged the appointment of one of the Göttingen seven to the University of Leipzig. In the 1860s, he turned his attention to improvements in education. With the support of parliament, he raised teachers' salaries, founded teaching seminars, and fought the church for control over the schools. Moreover, convinced that Saxony's further transition to a modern industrial state depended upon support for science education (with the exception of certain regions in Prussia, Saxony was the most industrialized of all German states), he made substantial investments in the non-classical secondary schools, and began the construction of new teaching and research laboratories at the University of Leipzig. The most famous of these—Carl Ludwig's physiology laboratory—was completed in 1868, along with a new chemistry laboratory. Other institutes followed soon after the war.

Thus Baden's support of the experimental sciences in the 1850s and early 1860s, although not unique, was precocious. The relative harmony that reigned between monarch, ministry, and parliament, and their shared support for political and economic liberalism, provided a more conducive environment for reforming the universities. Two years after Bunsen joined Heidelberg's philosophy faculty, he orchestrated the appointment of his close friend, Gustav Kirchhoff, a young experimental physicist with whom he had worked closely in Breslau. Bunsen held him to be the smartest of the young men who had studied under Magnus in Berlin, and the best mathematical physicist in Germany.[56] Kirchhoff shared, moreover, Bunsen's political views. Throughout their years in Heidelberg, both men traveled in liberal circles (their friends included Häusser, Gervinus, Vangerow, von Mohl, and later Helmholtz) and fought for the appointment of other professors who shared their views on science and politics.

Bunsen's attempt to complete the triumvirate and bring a young experimental physiologist to Heidelberg was, however, less successful. Actually, plans to hire a physiologist preceded Bunsen's tenure at the university, but for several reasons they failed. In contrast to the appointments in chemistry and physics, the hiring of an experimental physiologist involved the creation of a new position rather than the replacement of an "old-style" scientist with an experimentalist. Thus, necessary funds had to be available. But financial considerations were not the only hinderance. Several members of the medical faculty, foremost the conservative-minded professor of surgery, Maximilian von Chelius, were also strongly opposed. The battles that ensued, and they lasted until 1856 when Friedrich became Grand Duke and silenced the conservative opposition, form the subject of the next chapter. They provide an exemplary tool for unraveling the various interests—political, disciplinary, and in the case of physiology, medical—

surrounding the institutionalization of the experimental sciences, demonstrating that much more than the dynamics of the academic market were at play.

Notes

1. Frank R. Pfetsch, *Zur Entwicklung der Wissenschaftspolitik in Deutschland, 1750–1914* (Berlin, 1974), p. 52; Wolfram Fischer, "Wissenschaft, Technik und wirtschaftliche Entwicklung in Deutschland seit dem 18. Jahrhundert," *Berliner wissenschaftliche Gesellschaft e.v. Jahrbuch,* 1 (1977/78): 107–128, p. 121.

2. Peter Borscheid, *Naturwissenschaft, Staat und Industrie in Baden, 1848–1914* (Stuttgart, 1976). I expand on Borscheid's thesis on pp. 97–105.

3. Wolfram Fischer, *Der Staat und die Anfänge der Industrialisierung in Baden 1800–1850. Vol. 1: Die staatliche Gewerbepolitik* (Berlin, 1962), p. 27.

4. Walter Schöler, *Geschichte des naturwissenschaftlichen Unterrichts im 17. bis 19. Jahrhundert* (Berlin, 1970), p. 221; Friedrich Paulsen, *Geschichte des gelehrten Unterrichts auf den deutschen Schulen und Universitäten,* 2 vols. (Leipzig, 1897), vol. 2, p. 517.

5. Loyd E. Lee, *The Politics of Harmony. Civil Service, Liberalism, and Social Reform in Baden, 1800–1850* (Newark, 1980), pp. 171–172.

6. Lothar Gall, "Gründung und politische Entwicklung des Großherzogtums bis 1848," in *Badische Geschichte,* ed. Landeszentrale für politische Bildung Baden-Württemberg (Stuttgart, 1979), pp. 11–36, here p. 33; Friedrich von Weech, *Badische Geschichte* (Karlsruhe, 1890), p. 558; Karl Stiefel, *Baden 1648–1952,* 2 vols. (Karlsruhe, 1977), vol. I, p. 272; "Friedrich von Blittersdorff," in *BB,* 2: 87–103.

7. Stiefel, *Baden,* vol. I, pp. 272–273; Weech, *Badische Geschichte,* pp. 558–565; Gall, "Gründung und politische Entwicklung," p. 33; "Alexander von Dusch," in *BB,* 1: 197–204; "Johann Baptist Bekk," in ibid., 1: 61–69.

8. Franz X. Vollmer, "Die 48er Revolution," in *Badische Geschichte,* ed. Landeszentrale für politische Bildung Baden-Württemberg (Stuttgart, 1979), pp. 37–64, here pp. 38–39. Also Theodore S. Hamerow, *Restoration, Revolution, Reaction, Economics and Politics in Germany, 1815–1871* (Princeton, 1958), chap. 3.

9. Vollmer, "Die 48er Revolution," p. 38. Baden had a population density of 88 persons per square kilometer in comparison to 56 per square kilometer in Prussia. See Fischer, *Der Staat und die Anfänge der Industrialisierung,* p. 328.

10. Fischer, *Der Staat und die Anfänge der Industrialisierung,* p. 381; Hamerow, *Restoration, Revolution, Reaction,* chap. 3.

11. Hugo Ott, "Die wirtschaftliche und soziale Entwicklung von der Mitte des 19. Jahrhunderts bis zum Ende des Ersten Weltkriegs," in *Badische Geschichte,* ed. Landeszentrale für politische Bildung Baden-Württemberg (Stuttgart, 1979), pp. 103–142, here pp. 103–106; Hamerow, *Restoration, Revolution, Reaction,* p. 76; Fischer, *Der Staat und die Anfänge der Industrialisierung,* p. 390.

12. See Fischer, *Der Staat und die Anfänge der Industrialisierung,* p. 386.

13. On Mathy, see "Karl Mathy," in *BB,* 2: 45–69; Erich Angermann, "Karl Mathy als Sozial- und Wirtschaftspolitiker (1842–48)," *Zeitschrift für die Geschichte des Oberrheins,* 103 (1955): 499–622.

14. Weech, *Badische Geschichte,* pp. 567–568.

15. Günter Richter, "Revolution and Gegenrevolution in Baden 1849," *Zeitschrift für die Geschichte des Oberrheins,* 119 (1971): 387–425. Lothar Gall, *Der Liberalismus als regierende Partei* (Wiesbaden, 1968), pp. 56–62. Gall speaks, in fact, of "restrictions" alone; he denies that a true reaction occurred in Baden. Richter challenges this interpretation in his article, see p. 424.

16. Gall, *Der Liberalismus als regierende Partei,* p. 61.

17. Leopold's older son, Ludwig, was mentally retarded and thus incapable of succeeding his father. Friedrich ruled as Prince Regent until his brother's death in 1856, when he acquired the title of Grand Duke.

18. Alfred Girlich, *Die Grundlagen der Innenpolitik Badens unter Großherzog Friedrich I. Entwicklung und Verwirklichung der Idee einer Volkserziehung* (Diss. Heidelberg, 1952), p. 100; Gall, *Der Liberalismus als regierende Partei,* p. 63; Hermann Oncken, ed., *Großherzog Friedrich I. von Baden und die deutsche Politik von 1854–1871. Briefwechsel, Denkschriften, Tagebücher* (Stuttgart, 1927), p. 2; Stiefel, *Baden, 1648–1952,* vol. 1, pp. 290–298.

19. Bernd Ottnad, "Politische Geschichte von 1850 bis 1918," in *Badische Geschichte,* ed. Landeszentrale für politische Bildung Baden-Württemberg (Stuttgart, 1979), pp. 65–85, esp. pp. 66–67.

20. "Die neuesten Verordnungen über das Volksschulwesen," *Karlsruher Zeitung,* 6 November 1851. For similar views, see the published account of the parliamentary proceedings of the lower house, in the *Karlsruher Zeitung,* 3 November 1850, and "Ueber die politische Bildung der Jugend," in ibid., 20 and 21 May 1853.

21. Cited in Fischer, *Der Staat und die Anfänge der Industrialisierung,* pp. 389–390.

22. "Die Volksschule in Hinsicht auf die Landwirthschaft," *Karlsruher Zeitung,* 19 February 1852.

23. Borscheid, *Naturwissenschaft, Staat und Industrie,* pp. 58–60.

24. Ibid., pp. 56–57. See also "Einrichtung einer landwirthschaftlichen Schule zu Karlsruhe," *Karlsruher Zeitung,* 17 September 1851.

25. "Einrichtung einer landwirthschaftlichen Schule zu Karlsruhe."

26. Borscheid, *Naturwissenschaft, Staat und Industrie,* p. 57.

27. Ibid. The following is from pp. 50–53.

28. Ibid., pp. 9–71.

29. Ibid., pp. 16–27.

30. Ibid.; R. Steven Turner, "Justus Liebig versus Prussian chemistry: Reflections on early institute-building in Germany," *Historical Studies in the Physical Sciences,* 13, 1 (1982): 129–162.

31. Turner, "Justus Liebig versus Prussian chemistry."

32. Hermann von Helmholtz, "Ueber das Verhältnis der Naturwissenschaften zur Gesamtheit der Wissenschaft," Akademische Festrede gehalten zu Heidelberg am 22 November 1862 bei Antritt des Prorectorats. In Helmholtz, *Vorträge und Reden,* 5th ed., 2 vols. (Braunschweig, 1903), vol. 1, pp. 157–185. I discuss this speech in detail in Chapter 9.

33. Letter from Gmelin, 27 February 1851, BGLA 205/255.

34. Faculty senate to the ministry of interior, 30 March 1851, BGLA 235/3113.

35. Cited in Borscheid, *Naturwissenschaft, Staat und Industrie,* p. 62.

36. Ministry of interior to the state ministry, 6 June 1851, BGLA 235/3113.

37. Borscheid, *Naturwissenschaft, Staat und Industrie,* p. 62; Frederic L.

Holmes, "The Formation of the Munich School of Metabolism," in William Coleman and Frederic L. Holmes, eds., *The Investigative Enterprise. Experimental Physiology in Nineteenth-Century Medicine* (Berkeley, 1988), pp. 179–210.

38. Ministry of interior to the state ministry, 6 August 1852, BGLA 235/3113.

39. Georg Lockemann, *The Story of Chemistry* (New York, 1959), pp. 175–179; Susan G. Schacher, "Robert Wilhelm Eberhard Bunsen," *DSB*, 2 (1970): 586–590.

40. Lockemann, *The Story of Chemistry*, pp. 175–179.

41. Borscheid, *Naturwissenschaft, Staat und Industrie*, pp. 62–63.

42. Ministry of interior to the state ministry, 5 May 1852, BGLA 235/3113; Bunsen to the ministry of interior, 3 November 1853, BGLA 235/352.

43. Borscheid, *Naturwissenschaft, Staat und Industrie*, p. 64.

44. Ibid., p. 35ff.

45. Borscheid argues that investments in the 1850s represented a sharp break with the past. His exact words are: "Nach Jahrzehnten der öffentlichen Mißachtung waren die Naturwissenschaften plötzlich wiederum zum bevorzugten Förderungsobjekt der badischen Regierung geworden." See *Naturwissenschaft, Staat und Industrie*, p. 59.

46. See Chapter 2 of this book.

47. Building and economics commission to the ministry of interior, 4 December 1851, BGLA 235/354.

48. Jolly to the building and economics commission, 21 November 1851, BGLA 235/354.

49. "Ideen, politisch, und Ideologie; ideelle und materielle Interessen," in *Staatslexikon oder Encyclopädie der Staatswissenschaften,* eds. Carl von Rotteck, Carl Welcker, 15 vols. (Altona, 1834–1843), 8 (1839): 283–295; "Materielle Interessen," in F. A. Brockhaus, *Conversations-Lexikon der Gegenwart* (Leipzig, 1838–1841), 3 (1840): 557–564. The importance of material interests in nineteenth-century German thought is the topic of a paper by Timothy Lenoir, "The Politics of Material Interests" (unpublished manuscript).

50. "Erfahrung," in *Staatslexikon*, 5 (1837): 253–263, here p. 253. See also "Ideen, politisch, und Ideologie," and "Materielle Interessen."

51. "Die materiellen Interessen," *Karlsruher Zeitung*, 25 August 1852.

52. A classic statement of the scientific method's value as a tool for teaching critical thinking is Hermann von Helmholtz, "Ueber das Verhältnis der Naturwissenschaften zur Gesamtheit der Wissenschaft."

53. Schöler, *Geschichte des naturwissenschaftlichen Unterrichts*, p. 221; Paulsen, *Geschichte des gelehrten Unterrichts*, vol. 2, p. 517.

54. See Max Lenz, *Geschichte der königlichen Friedrich-Wilhelms-Universität zu Berlin*, 4 vols. in 5 (Halle, 1910–1918), vol. 3, pp. 154–163 (physiology), 278–296 (physics), 296–306 (chemistry). The only institute built in the 1850s at the University of Berlin was Rudolph Virchow's pathology institute. Nevertheless, even here expenditures were small. The institute consisted of little more than renovations and additions to the existent dissection house, with total costs running to a mere 14,000 taler. See ibid., pp. 165–176. For the physiology laboratory, see also Albert Guttstadt, *Die naturwissenschaftlichen und medicinischen Staatsanstalten Berlins. Festschrift für die 59. Versammlung deutscher Naturforscher und Aerzte* (Berlin, 1886), pp. 260–264.

55. "Johann Paul Freiherr von Falkenstein," *ADB*, 48 (1904): 489–494. See

also Timothy Lenoir's article, "Science for the Clinic: Science Policy and the For-
mation of Carl Ludwig's Institute in Leipzig," in William Coleman and Frederic L.
Holmes, eds., *The Investigative Enterprise. Experimental Physiology in Nineteenth-
Century Medicine* (Berkeley, 1988), pp. 139–178, esp. pp. 165–169.

56. Bunsen to Ludwig, 28 September 1851, Correspondence Bunsen, University of Heidelberg, Handschriftenabteilung, 2812, pp. 11–18.

6

The Battle for an Experimental Physiologist

When the University of Heidelberg created a separate chair for experimental physiology in 1858, it did so in response to a decade-long battle for the establishment of this discipline. The decentralized structure of the German university system may have fostered the relatively rapid establishment of the experimental sciences throughout Germany (as compared to other European countries), but the decision, as I have been arguing, to invest heavily in these subjects was based in part on a broader "ideology of the practical" that rated highly the exact method of the experimental sciences as a tool for teaching a critical approach to problem solving. In addition, other concerns, peculiar to physiology, contributed to the establishment of this discipline. For one, methodological changes, foremost the development of sophisticated instrumental techniques, encouraged specialization, making it increasingly difficult for one individual to assume responsibility for all the life sciences. In Heidelberg, as elsewhere, this generated discussions on the advisability of expanding the medical faculty and creating a new position for a physiologist. One of the strongest advocates of this expansion was Henle, who, by mid-century, was defining himself more and more as an anatomist and actively campaigning for the appointment of a physiologist who could take over his classes in physiology and teach the experimental method to students. In his efforts he received strong support from members of both the state health commission and the local medical society, who fought for the appointment of an experimental physiologist as part of their greater plans to reform educational and licensing requirements in the state. In the same way that impelling agricultural problems led to increased support for chemistry, medical concerns defined the context in which experimental physiology became established in the university system.

Although the Baden government showed an interest in hiring an experimental physiologist in the early 1850s, a number of factors kept it from taking action until later in the decade. First, great investments in chemistry depleted the available funds, but, as I have already indicated, resistance on the part of several older members of the medical faculty played a role as well. Political differences colored their feelings toward the young experimentalists; but they disliked even more the tendency toward increased specialization. For them, the focus on sophisticated instruments and ever smaller areas of research challenged the earlier notion of *Wissenschaft* with which they still identified. In the somewhat conservative and financially constrained atmosphere following the revolution, these professors succeeded in having their way; not until political changes in 1856 brought in a more liberal-minded ministry did the tide turn. Thus, as we will see in this chapter, the successful establishment of experimental physiology represented a response to the specific, albeit varied, needs and wishes of several different groups.

Henle's Interest in Hiring a Physiologist

In the winter of 1848, even before tensions between Tiedemann and Henle had reached a peak, the latter had already begun making plans to bring a physiologist to Heidelberg. His preferred candidate was Carl Ludwig. Since 1846, when the young experimental physiologist had written to Henle, praising his *Handbuch der rationellen Pathologie,* the two men had remained in correspondence, sharing scientific, political, and professional ideas.[1] Henle was sympathetic to Ludwig's approach to the study of organic function, an approach the young experimentalist shared with his friends Emil du Bois-Reymond, Hermann Helmholtz, and Ernst Brücke. In 1847 the four young scientists had sworn an oath to reduce physiology to its chemical and physical foundations, creating an organic physics based exclusively on mathematical, physical, and chemical laws. Although, as Paul Cranefield has pointed out, the members of the "1847 group" did not fulfill their reductionist dreams, they did succeed in establishing a new methodological approach to the study of organic function based on active experimentation.[2]

In developing this new approach the young scientists relied heavily on sophisticated instruments and instrumental techniques. Du Bois-Reymond's astatic galvanometer and induction apparatus, Helmholtz's myograph, ophthalmoscope, and ophthalmometer, and Ludwig's kymograph and vacuum pump are only a few of the many instruments conceived of and often constructed by this new generation of physiologists. These instruments simplified conditions for experimenting on isolated organs, allowed better control of the phenomena, aided in the establishment of causal connections, and permitted exact measurements and graphical representation of organic functions. In addition, they required a mastery of mathematical skills and technical dexterity that clearly distinguished this methodological approach from the microscopical, chemical, and vivisectional skills of most anatomists.[3]

At the time Henle began showing an interest in bringing Ludwig to Heidelberg, the young physiologist had just completed the construction of an instrument that would eventually revolutionize the medical field—the kymograph. Ludwig had been studying the physical dynamics of body fluids, and was particularly interested in the relationship between pressure fluctuations in the main arteries and the thorax cavity. In order to establish pressure changes in the latter he had taken a tube attached to an expandable balloon, filled them with water, and sealed the tube hermetically within the chest wall of the test animal. To make the fluctuations visible he had then connected the tube to a U-shaped quicksilver pressure gauge. Measuring the blood pressure had been easier; here he had made use of a standard manometer invented by the Frenchman Poiseuille specifically for measuring arterial pulsations. By using these two techniques, Ludwig had been able to demonstrate the plausibility of a correlation between the two organic functions, but he wished to make a stronger statement. The solution ended up being technical and it made possible not only more sensitive readings, but the simultaneous recording of pressure fluctuations in the blood and thorax cavity as well.[4]

Ludwig's invention was straightforward. He placed a rod-shaped swimmer with a feather quill on top of the quicksilver in the pressure gauge, and positioned the quill against an evenly rotating drum. The result was a drawing that provided information on both the intensity of the pressure (the height) and the periodic variations (the width). By positioning the quill at the same point on the drum for different recordings, Ludwig could, moreover, compare graphs easily and describe with greater accuracy the degree to which correlations existed between different functions. This instrument thus offered the possibility of capturing in quantitative form what had previously been known only as vague patterns of behavior. The consequences for medicine would eventually be tremendous. The stethoscope may have made audible what remained invisible, but the kymograph promised to translate these invisible functions into visible forms. All these instruments came to symbolize to the physician "objective" sources of information that freed him from dependence on "subjective" patient accounts. The ever growing number of new diagnostic techniques not only increased medicine's status as an exact science; it also, as Pfeufer had pointed out, redefined the terms of entry into the elite medical profession, basing it less on "genius" and "intuition" than on familiarity with standard scientific and instrumental techniques.

As mentioned previously, the kymograph was only one of many instruments used by the younger generation of physiologists in their attempt to redefine their field and transform the study of organic function into an exact science. Henle, aware of these new developments, and conscious even more so of his inability to teach the entire area of anatomy and physiology, tried to bring Ludwig to Heidelberg in 1848. The young physiologist showed an immediate interest in the position. Although he was an associate professor in Marburg at the time, he had had difficulties with the conservative Kurhessen government since his university days in the 1830s, and matters grew only worse with the onset of the reaction following the failure of the Revolution of 1848.[5] Thus Ludwig had definite reasons for wanting to leave Marburg, but from his letters to Henle it is clear he also had particular interests in coming to Heidelberg. The young physiologist believed that a person, such as Henle, who had defined his own rational method as one that traced physiological and pathological facts "back to physical and chemical processes," would be interested in helping him and his friends establish a program of organic physics. He also valued the opportunity to work with someone whose energies focused both on bridging the gap between physiology and pathology, and on persuading the medical community of the necessity of this link. Ludwig realized that many physicians had yet to be convinced of the relevance of experimental research for medical theory and practice, and he appreciated Henle's importance here. "It had become obvious to me," he wrote in his first letter to Henle, "that we calculators and experimentalists would not be able to live at all without a person like you."[6] Not only did Henle raise questions that often provided the stimulus for physiological research, but through his journal, textbooks, and lectures, he had direct contact with the medical community.

Historians of physiology have tended not so much to challenge as to overlook the importance of the medical context for the history of their discipline.[7] Yet it is clear that Ludwig understood the significance of this context; nor was he alone. His friend Helmholtz, inventor of the ophthalmoscope, although interested primarily in questions related to physics, epistemology, and mathematics, also cultivated a connection with the medical community.[8] The motives of these young scientists were not merely self-serving ones, although Ludwig, Helmholtz, and others were acutely aware that institutional support for their subject would have to come from the medical faculties. Nevertheless, they perceived themselves to be part of a community of scientists whose goal was to demonstrate the superiority of inductive over speculative methods of inquiry for the acquisition of true knowledge about the natural world.[9] Practical medical applications of their work provided them with ideal ammunition in this struggle, in the same way that someone engaged in basic research receives confirmation of his or her theories when they are used to cure a fatal illness.

Ludwig had strong hopes that Henle would support this community. In a letter written in November 1848, he even suggested that Henle convert his *Zeitschrift für rationelle Medizin* into the voice of these "new powers": men who were doing exciting work in physiology, clinical medicine, and physics. "If someone would successfully focus these powers," he wrote, "then an enterprise might easily be created that would have no equal in brilliance." And Ludwig knew exactly where Henle would find these individuals:

> When I think of DuBois, Helmholtz, Brücke, Vierordt, Traube and E. Weber my heart beats for joy over such education and talent. When I include your microscopical and Liebig's chemical schools, then such a great number of young and brave powers . . . presents itself that one hardly knows what to do with all the wealth.[10]

Although a direct response to this proposal is not available, subsequent articles in the *Zeitschrift* suggest that Henle's interest in this experimental direction fell short of Ludwig's expectations. Moreover, in later years, although expressing great respect for the work being carried out in this field, Henle admitted a certain skepticism toward a purely experimental approach to the study of form and function.[11] As we have already seen, his "rational method" embraced several different scientific styles, having little to do with the emerging specialization implicit in the demands of the 1847 group. Henle supported experimental work, but not to the exclusion of other scientific approaches. Ludwig, on the other hand, fought hard to distinguish his style of research from the morphological tradition of the Göttingen school. In 1849 he wrote to Henle of his hope that the two of them would be able to convert Heidelberg into an "experimental college" that "would be in a position to offer strong competition to the Göttingers."[12] That Henle did not share Ludwig's vision is evident from the ease with which he transferred his allegiance back and forth between morphologists and "organic physicists" in the three years in which he attempted to convince the Baden government to hire a professor of physiology.

The first sign of Henle's lack of total commitment to the 1847 group came in 1850, after negotiations with Ludwig had fallen through.[13] At this point Henle, who was still intent on hiring a professor of physiology, directed his energies toward Carl von Siebold, then professor of anatomy and physiology in Freiburg and one of the leading comparative anatomists of the day.[14] Von Siebold had studied medicine in Berlin briefly (1823) before transferring to Göttingen, where he remained for the next three years working with Blumenbach and Hansmann. All of his subsequent publications (and by 1850 they totaled over one hundred) dealt with research in zoology and comparative anatomy; and in 1848 he began a journal with A. Kölliker entitled *Zeitschrift für wissenschaftliche Zoologie*.

Von Siebold's reputation as a morphologist did not, however, prevent Henle from identifying him as an experimentalist. Indeed, in a report Henle sent to the medical faculty, he stated explicitly that Siebold and he would together

> be able to create an institute whose operation surmounts the energy of a single individual, a zootomic-physiological institute in which the students would be involved in experimenting and investigating scientific questions, and where they would be educated for the special branches of our science.[16]

Nothing demonstrates better the different views Henle and Ludwig held regarding the nature and future of physiological research than this statement. Henle's approach to the study of organic function was eclectic at its core, a result of his having studied medicine at a time when a clear methodological split between anatomy and physiology did not yet exist. Both subjects, had, rather, focused on the use of the microscope. Henle was not, of course, unaware of the growing diversification in the field; he once even apologized to du Bois-Reymond for "still holding a high post in a field for which younger powers have earned fair claims."[16] Moreover, he knew only too well of the emerging tensions between the morphological and physicalist schools, having received several letters from Ludwig in which the young physiologist mentioned and discussed the differences between these two approaches.[17] Nevertheless, Henle's awareness did not translate into a commitment to one side of the battle or the other; nor did he reserve the word "experimental" for the approach to the study of organic phenomena associated with the 1847 group. Rather, Henle's concern in the early 1850s was simply to hire the best person available, and in his eyes, von Siebold was highly qualified to "take over physiology entirely or in part, thereby giving me the opportunity to dedicate more hours in the summer semester to applied anatomy, and to the subsidiary anatomical subjects, such as general, topographical, and pathological [anatomy], etc."[18]

When Ludwig heard of Henle's decision to bring von Siebold to Heidelberg he wrote a desperate letter sharing his concern and surprise. Aware of the importance of Henle's work and support for the future of experimental physiology, he expressed his dismay at the apparent abandonment of what he thought were common goals.

> I was grieved to death when Stannius brought me the news that you are now thinking of Siebold and are already in negotiations with him. In spite of the greatest admiration which I have for him, I stand nevertheless by the conviction that he will not help Heidelberg. What von Siebold can do for Heidelberg, you are already achieving more than once over.[19]

Ludwig then went on to promote his comrades-in-arm, Helmholtz and du Bois-Reymond, praising them both and comparing their talents in research, teaching, and politics. "When you have the choice between Helmholtz and du Bois-Reymond, then you are reveling in riches. And were I to have to decide between the two . . . I would take them both."[20]

Henle, disturbed that negotiations with von Siebold were taking so long, did inquire of Helmholtz and du Bois-Reymond whether they would be interested in a position at Heidelberg.[21] After receiving affirmative responses from both, he encouraged the medical faculty to submit a final report to the university faculty senate. In a fashion that would have been less than satisfying to Ludwig and the other young experimentalists, Heidelberg's medical faculty announced that its first choice remained von Siebold, "one of the first celebrities in comparative anatomy," but it added that if obstacles should stand in the way of hiring Professor Siebold, then, since the faculty knows of no one else who enjoys such a universally recognized reputation in both physiology and comparative anatomy, it would direct its proposal to one of the young scholars representing experimental physiology.[22]

Medical Interests in Experimental Physiology

This supportive though restrained recognition of the young experimentalists was overshadowed by the great enthusiasm expressed by the Baden health commission, a government committee subordinate to the ministry of interior.[23] Organized in 1803, the commission consisted primarily of physicians and had, as part of its responsibilities, control over the state medical examination and the granting of medical licenses. Moreover, it had a say (albeit only in an advisory capacity) in the kind of education and training offered to medical students. In June 1852 it came out strongly in support of the new experimental sciences. In a recommendation sent to the ministry of interior, it pointed out that Siebold was "more zootomist than physiologist" and thus not able to represent the latter science in the necessary fashion:

> To stay in the spirit of the times it is necessary to focus on cultivating the exact method in true scientific research and to train students more in the method of examining and utilizing natural objects. This being so, he [Siebold] would not teach the subject of physiology in an up to date fashion . . . and another teacher, acquainted with the exact method and capable of heading a physiological institute with success, must be called in his place.[24]

The health commission was echoing a general concern of physicians with the kind of education being offered to medical students. In Baden, state-employed physicians had formed a local medical organization in 1835, private physicians in 1844, and both had consistently placed great importance on the natural sciences as a way to raise standards in the profession and improve physicians' social standing in society.[25] In their local journals, physicians pleaded with their colleagues to end the pettiness, bickering, and competition that divided the profession, hurt its image, and weakened its collective strength. Instead, they argued, physicians must share their knowledge and experience, uniting around the common goal of promoting *Wissenschaft*. In this way medical care would improve, and physicians would form a united front capable of protecting their own interests.

For private physicians, who did not have the security enjoyed by their state-employed colleagues, the issue of financial security took center stage. This concern led some to argue for the advantages of making all physicians employees of the state, but most contributors to the organizations' journal, *Mittheilungen des badischen ärztlichen Vereins,* rejected such a move. In fact, they advocated even greater freedom from the duties imposed on them by the government, arguing for the "release of physicians from the government's tutelage and supervision."[26] In particular, they wanted to end their obligation to treat all individuals who requested their assistance, regardless of the person's ability to pay (the so-called *Kurierzwang*). Few, however, advocated total autonomy. Rather, members of the organization wanted the government to identify them as the true representatives of physicians in private practice, and consult them in all medical matters. Foremost, they wanted to work with the government to restructure the medical system.

One of their major goals was to convince the government to raise the qualifications necessary for practicing medicine. In the 1840s there were nine categories of health practitioners in Baden, each with different skills and educational backgrounds.[27] Officially the medical responsibilities of each group were carefully specified, but in practice boundaries were often crossed and competition for patients occurred. Academically trained physicians responded to this pressure by demanding the improvement and codification of educational requirements, and the establishment of a single medical examination and a single license for practice. Their targets were the existing examination and licensing regulations, which had been set down in 1803 during the reorganization of the state and had received only minor modifications over the years.[28] In these regulations it stated that the student had absolute freedom to study what he wanted (*Lernfreiheit*), meaning that a set curriculum could not be established. The length of medical studies was set at three and a half years, but to qualify for the state medical examination the student had only to fulfill the ambiguous requirement of having acquired "a thorough knowledge of the natural sciences and medicine."[29] Given by the health commission, this examination consisted of three separate units—internal medicine, surgery, and obstetrics—and tested for theoretical knowledge alone. The student could take any part independently of the others, and passing any of the units entitled him to practice medicine in that area. The only exception was for those wishing to practice obstetrics—they had to possess a license in either internal medicine or surgery as well.[30] The laxity of these criteria was compounded further by the fact that students had three chances to pass the examination before being denied the right to apply for a license. Only for a position as state physician were the criteria somewhat more stringent. Then the government required possession of all three licenses and two years of practice.[31]

In 1848 several local branches of the state medical society banned together and submitted a plan for reforming medical education to the ministry of interior.[32] They suggested that the examination be divided into two parts, one in the natural sciences and the other in medicine. The former was to be given at an earlier time, preferably prior to the study of medicine proper. This would release the student from the pressures of having to prepare for a single examination covering all aspects of science and medicine. Instead he could focus initially on preparatory courses, and then concentrate on his practical studies. Still, the final examination was to test the student in both theoretical knowledge and practical skills. In addition, the society advocated the abolishment of the classifications of physician, surgeon, and obstetrician, favoring a single license for all three subject areas.

Baden physicians were not alone in their demands for reform. Throughout the German states academically trained physicians joined together in the 1840s to form medical societies and fight for the standardization of stricter educational requirements and the abolition of the tripartite medical examination.[33] The motivations behind these demands were manifold. As Magali Sarfatti-Larson has argued in her general study of professionalization, standardization is a crucial step in the emergence of professions. Since one goal of professional groups is to gain a monopoly over their particular area of expertise, it is essential that they be able to distinguish their product clearly from those of their competitors. In the case of a product that is a professional service, this can only occur through the standardization of the professionals themselves, that is, through the establishment of a set program of education.[34] Thus hopes of limiting competition with unlicensed medical practitioners as well as with individuals licensed only in surgery or obstetrics played a significant role in the fight for educational reform. Moreover, the demand for unification, focused on a common educational background, reflected as well a strategy for raising standards in the profession, upgrading medical care by requiring that all physicians receive training in the natural sciences and surgery, and, thus, by establishing competence in a particular body of knowledge and special techniques, legitimating claims to a monopoly over the medical domain.[35]

Larson and others interested in professionalization strategies also emphasize the degree to which the success of a particular group depends on the support and protection of the ruling elite, the elite often being the state government.[36] The bond is marked, however, by a tension between the professionalizing group's desire for autonomy and the government's tendency toward bureaucratic control. Not surprisingly, national differences exist in the balance between these two forces. In the German states, the various governments played a greater role in the professionalization of physicians than in countries such as England and the United States, reflecting, I may add, greater government intervention in such areas as industry and education as well. Not only did physicians show a willingness to work together with governments to raise standards in their profession, governments also helped regulate educational and licensing requirements.[37] Nevertheless, I wish to suggest that national differences may have been more one of degree than kind. The passage of legislation in the various German states represented a long process that occurred in several stages, and private physicians had to fight, just as their American counterparts had, to convince their governments to grant them these privileges. The existence of a medical police in Germany does not challenge this. Although these medical practitioners were state employed, they did not enjoy a monopoly over health care; rather they shared responsibilities with surgeons, apothecaries, midwives, and a slew of other medical personnel. Moreover, although the state positions provided secure employment, state-employed physicians could hardly be considered a professional elite. Their pay was so poor that many had to supplement their income through private practice, and they had little say over the content and extent of their duties—something that led them to organize in the 1830s and fight for greater control.

On the other side, state governments in the United States were by no means absent in the professionalization process. In fact, in the second half of the nineteenth century the American Medical Association turned to the state legislatures, trying to convince them to reinstate licensing laws (many states had had such laws in the pre-Jeffersonian period). Initially the AMA had little success, but in the 1870s and 1880s most states began regulating medical practice, passing licensing laws that were crucial to physicians in their attempt to gain a monopoly over the medical market.[38] Ultimately, the AMA turned into an extremely powerful self-regulatory organization, whereas the creation of a German national health insurance system subjected physicians to greater government regulation. But these outcomes reflect long historical processes; the paths did indeed diverge, but in the mid-nineteenth century German and American physicians had similar desires for self-control, and, to a significant extent, similar strategies as well.

The central problem for physicians in the period before the bacteriological and therapeutic breakthroughs was to convince governments of their rights to privileges. At mid-century they could hardly claim greater effectiveness than their competitors, but by arguing for stricter educational requirements based on increased work in the laboratory and clinic, they were promising to acquire those skills that would let them join the slowly emerging elite of scientists. This was not, however, a strategy designed purely for the acquisition of power and prestige. What is often neglected in studies on professionalization is an appreciation of the conviction shared by members of the group that their training does, or will, qualify them, and them alone, as experts in their field. Physicians around mid-century may have been motivated by a desire to reduce competition in the medical domain, but their goal was to acquire skills that would render them superior to their competitors; and there is little doubt that they saw increased training in the laboratory and clinic as a means of acquiring just that edge.[39]

In the 1840s physicians throughout the German states had little luck in convincing their various state governments to set down new licensing and educational requirements.[40] Baden was no exception. Although the suggestions of its local medical society provided the framework for new medical regulations established in 1858, very few changes were made before that time. The reform plans had been written in the spirit of the revolution of 1848, and with the failure of the latter the hopes for medical reform were temporarily crushed.[41] The medical society succeeded, however, in adapting to the new political atmosphere. As early as November 1849, just a few months after Prussian troops marched into Karlsruhe, it published an article in its journal on the reasons physicians had participated in the recent uprisings. The revolution, earlier seen as a way to build a society based on freedom, prosperity, and education, was now likened to "an epidemic whose miasma penetrated all." Physicians, argued the author, had taken part in the uprisings in especially large numbers because they had had very little to lose. Subjected to excessive competition, they lacked work and financial security; totally dependent on community patronage, they lacked the freedom to oppose popular opinion. They had thus been swept along by revolutionary rhetoric. To prevent this happening again, the author concluded, physicians needed strength and independence which could be acquired only through a "true scientific character and an established professional organization [*feste Standeseinrichtung*]."[42]

In December 1849, Robert Volz, editor of the local physicians' journal and president of one of the society's local branches, wrote directly to the minister of interior requesting recognition and support from the state. He received a reply shortly thereafter in which the ministry acknowledged the importance of the society and explained its plan to establish a commission, composed in part of representatives of the medical society, to review plans for a reform of the medical system. A few months later Volz announced his intent to "follow the repeatedly outspoken requests of the society . . . to dedicate its newspaper more to science than has previously been the case."[43] The withdrawal from politics into scientific work and educational reform was not an uncommon strategy within academic circles during the period of reaction. Volz's decision met, most importantly, with the approval of the government health commission, and one year later he was invited to join their ranks.[44]

Not until 1858 did the efforts of physicians to reform the Baden medical system succeed. Although the reasons for this delay are unclear, physicians themselves, observing successful attempts by other groups to organize (such as foresters, innkeepers, and brewers), bitterly attributed their own failure to the fact that they did "not manage millions [of gulden] and [did] not have taxable goods [*kein Steuerkapital repräsentiren*]."[45] The state was, indeed, preoccupied with regulating standards for other professional groups in the post-revolutionary period, especially the school teachers, and this may have prevented more immediate action in the case of physicians.[46]

Nevertheless, the government did follow the advice of both the health commission and Henle and begin to pursue the appointment of a physiologist. It had, in fact, begun to consider Helmholtz and du Bois-Reymond for this position when a number of events occurred that forced a change of plans.[47] In the beginning of June Pfeufer decided to accept a position in Munich, and the search for his replacement took precedence over the appointment of a professor of physiology.[48] Pfeufer's decision to leave Heidelberg reflected professional and political concerns. In Munich he had been offered charge of a hospital with 144 beds, certainly a great improvement over the small clinic he had in Heidelberg. But the decision to leave had not been an easy one, and the political atmosphere in Baden, particularly the in-fighting among the members of his own faculty, may have been the deciding factor. His circle of friends—Häusser, Gervinus, Jolly, Vangerow, Mittermaier, and, of course, Henle—had belonged to the core of the liberal movement during the tumultuous years of the revolution, most of them having participated in the publication of the short-lived liberal newspaper, the *Deutsche Zeitung*. Pfeufer, moreover, had been a member of a seven-person commission chosen in March 1848 to deliver a petition of liberal demands to parliament, and in April he had represented Baden in the Frankfurter *Vorparlament*.[49] The fact that he had belonged to the moderate branch of the liberal group and had been outspoken in his opposition to the more radical republicans did not, however, make much difference to the conservative members of his faculty, foremost Chelius. As a result, when Munich made its offer, Chelius persuaded the medical faculty not to encourage the government to make a counteroffer, and this in spite of Pfeufer's unquestionable popularity and talent. Henle (perhaps not the most unbiased source) interpreted this as a political maneuver on the part of the other members of the faculty and began to grow concerned about the security of his own position. In a letter to du Bois-Reymond, he described his predicament:

> To all the open wounds from which we are suffering, yet another one, the worst one, has come—the loss of Pfeufer. This is so nasty because it exposes the system. Pfeufer was let go without making an attempt to keep him here, not even for the sake of decency. Pfeufer and I were hired by the only energetic curator [Dahmen] in order to put a stop to the sons who were intending to take over the business of their fathers. He [Dahmen] was in Heidelberg for a short while but the clique got rid of him long ago. They have taken care of Pfeufer, soon they will also try to get rid of me and I must search out every opportunity to get away from here in order not to decay in the scientific wasteland which is being produced here.[50]

In 1852 Henle entered negotiations with Rudolph Wagner for a position as professor of anatomy at the University of Göttingen. His concern with the political situation, but also his wish to focus on anatomy alone, had led him to take this action. "After the fragmentation of my energy which I have had to endure for years," he wrote Wagner in June, "a professorship would be all the more desirable for me, the more it would allow me to concentrate exclusively on general and special anatomy."[51] In fact, Henle had already decided to stop teaching physiology even if he were to remain in Heidelberg, but this was not necessary—in July 1852 he received an offer from Göttingen that he accepted immediately.[52] Further discussions surrounding the appointment of a physiologist were now tied up as well with the need to fill two vacancies in the medical faculty.

Henle's and Pfeufer's departure signified the end of an era when the link between physiology, pathology, and clinical medicine had been exceptionally strong. Yet Henle and other "physiological pathologists" did not abandon physiology without leaving their mark on the field. Through research, textbooks, and journals, they had helped redefine this science, weakening its association with earlier more philosophical systems. Moreover, their fight to create a scientific medicine based on physiology had cast this science within a medical context. For them, physiology and pathology had represented two sides of one coin. Indeed, most of them had taught not only anatomy and physiology, but pathology and pathological anatomy as well, in addition to working closely with clinicians. Their research problems as well as the relevance of their work had been defined totally within a medical milieu. Years later, Henle would even describe his own reform efforts as having focused on the introduction of microsopical and chemical techniques into the clinic.

The next generation would view the relationship between physiology and medicine differently. As we have seen, du Bois-Reymond and his colleagues shifted priority to the establishment of an autonomous physiological science by exploiting the experimental techniques of the physical sciences. One consequence was a greater distinction between physiological and pathological subjects. Henle, for example, was the last professsor at Heidelberg to teach both general pathology and physiology, and after he left the university even pathological anatomy became the responsibility of the clinician. But the link between physiology and medicine, while no longer as direct, was not questioned. As we have already seen, several of the young physiologists (du Bois-Reymond was the exception) appreciated the extent to which the success of their own program depended on nurturing the medical context. The questions they asked and the problems they pursued may not have been motivated by strictly medical concerns, yet they did not fail to appreciate and exploit the importance of the experimental method for the establishment of a medical science. By the 1850s, largely because of the work carried out by Henle and other physiological pathologists, they began to find a receptive audience among the academically trained members of the medical community. This was reflected quite clearly in the discussions surrounding Henle's replacement; the question of whether to hire an experimental physiologist occurred squarely within a medical context.

The Search for Pfeufer's and Henle's Replacements

As soon as Henle announced his intended departure, the ministry of interior wrote to the state ministry, painting a bleak picture of the university's future if changes were not made immediately in the medical faculty. "The number of students of medicine at the University of Heidelberg," it wrote,

> has decreased greatly in the last years, and the study of this science [medicine] is itself in visible decline. The causes lie for the most part in the personal and factional relationships about which one could, until now, only complain but not change.
>
> However, the time may have come to pave a better path; but at the same time the situation has reached such a point that if a long-lasting unfavorable crisis for the medical faculty . . . and thus for the university, is to be avoided, then every step must be taken to revitalize the faculty as quickly as possible through the attraction of excellent men.[33]

The falling enrollments suffered by the University of Heidelberg did not reflect a general trend in medical schools at the time. On the contrary, enrollments in the medical departments of German universities increased steadily until 1854, after which they reached a plateau until the end of the decade.[54] In 1830 Heidelberg may have been able to draw 10 percent of these students, and in 1840 still 8 percent, but after the revolution only 5 percent continued to choose this university, a statistic that frightened the ministry.[55]

When the ministry of interior wrote the above report, it had already begun its search for Pfeufer's replacement, selecting ultimately Karl Ewald Hasse. Hasse (1810–1902) had received his medical degree from Leipzig, after which he had spent two years learning the new diagnostic techniques in Paris, Vienna, and Prague.[56] In 1836 he returned to Leipzig to work as an assistant in the university's medical clinic, teaching the skills he had acquired in auscultation, percussion, and pathological anatomy. He remained there seven years, being promoted to associate professor in 1839. In 1843 he decided to move to Zurich when the university offered him Pfeufer's old position as full professor of pathology. In the following years, Hasse received several offers from other universities, including Breslau and Halle, but not until Heidelberg asked him to follow in Pfeufer's footsteps once again did he decide to leave Zurich. His decision to move seems to have been based on the expectation that Heidelberg would provide a better environment for carrying out scientific research. In August 1852 Hasse accepted Heidelberg's offer. His responsibilites were to teach general and special pathology and therapeutics, and to direct the medical clinic. Moreover, he took over responsibility for the teaching of pathological anatomy, institutionalizing the link between this subject and the clinic that he had learned to appreciate while studying in Paris and Vienna.[57]

With Pfeufer's replacement settled, the members of the ministry of interior turned to the question of filling Henle's position, acknowledging the greater difficulty of this task given the unresolved question of whether to hold the position intact or hire two professors, one for anatomy and the other for physiology. They did not, however, hesitate to express their conviction that the two subjects had to be separated:

> We believe that there must be one *Ordinarius* for anatomy and one *Ordinarius* for physiology, and that the anatomical and physiological institutes must be separated from one another. The directorship of the former should rest with the first, the directorship of the physiological institute, however—which must, of course, first be built in Heidelberg—should be transferred to the latter. Both positions should be filled with excellent talents; for physiology, namely, a man must be won who is devoted to the exact method. Because of the direction which the entire course of medical studies has taken in our day, it is our conviction that physiology must be taught in its entirety and in a totally satisfactory fashion at a university that wants to enjoy high repute and attendance.[58]

In 1852 the ministry of interior, backed by the health commission, spoke out for the creation of a separate chair and laboratory for physiology. These demands did not come directly from the physiologists themselves. In fact, in 1855 Ludwig accepted a position in Vienna for physiology and zoology, and in the same year Helmholtz went to Bonn as professor of anatomy and physiology.[59] This is not to say that the young experimentalists did not fight for the establishment of their own discipline, but in the early 1850s they were not yet in a position to make concrete demands. Baden's interest in supporting this new science was not, therefore, a response to conditions being set by potential candidates. Nor, one must add, can this be explained by the concrete contributions made to therapeutics. Instead the source of interest must be sought in the state's general commitment to the experimental sciences that characterized its educational policies in the 1850s, and its conviction that instruction in the exact method would greatly improve medical education.

At this point, however, the members of the medical faculty made an about face and opposed the hiring of a physiologist. In a letter to the ministry they expressed their conviction that it would be "the most appropriate for [medical] studies and for the anatomy institute, as well as for the science itself, when anatomy and physiology would remain united and represented by one well-acknowledged talented teacher." The person they suggested was Friedrich Arnold, professor of anatomy and physiology in Tübingen and someone who "makes proper allowances for the experimental direction in physiology without indulging in the one-sidedness that is evident among many others."[60]

Although the reasons for this change of faith are not stated explicitly, personal and political motives obviously made up the lion's share. With Henle and Pfeufer gone, the senior members of the faculty—Chelius, Puchelt, Nägeli—constituted a politically conservative group, and they took advantage of their unity to block the appointment of an individual who would immediately join the liberal ranks of the university and divide the faculty once again.[61] Thus, in much the same way that Henle and Bunsen tried to hire individuals of their own political persuasion and scientific style, Chelius and his colleagues sought to fashion the medical faculty after their own image. Indeed, they went so far as to try and establish family dynasties: in 1835/36 Nägeli's son began lecturing at the university, being promoted to assistant professor in 1839; in 1841 Puchelt's son also began teaching; and in 1852 Chelius's son, who had been lecturing since 1847, was promoted to assistant professor.[62] Henle, disgusted by these manipulations and maneuverings, decried the excessively pliable ministry, even imagining it to be brainwashed by Chelius.[63] All this suggests that the faculty's earlier willingness to consider an experimental physiologist had represented a compromise imposed on it by Henle and Pfeufer, and that its recent antagonism toward the same group stemmed from a desire to hire individuals of its own scientific style and political convictions. As we will see, Arnold fit the bill perfectly.

The members of the ministry of interior were not pleased with this turn of events. In a report sent to the state ministry they supported Arnold, praising his skills as an anatomist, but expressing their concern that he would not teach physiology "in the necessary way." They decided, however, to support the medical faculty's decision for two reasons. They had no desire to generate discord by acting against the wishes of the faculty. But more important, funds were lacking. The balance from the university budget of 2650 gulden had been exhausted by Bunsen's salary of 2700 gulden. That left the money freed by Henle's and Pfeufer's departure, which totaled 3800 gulden, and from this 2500 had already been promised to Hasse. Added to the remaining 1300 came another 1900 acquired by transferring Gmelin's pension from the university to the state budget. Thus a total of 3200 gulden were available, from which 2800 would go to Arnold. With only 400 gulden remaining, a professor for physiology could obviously not be lured.[64] Physiology, while important, was still low on the academic totem pole in 1852.

Friedrich Arnold (1803–1890)

Friedrich Arnold was hired on 30 July 1852.[65] This was not his first appointment at the University of Heidelberg. Between 1821 and 1825 he had studied medicine there before becoming prosector in the anatomy institute under Tiedemann. In the nine years he spent at the univeristy (in 1834 he was promoted to assistant professor) Arnold alternated courses in osteology, syndesmology, and the anatomy and physiology of the nervous system and sense organs, with surgical anatomy and instruction in dissection.[66] In 1835 he accepted a position as full professor of anatomy and physiology in Zurich, in 1840 he moved to Freiburg im Breisgau, in 1845 to Tübingen, and in 1852 he returned to Heidelberg. For the next six years, until Helmholtz's appointment in 1858, he taught all anatomical and physiological subjects, after which he focused solely on anatomy. He held this position until his retirement in 1873 when he was replaced by his son-in-law Carl Gegenbaur.

As part of the negotiations in 1852 the ministry of interior spelled out in exact detail the specific courses Arnold was to teach, an unusual procedure that most likely reflected the ministry's concern that physiology be well represented. In the winter semester Arnold was expected to offer lectures on "microscopical anatomy and special physiological anatomy" as well as practical exercises in dissection; in the summer, experimental physiology and developmental history in addition to "exercises in microscopical and physiological work." Moreover, it was his responsibility to "set up a physiological cabinet with a laboratory according to present standards in physiology."[67] The medical faculty requested specifically that in this matter all of Arnold's demands be met: they did not want "the physiological institute at this university to stand behind the institutes at other universities."[68]

Arnold set up his "laboratory" in the anatomy building, for the most part in those rooms Henle had previously allotted to physiology.[69] In the small lecture room arranged by Henle for physiological and microscopical anatomy (650 sq. ft.) he now set up his instruments, using the space for his own laboratory work and instruction. The room could not accommodate many students, nor was it intended for this purpose. It contained one large and two small tables for physiological experiments, three tables for microscopical demonstrations and exercises, one table each for a balance and thermometer, for quicksilver and water basins, and for chemical experiments. The room previously occupied by the physiological assistant was now converted into a small chemical kitchen (200 sq. ft.) for those experiments that could possibly cause damage to the instruments. And last, the "laboratory" had two small rooms for test animals, and a stall and two basins in the garden for keeping dogs, rabbits, larger animals, and frogs.

The government allotted Arnold 500 gulden to buy the necessary instruments and equipment, a sum that du Bois-Reymond, carrying on his battles with the Prussian ministry for recognition of his science, would most certainly have envied.[70] From Henle, Arnold had inherited nothing more than a galvanometer, various tools for cutting bones and nerves, a middle-sized balance with weights, a case with compasses and measuring sticks, a thermometer, and eleven microscopes. What he then bought or built totaled almost 100 instruments, many of which permitted the analysis and measurement of the physical and chemical properties of organic function. Some of the more important purchases included:[71]

1. An air pump with five different bell jars for creating rarified air or a vacuum
2. Four endosmeters for ascertaining the diffusion capacities of membranes
3. An induction apparatus for creating high tensions
4. Various diffusion apparatus (for gases, fluids, etc.)
5. Various fistula apparatus for collecting digestive products
6. A spirometer for measuring the capacity of the lungs
7. A kymatograph (a variation on the kymograph)
8. A suction pump and pressure pump
9. A stereoscope
10. An ophthalmoscope

The acquisition of these instruments marked a significant turning point in the institutionalization of experimental physiology at the University of Heidelberg. Traditionally, historians have focused on the creation of new faculty positions and scientific institutes as the signs of the successful institutionalization of a new scientific field. These are, to be sure, reliable signs, but they often reflect the culmination of a much longer process in which a scientific specialty gradually acquires financial and institutional support. In the case of Baden, political and economic factors had delayed the hiring of an experimental physiologist in 1852, but this had not meant a lack of interest in this science. The government had granted Arnold a considerable sum of money for the purpose of outfitting a "modern" laboratory. Thus by 1852, six years before Heidelberg hired an experimental physiologist, the application of the instruments and techniques of physics to the study of organic function had acquired an institutional setting at the university.

Nonetheless Arnold's style of research and teaching differed from that of the young experimentalists. In a report published in 1858, Arnold provided detail on several experiments, and thus on the kind of research conducted by him in his laboratory during the five years he taught physiology.[72] Two of the five topics he discussed fall under the category of physiological chemistry: he examined bile production in dogs as a function of different forms of nutrition, different body weights, and different times of the day; and he examined the digestion of animal protein both in vivo and in vitro. The other three experiments carried out in his laboratory concentrated on the mechanical properties of various organic structures. Here he studied the irritability of the frog heart and joint muscles in a vacuum, and specifically the effect of mechanical and electrical stimuli, of muscle respiration (the uptake of oxygen and release of carbon dioxide), and of the loss of moisture on muscle irritability. In another series of experiments he compared imbibition in the calf muscle of a living frog with that in an isolated muscle, paying particular attention to the effect of bloating on the muscle's ability to respond to mechanical and electrical stimuli. And last he dealt with respiration capacity in human beings, and the role of the pectoral muscle in this process.

All the information on Arnold's laboratory can be found in the above-mentioned report. Published in 1858—the year the university decided to hire an experimental physiologist—this book is Arnold's account of the manner in which he had represented the subject. In this regard it is interesting to note the research topics he deemed particularly worthy of mention: physiological chemistry and the mechanical properties of organic structures. Based on this alone it would be difficult to distinguish him from Carl Ludwig or Ernst Brücke. But in contrast to the young experimentalists, Arnold did not employ sophisticated instruments beyond the air pump, multiplicator, and spirometer. Rather, most of the studies relied on vivisectional techniques, and it was here in the inset of fistulas, the binding of arteries, and the laying bare of muscles that Arnold was at his best. The anatomist qua physiologist had indeed purchased a multitude of instruments that marked his recognition of the physicalist direction in physiological research, but unlike the young experimentalists who spent many of their university days learning to construct and use these sophisticated instruments, Arnold had acquired training in anatomical dissections and the preparations of nerves, muscles, and other tissue structures. As the philosopher-psychologist Wilhelm Wundt wrote of his uncle and first professor of physiology:

[He] belonged, like Johannes Müller and the brothers Heinrich and Eduard Weber, to an older generation for whom physiology was still essentially a subject subsidiary to anatomy. For all that, Arnold still occupied an important position in [this subject]. This was so because he used a method with great skill, namely vivisection, which was of particular importance for future physiological work. However, this was a side [of physiology] which was by nature limited to the lecture. [Arnold] lacked the physicalist training necessary for the establishment of an independent physiological science.[73]

Arnold's aptitude as an anatomist and vivisectionist was not in question. Indeed, even an enemy of his—Philip Jolly in the philosophy department—admitted so much in a letter to Henle, describing the respect Arnold had earned for his knowledge of particular anatomy (*spezielle Anatomie*).[74] His performance as a physiologist, on the other hand, drew criticisms immediately and from several directions. The Baden health commission soon lamented the appointment, and students refused to attend his classes in physiology.[75] As Wundt implied, Arnold's poor background in physics and mathematics, his lack of skill in instrumental techniques, and his ambivalence toward the establishment of an autonomous discipline of physiology all indicated his indifference toward the new direction physiological research had taken. Perhaps more upsetting to the students and government officials, his pedagogical views seemed less than modern as well. Unlike his younger contemporaries who emphasized the importance of having students carry out their own experiments and work directly with the material at hand, Arnold believed that demonstrations conducted by the professor sufficed.[76] With this rationale he offered a class in experimental physiology every semester that met in the hour just prior to his lecture course and was adorned with experimental demonstrations. These lecture-demonstrations covered every aspect of the science from diffusion to developmental history and were, according to Arnold, "imperative for the study of medicine in our day." But they could not, he added, be replaced by practical exercises in the physiology laboratory, "because only very few medical students can spare the necessary time [for practical work]."[77]

Arnold belonged, as his nephew Wundt pointed out, to an older generation of physiologists. This was true both in his scientific approach to the study of form and function, and in his pedagogical ideas. His indifference toward practical exercises in the laboratory and hands-on experience demonstrated his indifference as well toward an ideology of scientific research and education that found ever more advocates in the post-revolutionary period. For some, the popularity of laboratory training resulted from its association with an anti-authoritarian educational philosophy. It meant that students acquired knowledge not only from their professors, but through their own independent work as well. Helmholtz, for example, argued that mathematics and the sciences, more than any other subjects, taught the youth to derive their own conclusions and trust their own deductions, rather than rely on arbitrary rules and regulations.[78] The compatibility of this claim with political liberalism is obvious—both stress the importance of independent thinkers who have the mental skills to make judicious judgments, but this is not the only, and perhaps not even the most important reason for the increased status and respect accorded to scientific training in the 1850s. Rather its total identification with the politics of material interests guaranteed its success. Although based more on promises than goods delivered, faith had grown that practical exercises in the laboratory would someday translate into material benefits. Of course, all practical benefits did not lie in the far-distant future. Gains made in certain branches of the economy, whether in agriculture, transportation, or industry, raised hopes in other areas, such as medicine, that the experimental sciences would also bring improvements—in health care, of course, but also in the social status of physicians. In the 1850s the direct utilitarian value of laboratory training seemed to be of less importance than the pedagogical value of learning the exact method of the experimental sciences through direct involvement in laboratory research.

Four years after Arnold began teaching at Heidelberg, the Baden government underwent political changes that returned several reform-minded ministers to office. In this year the mentally ill Leopold died, and Prince Friedrich, regent since 1852, became Grand Duke of Baden. As we have already seen, despite the dominance of a conservative ministry in the early 1850s, Friedrich's liberal tendencies had helped prevent the onset of a true reaction in Baden. With his ascendancy to the throne, Friedrich began to give more expression to his constitutional and liberal ideas. Although liberals would not become "the ruling party" until 1860, Friedrich made some immediate changes in his cabinet, one of which was to have far-reaching consequences for university politics: In 1856 Franz Freiherr von Stengel (1803–1870), the person who had played a major role in hiring Henle and Pfeufer in 1843, was named president of both the ministry of justice and the ministry of interior.[79] Now, thirteen years after his initial reform work, von Stengel turned his attention once again to improving university education. One of his top priorities was the reorganization of the medical faculty at the University of Heidelberg.

Notes

1. Ludwig to Henle, 19 July 1846, in Astrid Dreher, *Briefe von Carl Ludwig an Jacob Henle aus den Jahren 1846–1872* (Diss. Heidelberg, 1980), p. 43. Unfortunately this book consists of Ludwig's letters to Henle alone. I have not been able to locate Henle's responses.

2. Paul F. Cranefield, "The Organic Physics of 1847 and the Biophysics of Today," *Journal of the History of Medicine*, 12 (1957): 407–423.

3. For a discussion of the extent to which the growth in technical culture supported by an industrializing society influenced this research style, see Timothy Lenoir, "Social Interests and the Organic Physics of 1847," in E. Ullmann-Margalit, ed., *Science in Reflection* (Dordrecht, 1988), pp. 169–181. Also see Joseph Ben-David's comments in the same volume.

4. Ludwig's work is discussed in Heinz Schröer, *Carl Ludwig. Begründer*

der messenden Experimentalphysiologie (Stuttgart, 1967), pp. 104–114; Stanley Joel Reiser, *Medicine and the Reign of Technology* (Cambridge, 1978), pp. 100–101.

5. Schröer, *Carl Ludwig,* esp. pp. 43–48.

6. Ludwig to Henle on 19 July 1846 and on 27 March 1849, in Dreher, *Briefe von Carl Ludwig,* pp. 44 and 71, respectively.

7. See, for example, Karl E. Rothschuh, *History of Physiology* (New York, 1973): Thomas S. Hall, *History of General Physiology,* 2 vols. (Chicago, 1969).

8. See Chapter 7 of this book, as well as my article, "Hermann von Helmholtz and the German Medical Community," in David Cahan, ed., *The Borders of Science: Essays on Hermann von Helmholtz* (Berkeley and Los Angeles, forthcoming, 1993).

9. The clearest statement of this is in Hermann von Helmholtz, "Ueber das Verhältnis der Naturwissenschaften zur Gesamtheit der Wissenschaft," Akademische Festrede gehalten zu Heidelberg am 22 November 1862 bei Antritt des Prorectorats. In *Vorträge und Reden,* 5th ed., 2 vols. (Braunschweig, 1903), vol. 1, pp. 157–185.

10. Ludwig to Henle on 22 November 1848, in Dreher, *Briefe von Carl Ludwig,* p. 57.

11. Henle to Pfeufer on 11 December 1853 and 17 April 1854 in Hermann Hoepke, *Der Briefwechsel zwischen Jakob Henle und Karl Pfeufer, 1843–1869* (Sudhoffs, Archiv. Beihefte 11) (Wiesbaden, 1970). Ludwig cites a portion of a letter sent to him by Henle on 14 April 1854 in which the older scientist expressed this skepticism, in Dreher, *Briefe von Carl Ludwig,* p. 121.

12. Ludwig to Henle on 1 January 1849, in Dreher, *Briefe von Carl Ludwig,* p. 61.

13. Henle's difficulty in convincing the Baden government to act quickly and hire Ludwig led the young experimentalist to accept an offer from Zurich. Although the exact reasons for Baden's hesitation are not clear, political problems probably played the greatest role. In the years just following the revolution the government did not respond favorably to individuals who had sympathized with— or, in Ludwig's case, participated in—the recent uprisings. Ludwig came up against difficulties in Marburg, Heidelberg, and in Königsberg, where he had also applied for a position that eventually went to Helmholtz. Only Zurich, the home of many German political dissidents, did not seem troubled by the young physiologist's political views. The letters in which Ludwig discusses a possible call to Heidelberg are all in Dreher, *Briefe von Carl Ludwig:* 1 January 1849, 27 March 1849, 7 July 1849. See also a letter from Henle to Emil du Bois-Reymond in which he mentions his earlier interest in Ludwig, 28 March 1852, Darmstaedter Collection, SPK 3c1844(4). Ludwig's call to Zurich is mentioned in Schröer, *Carl Ludwig,* pp. 45–48.

14. Heidelberg's interest in von Siebold is discussed in Henle to the medical faculty, 27 February 1850; faculty senate to the ministry of interior, 2 March 1850; and medical faculty to the faculty senate, 1 March 1850; all in BGLA 235/3133. On von Siebold, see E. Ehlers, "Carl Theodor Ernst von Siebold. Eine biographische Skizze," *Zeitschrift für wissenschaftliche Zoologie,* 42 (1885): i–xxxiv; Richard Hertwig, *Gedächtnißrede auf Carl Theodor von Siebold gehalten in der öffentlichen Sitzung der königlichen Akademie der Wissenschaften zu München am 29 März 1886* (Munich, 1886); Armin Geus, "Carl Theodor Ernst von Siebold," *DSB,* 12 (1975): 420–422.

15. Henle to the medical faculty, 2 February 1850, BGLA 235/3133.

16. Henle to du Bois-Reymond, 28 March 1852, Darmstaedter Collection, SPK 3c1844(4).

17. The letters are in Dreher, *Briefe von Carl Ludwig*, on 22 November 1848, 1 January 1849, 27 March 1849, 9 August 1849, 20 October 1850, 14 July 1851.

18. Henle to the medical faculty, 27 February 1850, BGLA 235/3133. Henle was not alone in thinking this. At the same time that Heidelberg showed an interest in von Siebold, Breslau made him an offer to replace the recently deceased Purkyne as professor of physiology.

19. Ludwig to Henle on 3 November 1851, in Dreher, *Briefe von Carl Ludwig*, p. 105. Hermann Friedrich Stannius was professor of comparative anatomy and physiology in Rostock from 1837 until 1862.

20. Ibid.

21. Negotiations with von Siebold dragged on, in part because of financial difficulties, in part because of political differences, and last because the university had given priority to finding a new professor of chemistry. See minutes of the medical faculty from 25 January 1851, in *Acten*, 1851, III, 4a, 94, Universitätsarchiv Heidelberg. Henle discusses his negotiations with du Bois-Reymond and Helmholtz in a letter to du Bois-Reymond, 28 March 1852, Darmstaedter Collection, SPK 3c1844(4). See also Helmholtz to du Bois-Reymond, 16 July 1852, in Christa Kirsten, et al., eds. *Dokumente einer Freundschaft. Briefwechsel zwischen Hermann von Helmholtz und Emil du Bois-Reymond 1846–1894* (Berlin, 1986), pp. 134–35.)

22. Medical faculty to the faculty senate, 14 May 1852, BGLA 235/3133.

23. For information on the health commission, see Karl Stiefel, *Baden 1648–1952*, 2 vols. (Karlsruhe, 1978), vol. II, p. 1284; and BGLA 235/27692 and 236/15027.

24. Health commission to the ministry of interior, 23 June 1852, BGLA 235/3133.

25. The formation of local medical societies is discussed in Alfons Fischer, *Geschichte des deutschen Gesundheitswesens*, 2 vols. (Berlin, 1933), vol. 2, pp. 368–388. Both Baden medical societies published medical journals. The journal of the state-employed physicians began in 1836 under the title, *Annalen der Staatsarzneikunde;* that of the private physicians began in 1847 under the title *Mittheilungen des badischen ärztlichen Vereins.*

On professional strategies among physicians in Germany, see Claudia Huerkamp, *Der Aufstieg der Ärzte im 19. Jahrhundert* (Göttingen, 1985); E. Ackerknecht, "Beiträge zur Geschichte der Medizinalreform von 1848," *Sudhoffs Archiv,* 25 (1932): 61–109, 113–183; Fischer, *Geschichte des deutschen Gesundheitswesens*, vol. 2, pp. 368–388.

26. See, for example, "Freiburger ärztlicher Bezirksverein," *Mittheilungen,* 1849, Jg. 3, Nr. 3, pp. 16–21, here pp. 16–17.

27. Fischer, *Geschichte des deutschen Gesundheitswesens*, vol. 2, p. 371.

28. Kurfürstliche Badische General-Sanitäts-Commission, *Badische Medicinal-Ordnung* (Karlsruhe, 1807); Großherzogliche badische Sanitäts-Commission, *Entwurf einer neuen Medicinalordnung für das Großherzogthum Baden* (Karlsruhe, 1840); C. A. Diez, *Zusammenstellung der gegenwärtig geltenden Gesetze, Verordnungen, Instructionen und Entscheidungen über das Medicinalwesen und die Stellung und die Verrichtungen der Medicinalbeamten und Sanitätsdiener im Großherzogthum Baden* (Karlsruhe, 1859).

29. This ambiguous requirement was first set down in 1828. See *RB*, 5 August 1828; Diez, *Zusammenstellung*, p. 6. The regulations in need of reform are discussed in a letter from the ministry of interior to the state ministry, 8 January 1858, BGLA 233/31847.

30. Eberhard Stübler, *Geschichte der medizinischen Fakultät der Universität Heidelberg, 1326–1925* (Heidelberg, 1926), pp. 280–281.

31. The requirement for state physicians was set down in 1841. See *RB*, 5 July 1841; Ministry of interior to the state ministry, 8 January 1858, BGLA 233/31847.

32. This is discussed in *Mittheilungen*, 22 November 1848 (Nr. 22), pp. 165–167.

33. See Fischer, *Geschichte des deutschen Gesundheitswesens*, pp. 368–387; Huerkamp, *Der Aufstieg der Ärzte*.

34. Magali Sarfatti Larson, *The Rise of Professionalism. A Sociological Analysis* (Berkeley, 1977), especially the introduction. For the application of Larson's model to the professionalization of physicians in Germany, see Huerkamp, *Der Aufstieg der Ärzte*.

35. The Baden medical society had, in fact, petitioned the government for greater independence from the state, while simultaneously requesting that an official edict be passed requiring all private physicians to join the society. Mentioned in a report from the ministry of interior to the state ministry, 21 September 1849, BGLA 233/31847.

36. See Larson, *The Rise of Professionalism*. See also Eliot Freidson, *Professional Powers: A Study of the Institutionalization of Formal Knowledge* (Chicago, 1986).

37. Claudia Huerkamp, "Ärzte und Professionalisierung in Deutschland. Überlegungen zum Wandel des Arztberufs im 19. Jahrhundert," *Geschichte und Gesellschaft*, 6 (1980): 349–382, here p. 360. See also Charles E. McClelland, *The German Experience of Professionalization: Modern Learned Professions and their Organizations from the Early Nineteenth Century to the Hitler Era* (Cambridge, 1991).

38. Ronald L. Numbers, "The Fall and Rise of the American Medical Profession," in *Sickness and Health in America*, eds. Judith Walzer Leavitt, Ronald L. Numbers, 2nd ed. (Wisconsin, 1985), pp. 185–196.

39. See, for example, "Wie sollen die Aerzte gebildet werden?," *Mittheilungen*, 12 May 1852 (Nr. 9), pp. 65–69.

40. Ackerknecht, "Beiträge zur Geschichte der Medizinalreform;" Fischer, *Geschichte des deutschen Gesundheitswesens*.

41. "Unsere Aufgabe im neuen Jahr," in *Mittheilungen*, 1 January 1845 (Nr. 1), pp. 1–8; "Revolution," *Mittheilungen*, 14 July 1849 (Nr. 13), pp. 93–95.

42. "Ein Wort über die Betheiligung der Aerzte an der Revolution," *Mittheilungen*, 24 November 1849 (Nr. 20), pp. 149–156.

43. Statement by Franz Bils in *Mittheilungen*, 27 February 1850 (Nr. 4), p. 32.

44. These events are described in *Mittheilungen*, 12 February 1850 (Nr. 3), pp. 17–20. The first line of the letter from the health commission to Volz reads: "Man vernimmt mit Wohlgefallen, daß das Vereinsblatt mehr als bisher geschehen, der Wissenschaft gewidmet werden will . . ." For biographical information on Volz, see BGLA 76/8137.

45. "Reform" in *Mittheilungen,* 10 February 1858 (Nr. 3), pp. 18–19.

46. See "Vergleichung der Budgets-Sätze mit den Rechnungs-Resultaten für die Etats-Jahre 1849–1860," in *Verhandlungen.*

47. See Henle to du Bois-Reymond, 28 March 1852, Darmstaedter Collection, SPK 3c1844(4); and two letters from Helmholtz to du Bois-Reymond, 20 June 1852 and 16 July 1852, in Kirsten, *Dokumente einer Freundschaft,* pp. 131–132 and 134–135, respectively.

48. Ministry of interior to state ministry, 4 June 1852, BGLA 235/3133.

49. For Pfeufer's decision to leave Heidelberg, see Werner Goth, *Zur Geschichte der Klinik in Heidelberg im 19. Jahrhundert* (Diss. Heidelberg, 1982), p. 181; for information on the moderate liberals and Pfeufer's relationship to them, see Josef Kerschensteiner, *Das Leben und Wirken des Dr. Carl von Pfeufer* (Augsburg, 1871), p. 20; Thomas Nipperdey, *Deutsche Geschichte 1800–1866. Bürgerwelt und starker Staat* (Munich, 1983), pp. 387–388.

50. Henle to du Bois-Reymond, 28 March 1852, Darmstaedter Collection, SPK 3c1844(4). Henle expressed similar sentiments in a letter to Rudolf Wagner on 21 July 1852, in Hans-Heinz Eulner, Hermann Hoepke, eds., *Der Briefwechsel zwischen Rudolph Wagner und Jacob Henle, 1838–1862* (Göttingen, 1979).

51. Henle to Wagner on 26 June 1852, in Eulner, *Der Briefwechsel zwischen Rudolph Wagner und Jacob Henle,* p. 41.

52. Henle to Wagner on 1 July 1852 in ibid., pp. 47–49; Wagner to Henle on 4 July 1852, in ibid., pp. 50–51.

53. Ministry of interior to the state ministry, 23 July 1852, BGLA 235/3141.

54. Franz Eulenberg, *Die Frequenz der deutschen Universitäten von ihrer Gründung bis zur Gegenwart* (Leipzig, 1904), p. 255.

55. Ministry of interior to the state ministry, 23 July 1852, BGLA 235/3141.

56. For biographical information, see Dr. v. Ziemssen, "Feuilleton, Karl Ewald Hasse," *Münchener medicinische Wochenschrift,* 44, 1 (1897): 282–283.

57. See the medical faculty's recommendation, 14 May 1852, BGLA 235/3133; ministry of interior to the state ministry, 23 July 1852, BGLA 235/3141; 7 August 1852, BGLA 235/3133.

58. Ministry of interior to the state ministry, 23 July 1852, BGLA 235/3141.

59. Schröer, *Carl Ludwig,* p. 62. Leo Koenigsberger, *Hermann von Helmholtz,* 2 vols. (Braunschweig, 1902), vol. 1, p. 257.

60. Medical faculty to the ministry of interior, 26 July 1852, BGLA 235/3141.

61. That personal and political tensions had split the medical faculty in two is discussed by the ministry of interior in a report sent to the state ministry, 23 July 1852, BGLA 235/3141.

62. All the promotions are listed in the *Anzeige.* See also Henle to Wagner on 21 July 1852 in Eulner, *Der Briefwechsel zwischen Rudolph Wagner und Jacob Henle,* pp. 62–65; Henle to du Bois-Reymond, 28 March 1852, Darmstaedter Collection, SPK 3c1844(4).

63. Henle to Wagner on 7 July 1852, in Eulner, *Der Briefwechsel zwischen Rudolph Wagner und Jacob Henle,* p. 53.

64. Ministry of interior to the state ministry, 23 July 1852, BGLA 235/3141.

65. "Friedrich Arnold," in *BL,* 1 (1962): 210–211.

66. *Anzeige,* 1825–1834.

67. Minutes of the medical faculty on 7 August 1852, in *Acten,* 1852, III, 4a, 95. Also ministry of interior to the state ministry, 23 July 1852, BGLA 235/3141.

68. Minutes of the medical faculty on 9 September 1852 in *Acten,* 1852, III, 4a, 95.

69. For Henle's institute, see Chapter 4. Arnold describes his laboratory setup in Friedrich Arnold, *Die physiologische Anstalt der Universität Heidelberg von 1853 bis 1858* (Heidelberg, 1858), pp. 7–10.

70. Arnold, *Die physiologische Anstalt,* p. 1. For du Bois-Reymond's struggle for funding, see Axel Genz, *Die Emanzipation der naturwissenschaftlichen Physiologie in Berlin* (Diss. Magdeburg, 1970).

71. Arnold, *Die physiologische Anstalt,* pp. 10–13.

72. Ibid., pp. 89–154.

73. Wilhelm Wundt, *Erlebtes und Erkanntes* (Stuttgart, 1920), pp. 73–74. For an assessment of Arnold's research skills, see also Hermann Hoepke, "Zur Geschichte der Anatomie in Heidelberg," *Sonderdruck aus Ruperto Carola,* 67/68 (1982): 115–122. Henle mentioned Arnold's ineptness with instruments in a letter to Wagner on 10 September 1853, in Eulner, *Der Briefwechsel zwischen Rudolph Wagner und Jacob Henle,* pp. 86–87.

74. Jolly to Henle, 14 or 16 January 1853, University of Heidelberg, Handschriftenabteilung, Nr. 4018. Jolly taught physics at Heidelberg until 1854 when he went to Munich and was replaced by Kirchhoff.

75. Mentioned in Jolly's letters to Henle on 14 or 16 January 1853, 25 March 1853, and 10 October 1855, all in ibid.

76. Arnold held such demonstrations to be of great importance, but unlike his younger contemporaries, he did not believe the students had to perform scientific exercises themselves. See Arnold, *Die physiologische Anstalt,* p. 5.

77. Ibid., pp. 5–6.

78. See Chapter 9 of this book.

79. Von Stengel's career in the Baden government had begun in 1832, when he became secretary of the ministry of interior. Ludwig Winter, then president of the ministry, recognized the talents of the young man and promoted him to assessor (1835) and then to ministerial advisor (1837). In this capacity he assisted Nebenius in organizing educational affairs. In 1848 he joined the liberal Dusch-Bekk government as minister in the department of justice, and remained in office after the revolution, moving to the state department. In 1848 he had also been elected to represent the University of Heidelberg in the upper chamber of parliament, remaining in this capacity until Friedrich promoted him to president of the ministries of interior and justice in 1856. See Lothar Gall, *Der Liberalismus als regierende Partei* (Wiesbaden, 1968), pp. 58–80; Friedrich von Weech, *Baden in den Jahren 1852 bis 1877* (Karlsruhe, 1877). Also, for Stengel's role in hiring Henle and Pfeufer, see Chapter 3 of this book.

7

The Institutionalization of Experimental Physiology

Grand Duke Friedrich's rise to power and his appointment of Franz Freiherr von Stengel to the ministry of interior had a significant impact on university politics. Although Baden had not experienced a severe reaction, support for political liberalism in the 1850s had waned in comparison with the *Vormärz* period, and this had influenced university appointments. The indifference of the government toward Henle's and Pfeufer's departure, and its appointment of Arnold, must all be understood within the context of the political debates between liberals and conservatives that had figured so prominently in the early 1850s. The year 1856 signaled a change in the political atmosphere and, by association, in the government's attitude toward the university. At a time when conservatives dominated most German state ministries, von Stengel was allying himself with liberal faculty members, working with them to reform the university. One of the first problems he tackled was the reform of the medical faculty.

By 1856 the popularity of the medical faculty had reached an all-time low. Indeed, the fear the ministry of interior had expressed in 1852 that a crisis would occur if the University of Heidelberg did not take radical measures to revitalize its medical faculty had proven justified. Between 1852 and 1854 enrollments had dropped precipitously, with an average of only forty-five local and fifty-three foreign medical students per semester.[1] Although enrollments had begun to increase in 1854, the ministry knew this reflected the large number of students coming to study chemistry—until 1864 they were required to enroll in the medical faculty.

Several factors seemed to be contributing to the unpopularity of the medical faculty. Arnold, praised for his knowledge of special anatomy, had less success in his lectures on general anatomy and physiology, and rumor had it that students were leaving Heidelberg to study these subjects elsewhere.[2] Chelius, Puchelt, and Nägeli were all getting old, although only Puchelt showed any signs of retiring. But what seemed to concern von Stengel most was Karl Hasse's announcement of his intended departure.[3] In the four years Hasse had taught pathology in Heidelberg, he had never felt part of the medical faculty. According to Philipp Jolly, who kept up an active correspondence with Henle during these years, the central problem rested in the division of the university faculty into two camps: a more powerful conservative group, led in part by Chelius, and a dwindling minority of liberal-minded professors, to which Hasse, Bunsen, and he belonged. Hasse, Jolly remarked, had not stood a chance against Chelius, who had the academic hospital under his control.[4] Frustrated with this situation, Hasse decided in 1856 to accept an offer from the University of Göttingen.

Von Stengel had no question about where his own allegiances lay. He blamed Chelius for the tensions that had torn apart the faculty in the preceding years, holding him responsible for the "demise" of a faculty that had "once been so well-known and respected."[5] In searching for ways to improve the faculty he relied almost exclusively on the advice of members of the liberal faction in the university—foremost Hasse and Bunsen. He, like they, wanted students to be educated in the most recent scientific and clinical techniques. As we have seen, his commitment to the sciences dated back to the 1840s, when he orchestrated the appointments of Henle and Pfeufer.[6] Von Stengel's motivations had never rested solely with the prestige of the university and its enrollment figures; he also wished to modernize the medical curriculum so as to train better doctors. When, for example, in 1856 he explored the possibility of creating a separate chair for experimental physiology, he relied heavily on the advice of the state health commission, in part because it consisted mostly of practicing physicians. As he made new appointments and initiated the construction of research and teaching institutes, he also revamped the medical curriculum and the procedure for medical licensing. Not that von Stengel cared little for the national and international prestige of the university. He wished as much as any minister of education to turn his state's university into a scientific center in Germany. But he was not simply following fashion. Instead he was convinced that support of the experimental sciences would better prepare students, and particularly medical students, for the problems ahead. And he believed one of the first things demanding attention was the appointment of an experimental physiologist.

Hiring an Experimental Physiologist

In May 1856, before Hasse departed, von Stengel solicited his advice on whether to bring a physiologist to Heidelberg. The young pathologist did not hesitate to sing the praises of this science. "Today," he explained, "physiology provides the fundamental basis for the study of medicine, and this is rightly so. In fact, enrollment depends largely upon the degree to which instruction in this science is adequately provided."[7] This confident response was enough to strengthen von Stengel in his conviction that action had to be taken immediately, and he instructed the members of his ministry to look more closely into the matter. Seeking professional advice, they turned to the state health commission, asking for an evaluation of the situation and suggestions for improvement.[8] The reply, not surprisingly, included an argument for the creation of a separate chair for physiology. Repeating and elaborating on its view from 1852, the commission used methodological, pedagogical, and institutional arguments to convince the state of the need to grant autonomous status to this experimental science at the University of Heidelberg.

"What was physiology," asked Franz Bils, director of the health commission and author of the report, "when it was still being taught by anatomists, pathologists, etc.? And what has it become since it has acquired its own teachers?" The question was not merely rhetorical; Bils proceeded to describe this subject's transition from a speculative body of knowledge to a modern science, a transition made possible by advances in chemistry, physics, microscopy, and mechanics. By following in the footsteps of these sciences, physiology had "itself become a natural science, that is, in the sense of an exact science." He then added,

> Here is a general answer to the ministry of interior's question. Namely physiology can be taught only by someone who is familiar with the exact sciences. The anatomist, even if he is very highly educated in his subject, is still engaged in a descriptive science, and this does not qualify him as a teacher of physiology. In physiology things must be explained; description is not enough. And if the [anatomy] teacher would nevertheless insist upon [teaching physiology] he would do so in contradiction to the spirit of physiology, even hampering its development.[9]

A reader who wanted or expected specific information on the advantages to medicine resulting from this transformation in physiology would be disappointed. Bils merely claimed that this science had grown more practical, citing as proof the "tendency among all better physicians to prepare the way for, and develop further, a physiological medicine." This had helped not only medicine; physiology had also acquired new "facts and points of view." To promote this union further, Bils recommended that someone with medical experience be hired for the position; he expressed his conviction of the intimate link between physiology and medicine by suggesting, moreover, that general pathology be included as well among the teaching responsibilities.

To communicate this knowledge to the students, Bils continued, the physiologist made use not only of lectures but of practical exercises as well. All students, he explained, should participate in these elementary exercises, and those who demonstrated particular talent, should, moreover, be encouraged to engage in independent research projects. When, however, it came to elaborating on the usefulness of these exercises, Bils could only offer his hope that the student "would be inspired to continue doing research after he entered practice," something, he emphasized, "that is to be highly valued."[10]

Bils may well have omitted mention of the concrete advantages to be gained from a knowledge of experimental physiology because therapeutics had, in truth, benefited very little from scientific research.[11] Nevertheless, Bils was not discouraged by the absence of tangible gains. Perhaps this was because diagnostics had not fared as poorly as therapeutics. One need only think of the use of chemical analysis, as in the identification of Bright's disease, as well as the invention of the stethoscope, spirometer, kymograph, and ophthalmoscope.[12] By 1850, these developments had already begun to bring a certain measure of objectivity to the diagnosis of disease, although the interpretation of the information uncovered often remained unclear. Bils' optimism, however, stemmed to a greater degree from the recent successes in physics, chemistry, and physiology, and he believed that medicine, by adopting the same experimental method, would also benefit. In a fashion reminiscent of Nebenius's support of laboratory instruction, he explained that "by the pursuit of a physiological problem, the young physician learns the method of investigation, which is as well the exact method of medical investigation."[13] That is, he believed that when the physician began to approach medical problems with the same critical eye as the scientist who tackled a problem in the laboratory, a medical "science" would prevail.

One should note that Bils envisioned two levels of engagement in the methods of medical science. On the one hand, the laboratory provided medical students with the opportunity to do routine exercises in experimental physiology. But it also catered to an elite group of talented students who had the privilege of being initiated into "the spirit of physiology." In other words, they learned the problem-solving method of the exact sciences. When we compare the pedagogical function of research as it was expressed in the 1830s with that of the 1850s, we see that at both times advanced research remained in the hands of the professors, assistants, and a small group—perhaps somewhat larger in the 1850s—of talented students. In this regard, little had changed; the activity remained associated with an elite. The radical difference came, however, in the kind of education offered to those who Pfeufer had called the *"Durchschnittsköpfe"*—the average students. In the 1830s these students had little, if any, opportunity to engage in practical exercises of any kind, whether in the laboratory or in the clinic. In the 1850s, on the other hand, laboratory work (and, as we will see later, clinical experience) was becoming an expected and required part of medical education.

The commission offered one last argument for physiology's autonomy that focused specifically on local circumstances at the University of

Heidelberg. Acknowledging the increasing importance of clinical material in the study of medicine, Bils pointed out that students were choosing large universities where clinical institutes provided ample opportunity for examining patients and performing autopsies. At this level, he explained, Heidelberg could never hope to compete, nor would this be an appropriate strategy. A small university had to concentrate on what it could do best, and this was to offer an excellent education in the theoretical sciences, among which physiology would take center stage.[14]

Given the decentralized structure of the German university system, and the tendency among students to attend a number of schools during their university education, this was an intelligent strategy. The health commission hoped students would prefer a small school environment for the first two years of their education, when theoretical courses made up the larger part of the curriculum. As we have already seen, "theoretical" no longer meant book learning and lectures. A small school could build laboratories and provide ample space and equipment for experimental studies. What it could not do was multiply the number of patients and corpses available for clinical and postmortem examination. This situation may help us to understand why, in contrast to Berlin where the university established a chair and research institute for pathological anatomy in 1856, Heidelberg did not grant full status to this subject until the late 1860s. On the other hand, it may also help to explain why Heidelberg was one of the first universities to grant institutional support to experimental physiology.[15] This, at least, was the logic behind the health commission's recommendation that Heidelberg focus on pre-clinical subjects. And certainly, if the state decided to accept this suggestion, one of the first orders of business had to be the hiring of a physiologist.

Having received the support of Hasse and the health commission, von Stengel now turned to Bunsen, well known for his politically liberal views and his support of the modern experimental sciences.[16] Bunsen replied immediately, recognizing the opportunity to bring another representative of the experimental sciences to Heidelberg and, presumably, to strengthen the liberal faction. His letter focused, of course, on the former alone:

> By a conscientious and unprejudiced deliberation of the circumstances at this university, it must appear not only desirable but also absolutely necessary to consider only those physiology professors who follow the new exact direction. This seems all the more imperative because this new direction, far from representing the specific view of a specific school, distinguishes itself much more from the older [schools] in that it does not simply take the fundamental principles of physiology from other natural sciences, but attempts instead to discover them for itself through the more critical method of independent experimental and mathematical investigations.[17]

Bunsen claimed to know of only four men who represented this new direction in physiology: Hermann Helmholtz, Ernst Brücke, Emil du Bois-Reymond, and Carl Ludwig. Although he praised all four, there was little doubt in his mind who among them was the best candidate. Helmholtz, he wrote, was by far "the most brilliant, most talented, and most generally educated," an excellent teacher whose lectures were less flashy than thorough, inspiring, and interesting.[18]

In addition to soliciting the advice of those he knew would support the appointment of an experimental physiologist, von Stengel followed the usual procedure and commissioned the university senate to contact the medical faculty and request the names of potential candidates.[19] He had anticipated trouble, but was surprised to receive a report from the medical faculty, indicating its realization that it could no longer prevent the hiring of a physiologist. The faculty's strategy was, however, to exert as much control over the successor as possible. Chelius, then dean of the faculty, began by emphasizing the success with which Arnold had taught experimental physiology during the previous years, explaining that Arnold "could not, in the interest of science and education, hand physiology over to a competitor who lacked the competence to represent the subject in its entirety in a dignified fashion."[20] Consequently, the number of potential candidates was limited. Here, as in Bunsen's letter, the four members of the 1847 group took center stage, but Chelius was more selective. Sharply criticizing du Bois-Reymond for his overspecialization, he claimed that the young physiologist's lectures were as specialized as his research and did not attract very many students. Ludwig and Brücke, on the other hand, he considered good, but doubted whether either would be prepared to leave Vienna. Helmholtz, however, seemed unhappy in Bonn, and Chelius looked favorably on the possibility of bringing him to Heidelberg. In fact he held Helmholtz to be the most capable of establishing a link between experimental physiology and medicine. Chelius had reason to believe this. Although it may seem strange today to think of Helmholtz in a medical context, he did actually have considerable medical experience. In exchange for a scholarship that had permitted him to study medicine, he had spent six years working as an army surgeon in Prussia. However, far more important for his medical reputation was his invention of the ophthalmoscope in 1850. Even Helmholtz referred to this invention later in life as the most important discovery for the purposes of furthering his career within university medical faculties.[21]

In June 1857 the members of the ministry of interior sent a report to the state ministry, summarizing the opinions of the medical faculty and Bunsen, and adding their own comments. They expressed surprise and relief that the medical faculty had agreed to the hiring of a highly qualified physiologist. While it is true, they added, that this was only out of consideration for Arnold, "still the opinion of the faculty concurs with the end result of our deliberations, although for totally different reasons, of course."[22] Agreement existed, moreover, as to who should be called. The different interests involved in the hiring of a physiologist—many of which had been medical—all pointed in the same direction. Helmholtz was the only person appropriate for the job.

Hermann Helmholtz's Early Career

Hermann Helmholtz (1821–1894) had greater medical training than most of his contemporaries who subsequently pursued careers as physiologists.[23] Unable to afford a university education, he had, at the age of seventeen, enrolled at the Berlin Königliches medizinisch-chirurgische Friedrich-Wilhelms-Institut (formerly called the Pépiniere), a medical school designed specifically for the training of military physicians, which gave promising young men of insufficient financial means the opportunity to pursue a medical career. The Prussian state financed their entire education, after which they were obligated to serve as military surgeons in the army for an eight-year period.[24] Although by 1838, when Helmholtz enrolled at the Institut, most of the classes took place at the University of Berlin, his course of study differed significantly from that of a university student. At the latter, students designed their own curriculum; at the former, they followed a strictly regimented schedule.[25] During the first of four years of instruction, they attended lectures on osteology, splanchnology, physics, botany, chemistry, physiology, general anatomy, and natural history. In the second year they continued to study these subjects, to which were added pathology and pharmacy, along with courses in anatomical dissection aimed at complementing their theoretical lectures. In the third year students advanced to general and special therapeutics, semiotics, surgery, and obstetrics. And in their fourth and final year, they attended the polyclinic and the surgical, medical, ophthalmological, and obstetrical clinics in the Charité hospital. Following this rigid four-year course of medical instruction, they spent a further year in the Charité doing rotation in the various wards. Although prohibited from treating their own patients, their duties were extensive. Under the supervision of the graduates of the Institut, they prescribed and administered medicines according to their superior's orders; wrote case histories; and supervised the nursing staff in all hygienic matters. Students of the Friedrich-Wilhelms-Institut received perhaps the best medical education and training then available in Germany.

Helmholtz's own interests, however, always rested in the natural sciences, and he took advantage of his association with the University of Berlin to pursue scientific research as well. Of greatest importance to him here was his contact with Johannes Müller, professor of physiology. Berlin hired Müller in 1833 to help reform its medical faculty and to lend more support to a new direction in scientific research, one that moved beyond simple observation to the "creation of new phenomena through experiment."[26] This new direction appealed to Helmholtz, too; in 1841 he decided to write a dissertation under Müller's supervision. For this purpose he scraped together his savings and bought his first instrument—a microscope. Without any sign of his later aversion toward microscopical research, Helmholtz investigated the structure of the nervous system in invertebrates, discovering that the nerve fibers have their point of origin in the ganglionic cells.[27] Müller, impressed with this work, offered him access to his anatomical museum and use of his instruments.

It was during this period as well that Helmholtz befriended du Bois-Reymond and Brücke, joining them in their pursuit of an organic physics. Yet unlike his colleagues, Helmholtz could not devote all his attention to the transformation of physiology into an exact science. In late September 1842, having completed his course work at the Institut, he began his year-long medical "internship" in the Charité, an experience Helmholtz found both difficult and challenging. His first assignment in the ward for internal diseases proved to be his most demanding. He began each day at seven o'clock, examining his own patients before making the rounds with his supervisor and other interns, at which time he reported on his findings and suggested appropriate therapeutic measures. The entire procedure lasted over four hours and occurred twice daily. During the remaining hours, he performed autopsies on the deceased and recorded the daily events in the hospital journal. His day did not end until eight o'clock in the evening.[28]

Helmholtz's letters to his family attest to the satisfaction he derived from this work, his only disappointment being that he had so little time to conduct his own research. During the fall of 1842 he accomplished little else than to put the finishing touches on his dissertation, which he defended on 2 November 1842. Entitled "The Structure of the Nervous System in Invertebrates," the thesis went beyond Helmholtz's initial study by demonstrating the link between ganglionic cells and nerve fibers in a host of organisms, both invertebrate and vertebrate alike.[29]

On 1 October 1843 Helmholtz's clinical internship ended and he was promoted to staff surgeon to the Royal Hussars at Potsdam and transferred to an army hospital there.[30] He remained in his native city five years, dividing his time between his medical responsibilities and scientific research. The former were clearly not overly demanding. Helmholtz managed to establish a small laboratory in the army barracks so as to conduct experiments in his spare time. During his Potsdam years (1843–1848) he focused particularly on the source of heat production during muscle contraction, conducting experiments that led ultimately to his articulation of the principle of the conservation of force. He soon recognized that the ability to explain animal heat as a function of the chemical transformations occurring within the muscles would greatly help his plans to create an "organic physics." Between 1843 and 1847 he showed experimentally that chemical changes occur in the muscle tissues during activity; that heat emission accompanies this process; and that this heat is brought to the muscles not by the nerves or blood but rather is produced in the tissues themselves. Having demonstrated these chemical physiological facts, he then analyzed and quantified this physiological process, deriving a mechanical equivalent for the amount of heat produced. This work formed the body of his paper, *Ueber die Erhaltung der Kraft,* which he completed in 1847.[31] By establishing the principle of the conservation of force, Helmholtz had effectively demonstrated the superfluousness of evoking any special life forces as explanatory principles.

Although Helmholtz's work on the conservation of force received a mixed review, few doubted he was a man of great promise. Apart from Müller's support, he now won that of the influential Alexander von Humboldt, who always had a keen eye for talented young scientists. When Brücke, who had been teaching anatomy at the *Kunstakademie* in Berlin, received a call to Königsberg as associate professor of physiology and pathology, von Humboldt arranged to have Helmholtz released from his military duties so that he could succeed Brücke.[32]

Helmholtz's tenure at the *Kunstakademie* lasted only one year. In the summer of 1849 Brücke moved to Vienna as professor of anatomy and physiology, and Helmholtz succeeded him once more. Thus, in the summer of 1849, at the age of twenty-nine, Helmholtz became associate professor of physiology and pathology at the Prussian university in Königsberg.

Helmholtz remained in Königsberg six years (1849–1855) during which time he continued his studies of nerve physiology (measuring the velocity of the nerve impulse), and also moved on to physiological optics and acoustics—two areas that occupied his attention for nearly twenty years. His interests centered on the physical foundations of sensory stimulation and the epistemological foundations of sense perception, yet in the process of researching and analyzing these topics he worked out certain physical and geometrical laws that permitted him to construct an instrument of great diagnostic importance to the medical community—the ophthalmoscope.

Helmholtz's Invention of the Ophthalmoscope and the Response of the Medical Community

To be specific, Helmholtz conceived the idea of the ophthalmoscope while preparing a lecture on optics for his students.[33] He wanted to describe the phenomenon, observed by both William Cummings, an English physician, and Ernst Brücke, wherein the human eye glowed in a dark room when light was directed at the eye and an observer stood near the light source. Neither Cummings nor Brücke had managed to see the inner structure of the eye; whenever they approached the eye closely so as to peer inside it, the glare from the light source diffused the entire pupil. While preparing his lecture, Helmholtz asked himself how an optical image is produced by the light rays reflecting back from the illuminated eye, a question that led him to analyze the rays' path. His discovery that they followed an identical path when entering and leaving the eye allowed him to explain Brücke's inability to see the internal structure: to do so he would have had to stand directly in the path of the light rays, thus blocking the light source.

It took Helmholtz merely eight days to circumvent the problem and invent an instrument that permitted him to see the retina and vessels within the living eye. He used a plane-polished glass surface that both reflects and transmits light, and thus acts as a partial mirror. By looking through this glass, which he placed at an angle, and using one surface to reflect light into the observed eye, he was able to eliminate the glare while allowing enough light to return so as to permit a clear view of the retina. Figure 7.1 gives a schematic demonstration of how the ophthalmoscope functions.

Here *C* is the plane-polished glass. A candle (*A*) illuminates the glass plate, whereby most of the light is reflected into the eye being observed (*D*). The rear of the eye (i.e., the retina) in turn reflects this light back along the same path by which the rays entered. Some light returns to *A* while some continues in a straight line (the reverse path of entry) through the glass plate and on to the observer (*G*). Since the latter must stand very close to the person being observed in order to see through the small opening of the pupil, the light rays entering the observer's eye converge, resulting in a blurred picture. To circumvent this problem, Helmholtz placed a concave lens (*F*) between the observer and the glass plate. His ophthalmoscope was complete.[34]

In December 1850 Helmholtz wrote his father expressing his surprise that no one had previously figured out how to construct such an instrument.[35] He reported that only the most elementary knowledge of optics had been necessary. Yet Helmholtz underestimated the mathematical knowledge needed to comprehend the geometrical optics on which the ophthalmoscope was based. Some of the physicians who voiced opposition toward the instrument (I discuss this in greater detail below) may have done so because of their inability to understand the physical and mathematical principles involved in the instrument's construction.

Yet Helmholtz's geometrical knowledge did not alone lead to the idea of the ophthalmoscope. As he himself later noted, his success resulted from his hybrid education: he knew more physics than physicians, and more physiology and medicine than physicists and mathematicians.[36] His medical studies had familiarized him with the practical problems confronting ophthalmologists, leading him to recognize the diagnostic potential of an instrument that would permit physicians to investigate changes in the retina. He wrote to his father:

> Until now a series of the most important eye diseases, included under the name "black cataract," have been *terra incognita*, because one could learn nothing about the changes in the eye either in the living or even after death. My invention will make the finest investigation of the internal structures of the eye possible. . . . Where possible, I shall examine patients with the chief ophthalmologist here and then publish the material.[37]

Helmholtz published the results of his work in 1851 in a small pamphlet entitled *Description of an Ophthalmoscope for the Investigation of the Retina in the Living Eye*. The medical community responded immediately. Among general practitioners, particularly older ones, some voiced opposition to the instrument. Helmholtz claimed that one colleague condemned

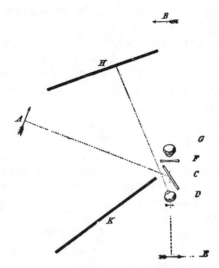

Figure 7.1   Schematic Drawing of the Path taken by Light as it Travels through the Ophthalmoscope. [*Source:* Thomas Hall Shastid, *The Description of an Ophthalmoscope, being an English translation of von Helmholtz's "Beschreibung eines Augenspiegels"* (Chicago, 1916).]

the ophthalmoscope as a dangerous instrument for letting too much light into the eye. Another, he added, believed that only those with poor eyesight needed the assistance of such an instrument.[38] Yet these hostile responses aside, the ophthalmoscope received extensive positive publicity in the scientific and medical journals soon after its invention. Although general practitioners probably did not use the ophthalmoscope in their routine patient examinations until the end of the century, it appealed immediately to a sizeable group of physicians with specialist interests in optometry and ophthalmology. By early December 1851 Helmholtz had received eighteen orders for his instrument. Between 1851 and 1856 at least sixteen books and eighteen articles were written on the ophthalmoscope. Several of these books aimed specifically at teaching physicians how to use the instrument: for example, *The Ophthalmoscope and Optometer for the Practicing Physician* (1852), by C. G. Th. Ruete, associate professor of ophthalmology at the University of Göttingen; and *The Use of the Ophthalmoscope, Including a New Instrument* (1853), by A. Coccuis, *Privatdozent* for ophthalmology at the University of Leipzig.[39] These specialists felt deeply indebted to Helmholtz and his instrument for their own recent successes. In 1854, for example, in a review of Helmholtz's work in the *Medicinische Centralzeitung,* the author adopted an ecstatic tone, characterizing Helmholtz as the "emancipator and liberator" of the field of ophthalmology.[40] And in the same year, Albrecht von Graefe, at the time a practicing ophthalmologist in Berlin and lecturer at the city's university, founded a specialist journal, *Archiv für Ophthalmologie,* in which he attributed the field's great upswing to Helmholtz's invention.[41]

If the ophthalmoscope was Helmholtz's most important contribution to the medical community, it was not the only one. He also did important work on accommodation—the process by which the eye adjusts its focus to maintain a clear picture of objects at different distances. He found that measurable changes in the cornea could be used as a reflection of pressure changes in the eye fluids caused by certain diseases, and he invented an ophthalmometer to permit such measurements. Aware of the medical significance of this work, Helmholtz published his results in von Graefe's *Archiv für Ophthalmologie,* the most important journal for specialists in eye diseases.[42]

Indeed, throughout his early career, Helmholtz appreciated and cultivated his connection to the medical community. He first presented his ophthalmoscope to the *Königsberger Gesellschaft für wissenschaftliche Medizin,* which elected him president in 1850. When, a few years later, he simplified the ophthalmoscope's external fittings, he published his results in Vierordt's *Archiv für physiologische Heilkunde,* a journal that reached a wide medical audience.[43] Moreover, while touring physiological institutes in Germany, he contacted members of the medical and scientific communities in order to demonstrate his instrument. The ophthalmologist Ruete, whom Helmholtz first met in Göttingen, was particularly pleased with what he saw. "For my trip," Helmholtz wrote his wife, "the ophthalmoscope has been splendid. I demonstrated it this morning and created a sensation here as well."[44]

Nowhere, however, was Helmholtz's interest in publicizing the medical significance of his work more obvious than in his *Handbuch der physiologischen Optik,* the first volume of which appeared in 1856. In 1854 he told his friend Adolph Fick, *Privatdozent* in physiology at the University of Zurich, that although he had decided against writing the *Handbuch* in a popular fashion for physicians, he did arrange it so that everything of medical significance was grouped together.[45] Thus, physicians, uninterested and usually unqualified to understand the mathematical parts, could easily focus on the sections that included an encyclopedic presentation of the anatomy of the eye, its dioptric, its various imperfections resulting in nearsightedness, farsightedness, and astigmatism, as well as a description of the ophthalmoscope and ophthalmometer. Helmholtz's success in reaching the medical community led von Graefe to hail the *Handbuch* as the bible of ophthalmology and the foundation for the newly emerging science of ophthalmology.[46]

Helmholtz's interest in encouraging close ties to the medical community derived from his appreciation of how physicians and physiologists could mutually benefit each other. Concerning the contributions physiologists made to medicine, Helmholtz could turn to his own invention of the ophthalmoscope, or Ludwig's invention of the kymograph. But more important, experimental physiology exemplified the proper methodological approach to the study of organic processes—whether healthy or diseased. As Helmholtz would later explain,

[The physician] must strive to know in advance what the result of his intervention will be if he proceeds in one way or the other. In order to determine in
advance what has not yet happened, or what has not yet been observed to
happen, there is no other method than to learn through observation the laws
governing phenomena; and these can be learned through induction—through
the careful search, production, and observation of those cases which fall under
the law.[47]

We have already seen the extent to which academically trained physicians embraced this vision of themselves as practitioners of the scientific
method. But if the medical community benefited from physiology, the
reverse was also true. Experimental physiologists were fighting for disciplinary autonomy, and they sought their institutional support in the university medical faculties. Several members of the 1847 group had appreciated the importance of maintaining a link between physiology and
medicine. As mentioned in Chapter 6, this had motivated Ludwig, early in
his career, to initiate a steady correspondence with Henle. Helmholtz, also
aware of the advantages that support from the medical community could
offer the experimental physiologists, admonished his friend du Bois-
Reymond, whose research and teaching concentrated on nerve physiology
to the exclusion of most other branches of physiology, to keep this concern
in mind. Indeed, Helmholtz believed du Bois-Reymond's difficulties in the
1850s in landing an appointment as professor of physiology issued from
his apparent indifference toward the medical community. "You can well
imagine," he wrote his friend,

> that men of practice lash out here and there at your lecturing style in physiol-
> ogy. . . . I will leave it to you to judge whether it is worth your while to
> further reduce the time you spend on animal electricity in physiology in order
> to acquire a better opinion from the [medical] faculty.[48]

Helmholtz's advice to du Bois-Reymond stemmed from his own, positive experience. Six years had passed since he had invented the ophthalmoscope and earned a reputation in medical circles. The ophthalmoscope, he
knew, had in many ways made his career. "For my place in the world," he
later wrote, "the construction of the ophthalmoscope was very decisive.
Among authorities and colleagues, I found, thereafter, such an appreciation of and benevolence toward my requests, that I was able to pursue the
inner drive of my intellectual curiosity much more easily."[49]

Helmholtz's Tenure at the University of Bonn

Helmholtz's high reputation in medical circles permitted him to define his
research projects however he wished, and even to move slowly away from
teaching routine medical courses. This became evident in 1855 when
Helmholtz expressed interest in leaving Königsberg for a position as professor of anatomy and physiology in Bonn. He desired this move for

personal and professional reasons: he was concerned about the adverse effects of the cold northern Prussian winters on his wife's health and believed Bonn would provide milder weather; he expected to have more scientific influence from Bonn than from Königsberg; and he wanted a slightly higher salary. But most important, he wanted to redefine his teaching responsibilities so as to exclude pathology. This marked his first shift away from the teaching of medical subjects proper. As he wrote in 1854 to Johannes Schulze, the Prussian minister of cultural affairs, he no longer felt fully capable of or interested in representing this subject:

> It has been my wish for a long time to be able to substitute general pathology, on which I lecture here, with anatomy, because the latter lies more within my interests than the former. I sense more and more by the questions and viewpoints that have recently arisen in pathology that the notions that I acquired during my earlier medical practice are no longer totally sufficient, and I must fear that this will grow worse every year.[50]

In the remainder of the letter Helmholtz elaborated on his knowledge of anatomy, emphasizing specifically the courses he taught at the *Kunstakademie* in Berlin, the anatomical nature of his dissertation research, and the instruction he had been giving at the University of Königsberg in the use of the microscope. He ended his letter, nevertheless, with the expressed wish that as professor of anatomy and physiology he would not have to neglect the latter subject, and added his hope that sufficient funds would be available for the purchase of instruments.

Helmholtz did not receive a reply to this letter and as the months drifted by he began to grow discouraged. Perhaps Schulze was suspicious of Helmholtz's true commitment to the subject of anatomy. In any event, nothing was done until Alexander von Humboldt intervened on Helmholtz's behalf in March 1855. Writing to Schulze, he praised the young professor, emphasizing the scientific contributions he had already made, and making his interest in Helmholtz's appointment clear.[51] Sure of the power he had in the Prussian ministry, Humboldt sent a letter to Helmholtz the same day expressing his confidence that an offer would arrive soon. It came on the 27th of March.[52]

Helmholtz's stay in Bonn was brief, lasting only three years. From the beginning he was disappointed in the institutional facilities for anatomy and physiology. The anatomy institute, he wrote du Bois-Reymond in October 1855, "is in a gruesome condition. Physiological instruments are few, and Budge has let these perish in dirt."[53] The budget for physiological experiments was, moreover, only fifty-four taler per year. Already in August he had written to the ministry explaining the absurdity of trying to teach physiology on such a small budget. It may, he explained, have been sufficient in earlier days, but it does not come near to covering expenses any longer.

> This science has progressed enormously in recent times, in particular through the introduction of physical methods of investigation that require complicated

and expensive instruments. It is no longer possible to give students an idea of the present standpoint in physiology without having a greater collection of instruments to use.[54]

Helmholtz fought with Budge and the ministry throughout the year, until the latter finally left Bonn. The future looked a little rosier now. Helmholtz was alone responsible for physiology and human anatomy, and expected he would be permitted to stop teaching microscopical and comparative anatomy, two subjects that had become a burden to him.[55] However, his expectation that a new anatomy institute would be built did not come to fruition, and his frustration with the poor institutional setup continued to grow. At this point the Baden ministry contacted Helmholtz to ask if he would consider a position in Heidelberg. In a letter to du Bois-Reymond in May 1857 he wrote:

> Bunsen wrote to me (and I believe you will be receiving a similar letter) that the Baden government is ready to make great sacrifices to attract a respectable physiologist to Heidelberg. The candidates are all pure full-blooded physicalists: Brücke, Ludwig, the two of us. The faculty, he wrote, will recommend both of us.[56]

Helmholtz had, however, little interest in the position. Although he was dissatisfied with his situation in Bonn, he was not yet ready to leave Prussia. He suggested to Bunsen that Heidelberg enter negotiations with du Bois-Reymond.

As we have already seen, the Baden government had serious reservations about du Bois-Reymond's specialization. It chose, therefore, to continue pursuing Helmholtz. At the end of May, Wilhelm Delffs, professor of chemistry in Heidelberg's medical faculty, arrived in Bonn to discuss possible terms of appointment. In a letter to du Bois-Reymond, Helmholtz described this encounter. He still had no desire to move to Heidelberg, but had decided to use these negotiations to improve his situation in Bonn. Nor did he feel guilty about using Heidelberg in this way: he had set such high terms—a salary of 3500 to 3600 gulden—that he "could not imagine the Baden ministry would spend so much money merely for a physiologist."[57]

Negotiations continued over the next several months; each time Heidelberg made an offer, Helmholtz turned it down. Von Stengel could have responded by entering negotiations with one of the other "organic physicists," but he chose instead to keep a watchful and hopeful eye on Helmholtz. In his opinion, no other candidate satisfied all the interests involved: Bunsen, although willing to consider one of the other physicalists, had expressed his definite interest in a qualified representative of the new experimental method, and he considered Helmholtz the best of the group; the medical faculty had made its preference for Helmholtz well known; and the health commission had expressed a similar interest in an experimentalist, adding its concern that someone with medical experience be hired. Although the commission did not mention any specific names,

Helmholtz certainly came closer to fulfilling these multiple wishes than any of the other physiologists.

Helmholtz was aware that Heidelberg had focused its interests solely on him, something he did not quite understand. In March 1858 he wrote to du Bois-Reymond to discuss the faculty's refusal to entertain any other candidate. As he explained:

> Among the faculty members there is, on the whole, great opposition toward the physicalist-physiologists. One does me the very questionable honor—I do not know why—of holding me to be less of a physicalist than the rest of our friends. Arnold, as I was told, had thus recommended me alone, perhaps in the hope that I would not accept. He has the legal right to teach physiology and could make great trouble for the government. For this reason, the government seems to have held back.[58]

At the end of October von Stengel wrote to Helmholtz once again. He knew that construction of a new anatomy institute in Bonn had not yet begun, and he hoped Helmholtz would change his mind.[59] This time von Stengel was almost successful, but new parliamentary elections in Bonn raised Helmholtz's hopes and he turned down the position once again. He added, however, that he might be willing to reconsider in the future. Von Stengel waited until January before writing again. This time Helmholtz decided to begin negotiations. The anatomical institute had not yet materialized, and, to make matters worse, he began to be blamed for the atrocious state of the institutional facilities. He claimed it was a question of honor that led him to take seriously Baden's offer. In February 1858 he began discussing specific terms of appointment with the Baden ministry.

Among Helmholtz's conditions were a physiological institute with work space for himself and students, a yearly endowment of 1050 gulden to pay for supplies, an assistant, a servant, and a salary of 3600 gulden.[60] On 17 February the members of the ministry of interior wrote to von Stengel, repeating Helmholtz's terms and adding their opinion that the stakes were far too high. Considering, they wrote, the costs of a new natural science institute, it might be wiser to hire someone, perhaps du Bois-Reymond or Ludwig, with more modest expectations. They felt that a salary of 3600 gulden "for a single and solitary subject, albeit a very important one, and one that is becoming increasingly more important, is nonetheless quite a lot."[61] Furthermore, they believed that the government could save funds by making provisional arrangements for the natural science institutes, at least until 1860/61, whereas Helmholtz's appointment would necessitate the immediate financing of a new laboratory. These hesitations had no effect on von Stengel. One day after receiving this report he wrote to Helmholtz agreeing to every term.[62]

In early March Helmholtz accepted the position, bringing to an end a process that had begun ten years earlier when the first cries for a physiologist had been heard in Baden. The process had been a long one, consisting of several stages and reflecting various interests. The young physiologists

themselves, interested in applying chemical and physical techniques to the
study of life, had developed a methodology that helped legitimize their
claims for disciplinary autonomy independent of anatomy. Their success
had depended not alone on their scientific skills, but on their articulation as
well of an approach to the study of nature that appealed to government
officials concerned with reforming the educational system. As we have
seen, the Baden government had turned to the experimental sciences in the
1850s both to solve specific agricultural problems and to teach new skills to
the next generation of teachers, physicians, and to some extent fledgling
scientists. Bunsen had been the first of the young generation of experimentalists to be appointed to the faculty at the University of Heidelberg, but
the government did not stop here. Two years later, in 1854, Baden also
hired the physicist Gustav Kirchhoff. Helmholtz's appointment was third
in a series, marking to some extent the fulfillment of Liebig's and Bunsen's
program to integrate the experimental sciences. But the decision to create a
chair for experimental physiology carried with it another dimension as
well. In the same way that agricultural problems had helped chemistry in
its fight for disciplinary autonomy, medical concerns played an important
role in physiology's success story. Events in Baden demonstrate this connection: in the years following Helmholtz's appointment the government
totally restructured the educational and licensing requirements for students
of medicine, guaranteeing that the future physicians of the state would
receive a modern education in the new methods of the experimental sciences.

Notes

1. Enrollment statistics are from *RB*, 1852–1856. For the ministry of interior's earlier warning, see Chapter 6.

2. Jolly to Henle, 14 January 1853, in Werner Goth, *Zur Geschichte der Klinik
in Heidelberg im 19. Jahrhundert* (Diss. Heidelberg, 1982), pp. 207–209.

3. Minutes of the medical faculty on 6 March 1856 in *Acten*, 1856, III, 4a,
99; medical faculty to the faculty senate, 18 March 1856, and university senate to
the ministry of interior, 19 March 1856, both in BGLA 235/3141.

4. Jolly to Henle (no date, but probably sometime around the end of 1853),
in Goth, *Zur Geschichte der Klinik*, pp. 214–216. Jolly mentioned this split in the
faculty in a number of letters, often referring to Chelius as "Barbifer maximus." See
ibid., pp. 207–219. Apparently the medical faculty, led by Chelius, had even tried
to push its own candidate for the vacant position in the physics department. The
government, however, supported Bunsen's choice of Gustav Kirchhoff. See Jolly to
Henle, 2 August 1854, ibid., pp. 217–219.

5. Ministry of interior to the state ministry, 23 January 1857, BGLA
235/29867.

6. See Chapter 3.

7. Hasse to von Stengel, 10 May 1856, BGLA 235/3141.

8. Von Stengel to the ministry of interior, 28 May 1856, BGLA 235/3141;

ministry of interior to the health commission, 28 November 1856, BGLA 235/29872.

9. Health commission to the ministry of interior, 10 December 1856, BGLA 235/29872.

10. Ibid.

11. Erwin A. Ackerknecht, *Therapeutics. From the Primitives to the Twentieth Century* (New York, 1973), chapters 10 and 11; Paul Diepgen, *Geschichte der Medizin,* 3 vols. in 2 (Berlin, 1951), vol. 2, 1, pp. 163–166.

12. Stanley Joel Reiser, *Medicine and the Reign of Technology* (Cambridge, 1978).

13. Health commission to the ministry of interior, 10 December 1856, BGLA 235/29872.

14. Ibid.

15. See Hans-Heinz Eulner, *Die Entwicklung der medizinischen Spezialfächer an den Universitäten des deutschen Sprachgebiets* (Stuttgart, 1970).

16. Shortly after Bunsen's arrival in Heidelberg, Jolly wrote to Henle that the chemist had immediately joined their group of friends in their struggle against the "ultramontanes." Jolly to Henle, 14 or 16 January 1853, University of Heidelberg, Handschriftenabteilung, Nr. 4018.

17. Bunsen to the ministry of interior, 28 May 1857, BGLA 235/29872.

18. Ibid.

19. Ministry of interior to the faculty senate, 7 May 1857, ibid.

20. Chelius to the faculty senate, 5 June 1857, ibid.

21. Helmholtz, "Erinnerungen (1891)," in Hermann von Helmholtz, *Vorträge und Reden,* 5th ed., 2 vols. (Braunschweig, 1903), vol. I, pp. 1–21, here p. 12. I elaborate on Helmholtz's relationship to the German medical community in "Helmholtz and the German Medical Community," in David Cahan, ed. *The Borders of Science: Essays on Hermann von Helmholtz* (Berkeley, forthcoming, 1993).

22. Ministry of interior to the state ministry, 23 June 1857, BGLA 235/29872.

23. Biographical information is from Leo Koenigsberger, *Hermann von Helmholtz,* 3 vols. (Braunschweig, 1902); R. Steven Turner, "Hermann von Helmholtz," in *Dictionary of Scientific Biography,* ed. Charles C. Gillespie, 14 vols. (New York, 1970–76), 6 (1972): 241–253.

24. On the Königliche medizinisch-chirurgische Friedrich-Wilhelms-Institut, see Dr. Schickert, *Die militärärztlichen Bildungsanstalten von ihrer Gründung bis zur Gegenwart* (Berlin, 1895).

25. Ibid., pp. 33–36, 48.

26. See Manfred Stürzbecher, "Zur Berufung Johannes Müllers an die Berliner Universität," *Jahrbuch für die Geschichte Mittel- und Ostdeutschlands,* 21 (1972): 184–226. The quotation is from p. 193.

27. Hermann Helmholtz, *De Fabrica Systematis nervosi Evertebratorum* (Med. Diss., Berlin, 1842). Reprinted in his *Wissenschaftliche Abhandlungen,* 3 vols. (Leipzig, 1882–95), vol. 2, pp. 663–79.

28. Helmholtz's attitude toward his internship is revealed in several letters to his parents on 7 October 1842, 8 December 1842, 19 December 1842, 16 January 1843, 8 February 1843, in David Cahan, ed. *Letters of Hermann von Helmholtz to his Parents 1837–1855* (Stuttgart, forthcoming 1993). Koenigsberger cites parts of some of these letters in *Hermann von Helmholtz,* vol. 1, pp. 47–52.

Rudolf Virchow's experience as an intern in the Charité was similar to Helmholtz's. See Virchow's letter to his father on 14 May 1843, in Marie Rabl, ed. *Rudolf Virchow. Briefe an seine Eltern 1839 bis 1864* (Leipzig, 1907), p. 64.

29. Helmholtz, *De Fabrica*.

30. Koenigsberger, *Hermann von Helmholtz*, vol. 1, p. 54.

31. Hermann Helmholtz, *Ueber die Erhaltung der Kraft* (Berlin, 1847). Helmholtz's experiments between 1843 and 1847 are published in "Ueber den Stoffverbrauch bei der Muskelaktion," *Archiv für Anatomie, Physiologie und wissenschaftliche Medicin*, 1845: 72–83; and "Ueber die Wärmeentwicklung bei der Muskelaktion," ibid., 1848: 144–164. Both are reprinted in his *Wissenschaftliche Abhandlungen*, vol. 2, pp. 735–744 and 745–763, respectively.

32. Koenigsberger, *Hermann von Helmholtz*, vol. 1, pp. 93–110.

33. Hermann Helmholtz, *Beschreibung eines Augenspiegels zur Untersuchung der Netzhaut im lebenden Auge* (Berlin, 1851). See also Koenigsberger, *Hermann von Helmholtz*, vol. I, pp. 133–143, and Stanley Joel Reiser, *Medicine and the Reign of Technology* (Cambridge, 1978), pp. 46–48.

34. Helmholtz, *Beschreibung eines Augenspiegels*, p. 47.

35. Cited in Koenigsberger, *Hermann von Helmholtz*, vol. 1, pp. 133–134.

36. Hermann Helmholtz, "Erinnerungen," p. 13.

37. Cited in Koenigsberger, *Hermann von Helmholtz*, vol. 1, pp. 133–134.

38. Helmholtz's comments are in "Das Denken in der Medizin" (1877), in his *Vorträge und Reden*, 5th ed., 2 vols. (Braunschweig, 1903), vol. II, pp. 167–190, here p. 179. For other discussions of opposition to the ophthalmoscope, see Reiser, *Medicine and the Reign of Technology*, p. 50; and George Gorin, *History of Ophthalmology* (Delaware, 1982), p. 129.

39. These and other works are listed in F. Heymann, "Die Augenspiegel, ihre Construktion und Verwendung," in *Schmidt's Jahrbücher der In- und Ausländer gesammten Medicin*, 89 (1856): 105–122.

40. *Medicinische Centralzeitung*, 1 November 1854, mentioned in *Mittheilungen*, 9 (1855): last page (no page number).

41. Albrecht von Gräfe, "Vorwort," *Archiv für Ophthalmologie*, 1 (1854): v–x. For a more detailed discussion of the ophthalmoscope's impact on the study of eye disease, see my article, "Helmholtz and the German Medical Community."

42. Hermann Helmholtz, "Ueber die Accommodation des Auges," *Graefe's Archiv für Ophthalmologie*," 2 (1856): 1–74.

43. Hermann von Helmholtz, "Ueber eine neue einfache Form des Augenspiegels," *Vierordt's Archiv für Physiologische Heilkunde*, 11 (1852): 827–852.

44. Helmholtz to his wife Olga, 6 August 1851, in Richard L. Kremer, ed., *Letters of Hermann von Helmholtz to his Wife 1847–1859* (Stuttgart, 1990), p. 51. See also Koenigsberger, *Hermann von Helmholtz*, vol. I, p. 149.

45. Koenigsberger, *Hermann von Helmholtz*, vol. I, p. 265.

46. Mentioned in Richard Greeff, "II. Historisches zur Erfindung des Augenspiegels," *Berliner klinische Wochenschrift*, 38, 48 (2 December 1901): 1201–1202.

47. Helmholtz, "Das Denken in der Medizin," p. 183.

48. Helmholtz to du Bois-Reymond, 26 May 1857, in Christa Kirsten, et al., eds. *Dokumente einer Freundschaft. Briefwechsel zwischen Hermann von Helmholtz und Emil du Bois-Reymond 1846–1894* (Berlin, 1986), pp. 171–173.

49. Helmholtz, "Erinnerungen," pp. 12–13.

50. Helmholtz to Schulze, 19 December 1854, cited in Koenigsberger, *Hermann von Helmholtz*, vol. 1, pp. 230–231.

51. Humboldt to Schulze on 24 March 1855, in ibid., pp. 249–250.

52. Humboldt to Helmholtz on 24 March 1855, in ibid., p. 250. The offer is reprinted in ibid., p. 251.

53. Helmholtz to du Bois-Reymond, 14 October 1855, in Kirsten, *Dokumente einer Freundschaft*, p. 157. Julius Ludwig Budge was also professor of anatomy and physiology at the University of Bonn until 1856.

54. Helmholtz to the Bonn ministry, 28 August 1855, Darmstaedter Collection, SPK, Fla 1847: Hermann von Helmholtz.

55. Helmholtz to du Bois-Reymond, 15 October 1856, in Kirsten, *Dokumente einer Freundschaft*, pp. 161–162.

56. Helmholtz to du Bois-Reymond, 18 May 1857, in Kirsten, *Dokumente einer Freundschaft*, pp. 167–169.

57. Helmholtz to du Bois-Reymond, 26 May 1857, in Kirsten, *Dokumente einer Freundschaft*, pp. 171–173.

58. Helmholtz to du Bois-Reymond, 5 March 1858, in Kirsten, *Dokumente einer Freundschaft*, pp. 176–178.

59. The following events are recounted in a letter from Helmholtz to an unknown person, 16 April 1858, in Darmstaedter Collection, SPK, Fla 1847: Hermann von Helmholtz.

60. Mentioned in a report from the ministry of interior to the state ministry, 17 February 1858, BGLA 235/29872.

61. Ibid.

62. State ministry to Helmholtz, 18 February 1858, ibid.

8

Experimental Physiology and the Medical Context

The institutionalization of experimental physiology at the University of Heidelberg occurred within a medical context. Helmholtz had been the favored candidate in part because of his reputation in medical circles, his position was in the medical faculty, and the same year of his appointment the government totally revamped the rules and regulations dictating the examination and licensing requirements for anyone wishing to practice medicine in the state. Academically trained physicians throughout Germany had been fighting since the mid-1840s to raise educational standards and tighten the examination and licensing requirements. One of their major goals was to replace the multiple categories of health-care practitioners with a single unified profession of highly trained physicians. Several states had already begun to comply. In 1852, for example, Prussia abolished its tripartite classification of physicians into doctors, surgeons of the second class, and surgeons of the first class, replacing it with a single category of university educated physicians.[1] In 1858 Baden followed suit, but it added a provision not yet required anywhere else: in stipulating the course of study university students were to follow, it made two semesters in the laboratory—one in chemistry and the other in physiology—a prerequisite for anyone wishing to practice medicine in the state.

The Medical Regulations of 1858

The medical regulations approved by the Baden government in 1858 replaced the prior laxity and vagueness in the state examination procedure with specific detail and an exact system of requirements.[2] First, it established four years as the absolute minimum period that a student had to attend the university before even qualifying for the state examination. Second, following the Prussian model, it abolished the tripartite classification of doctors, and concomitantly, the tripartite examination, requiring that all medical practitioners be trained in internal medicine and surgery in order to receive a license to practice. But the most significant change came in the examination itself. In accordance with the reform proposals of 1848, in which physicians had requested that a distinction be made between general scientific and medical subjects, the examination was divided into two parts: one in the natural sciences given after the first two years of study, and one in pathology and therapeutics coming at the end of one's studies. In order to even qualify for the first examination, students had to demonstrate that they had attended courses in anatomy, physiology, chemistry, botany, zoology, mineralogy, geology, and physics. But even this was not enough, for knowledge acquired in the lecture room no longer sufficed. The state also required all students to take two courses in dissection, and, in an unprecented move, dictated that they should spend one semester each in the physiology and chemistry laboratories as well. The examination itself tested for knowledge in all these subjects and consisted of both written and oral sections. The health commission retained jurisdiction over this examination, but the government assigned a special committee of university professors, newly appointed each time, to administer the actual test. This need for specialty knowledge was not challenged by the health commission.[3]

The remainder of the ruling focused on the last two years of study spent in "medical courses," and on the final test. To qualify for the latter students had to prove that they had attended classes in general and special pathology and therapeutics, comparative, pathological, and surgical anatomy, ophthalmology, psychiatry, surgery, obstetrics, pharmacy, pharmacology, state medicine, epidemiology of house pets, and the history of medicine. Moreover, they had to demonstrate that they had spent one year doing practical work in the medical, surgical, and obstetrical clinics. Again the examination was both oral and written, covering all the above subjects. In the oral section the students had to be prepared to answer questions on anatomy and physiology as well. In addition, a practical examination was included that tested the student's knowledge at the bedside and in the dissection room. The health commission, composed primarily of practicing physicians, retained full responsibility for this part of the examination.

These regulations, covering both examination and licensing requirements, marked an important turning point in the professionalization of physicians and the institutionalization of scientific medicine. The government's agreement to abolish the different classifications of health care practitioners and codify a standardized program of education provided physicians with the recognition and protection they needed in order to establish

claims of expertise in the medical domain. The regulations of 1858 signified not only the government's acceptance of the scientifically trained physician as the most qualified to assume responsibility for the health of the
state's citizens, but also its agreement to regulate the content of this training. By requiring students to pass an examination in the natural sciences
before moving on to medical courses, the government limited the students'
academic freedom in order to give institutional legitimacy to the principles
of scientific medicine: as of 1858 students had to have a command of
anatomy, physiology, and chemistry before being permitted to take medical courses where, presumably, they would be applying this knowledge to
the study of health and disease.

With these regulations, moreover, practical training became an institu-
tionalized part of the medical curriculum, and this not only in the clinic but
in the laboratory as well. During laboratory instruction, students were
introduced to common microscopical and chemical techniques, such as the
preparation of bone sections and injections, and the analysis of urine and
creatine. In addition, they engaged in physiological experiments proper,
inducing the contraction of frog legs, cutting superficial nerves, and sim-
ulating digestion. Unlike Müller's dissection courses in which the students
had been left to their own devices, hacking away at corpses without any
guidance, laboratory exercises here were well supervised. Two to three
hours of instruction were offered every week, and the laboratory, under the
watchful eye of an assistant, was open every morning from eight to twelve
o'clock to offer students the chance to pursue their own experiments.[4]

In contrast to training at the bedside, which served direct utilitarian
ends, laboratory courses focused on teaching the student how to tackle a
problem scientifically under simplified laboratory conditions. Physicians
believed that by isolating, controlling, and manipulating the phenomena,
students would learn to think inductively and establish causal connections.
This laboratory training was, however, only a preliminary step. Armed
with these critical abilities, students would then enter the clinic prepared to
test their hypotheses and tackle the complex signs and symptoms associated with disease. As the author of a lead article in the *Mittheilungen des
badischen ärztlichen Vereins* wrote, the student who learns the exact method
in the laboratory, will have "so cultivated his sense for the proper way of
looking at things . . . that the only task left would be to give instruction
on how to direct his experience through the great labyrinth of pathology
and therapy."[5] The young doctor would, presumably, be proceeding ratio-
nally.

That, at least, was the intent. The value of laboratory instruction for
medical students remained, however, considerably more ambiguous. Wilhelm Wundt, Helmholtz's assistant from 1858 to 1865, had responsibility
for directing the laboratory exercises and he himself questioned the government's decision to make physiological instruction a requirement. In his
autobiography, he complained that "the officials in Karlsruhe had obviously scarcely put the question to themselves as to how such a laboratory

course should be constituted, and even less what value it would perhaps have for future practitioners." "In reality," he added,

> the conviction of the uselessness of this course set in very soon, attendance diminished gradually, and I myself could not avoid concluding that exercises in experiments that were actually meant for physiologists alone were a relatively unnecessary endeavour.[6]

Even Helmholtz expressed some hesitations about the wisdom of this requirement. Shortly after his arrival in Heidelberg he wrote to du Bois-Reymond, characterizing the "legal regulation which turns the physiology course into a required course for Baden students" as an "overexaggeration of enlightened principles" and voicing his fears that "it could become very burdensome" for him.[7]

But Helmholtz soon found a solution to this problem: he made sure he would have little to do with routine laboratory instruction. Unlike Carl Ludwig, who involved himself directly in his students' work, attracting individuals from all over the world because of his interest and excellence in teaching techniques and methods, Helmholtz remained aloof from the routine drills conducted in his laboratory. These became the sole responsibility of his assistants: Wundt from 1858 to 1865, and Julius Bernstein from 1865 until Helmholtz's departure from Heidelberg in 1871.[8] Helmholtz distanced himself even further from his "medical" duties by requiring his assistant to teach his courses in microscopical anatomy, justifying this by his lack of histological knowledge and his tendency to get headaches from looking through the microscope.[9]

Helmholtz's reluctance to teach routine medical courses to run-of-the-mill students did not, however, reflect a disinterest in working with advanced medical students. On the contrary, he welcomed advanced students into his laboratory who were interested in clinical work in ophthalmology and ophthalmometry. Emanuel Mandelstamm, M. Woinow, and Hermann Jakob Knapp all came to Heidelberg, after studying with von Graefe in Berlin, to learn the theoretical underpinnings of their specialty. Knapp even stayed on to write his *Habilitation* on the curvature of the human cornea and to teach ophthalmology at the university.[10]

Still, Helmholtz's contact with medical students was greatly reduced during the years he spent at Heidelberg. In his teaching, he concentrated his lectures on subjects he enjoyed, alternating between a general human physiology course one semester and a more specialized course on the physiology of the sense organs during the following semester.[11] Much had changed since his days at the University of Königsberg, when he had been responsible for anatomy, pathological anatomy, and pathology, in addition to physiology. Experimental physiology had gained disciplinary autonomy, permitting Helmholtz (and others) to focus their time and energy on their specialized areas of interest. A paradoxical situation thus arose: the institutionalization of experimental physiology had occurred because of its perceived medical significance, yet that institutional home gave Helmholtz more license than ever to pursue his own interests, whether medical or not. Baden may have hired him and built a brand new laboratory as part of its reform of the medical curriculum, but for the first time in his career, Helmholtz did not have to teach routine medical courses at all. Indeed, in the thirteen years he spent at Heidelberg, his work took him further away from the medical context. This is most obvious in his research, where he turned more and more to questions of epistemology, aesthetics, and, ultimately, to mathematics and physics, finally leaving Heidelberg in 1871 to accept a position as professor of physics in the philosophical faculty at the University of Berlin.

Experimental Physiology and the Medical Community

The ambivalence surrounding experimental physiology's importance for medicine could be found not only among physiologists, but among physicians as well. In 1858, the year of Helmholtz's appointment, the Organization of German Scientists and Physicians met in Karlsruhe where Robert Volz held the opening address.[12] "We physicians," he began, "may consider ourselves as members of this organization by virtue of our profession; it is indeed an organization of natural scientists AND physicians."[13] Nevertheless, he reminded his audience, the link between medicine and science is only thirty years old, dating back to the foundation of the organization by Lorenz Oken in 1828. At that time the link reflected hopes for the future far more than it did reality. But, he added, much has changed since then, "not, as you all know, because of inventions and discoveries, but through the recognition of medicine's true foundation and through the altered method of investigation."[14]

Medicine, he went on, has traditionally depended on observations in its investigations, but the new method makes use of experiment to search after general laws. It may be more difficult and time consuming, but it also brings a greater degree of certainty. Nevertheless, he cautioned, as physicians our first task is to heal, and as such we cannot afford to totally abandon observation, for as helpful as the experimental method promises to be, direct benefits are not yet in our possession. Thus, he added, "although we recognize [the experimental method] as the correct method, and although it is the method that first raised medicine to a science, we cannot ignore [observation] and will most likely never be able to ignore it." The patient cannot afford to wait until the law describing his disease is found, and he will be "just as grateful to the physician for his recovery even if this did not follow an exact scientific course."[15]

Volz's recommendation was not to question the potential usefulness of the experimental method. Without it the modern physician would indeed have had few aspirations to being a scientist. Rather he dealt with this ambiguity by cautioning physicians not to expect miracles, while at the same time encouraging them to continue analyzing and measuring:

Even if the widest field lies fruitless before us, and much has still to be sowed, our task has nevertheless become clear to us, the path to reach it is known. It is the path that builds on laws, the path that traces the effects of electrical and magnetic forces back to a general measure, that determines the path of light and measures the size of its waves to the millionth part of a millimeter. But to attain such results, the physicist had to [take] a body (or a symptom) property by property, observing, examining, comparing, experimentally provoking, measuring, and weighing it in order to find ultimately the common laws its expressions obey.

We are also working on this task and its preliminary and more modest part devolves upon the medicine of our day. We must observe, weigh, and examine. But our time does not yet suffice for drawing conclusions. . . . Our medical research is still that of facts; that of our sons shall be of causes, of laws. In this way, substance will become motion, and physics physiology. Still, future physicians must always remember that the first goal of medicine is to heal.[16]

Volz's statement reveals the hopes and problems surrounding the role of the experimental method in the development of modern medicine. This method represented most importantly a particular way of approaching the study of health and disease that differed greatly from methods used earlier in the century. The analytic techniques of the physicist had become the model; the method was reductionist at its core. The task of the physician qua scientist was to reduce a complex of symptoms to its component parts, examine each part individually through a multitude of experimental techniques, derive laws explaining the behavior of the parts, and then demonstrate that the composite behavior (which was the disease itself) was nothing more than a function of the behavior of the individual symptoms.

This, at least, was the goal. But there was little doubt that physicians would have to wait a long time until such analyses were possible. Until that day, they would have to resort to other, less certain, sources of knowledge for diagnosing and treating patients. Volz and other physicians of the time accepted this discrepancy with an ease that has often led historians to the cynical conclusion that professional concerns alone motivated physicians in their fight for a medical science. While I do not wish to challenge this general interpretation, I want to argue that the story is considerably more complicated. An analysis that focuses purely on professional interests misses the fact that the world physicians fought for was also one in which they strongly believed. They were convinced that medicine would indeed benefit through a greater reliance on the scientific method. To be sure, the professional advantages to be gained through the "objectification" of medicine fueled this conviction, but it would be false to conclude that physicians were intentionally deceptive in order to acquire a monopoly over medical care. Rather they, like the young experimental physiologists and authors of the popular encyclopedias, believed that the experimental sciences would change society for the better. It is, of course, important for historians to demonstrate the extent to which the vision of society advocated by reformers or professionalizing groups often involves a more central role for the reformers themselves. But interpreting their vision as a mere reflection of self-interests is problematic, to say the least. The factors motivating reformers are, for one, usually more complex. But more important, such a "reductionist" interest model does not allow one to distinguish between different reform goals. On the contrary, it suggests that those advocating change do so simply because they have something to gain. The difficulties surrounding such a position are, I believe, evident.

German physicians in the second half of the nineteenth century did not believe that the tension between theory and practice had anything to do with the possible inappropriateness of the exact method for the study and treatment of disease; rather, if problems arose, it was because an exact science of medicine was still in its early stages of infancy. Whatever hindsight may have taught us, physicians at mid-century had many reasons to believe this. They were not, for example, without concrete signs of the advantages to be gained from this method. Although therapeutics may have remained relatively unaffected by this method, diagnostics had benefited considerably. This should not be underestimated. The inability to determine the cause of an ailment, particularly when an individual is in considerable pain, increases the stress and anxiety experienced by the afflicted person and family members. Knowing what is wrong always brings much relief, even if specific therapeutic measures are lacking. In this regard nineteenth-century physicians had gained much by the 1860s: they could diagnose specific diseases such as Bright's and Addison's disease; demonstrate that the "fevers" of the eighteenth century were actually distinct diseases such as malaria, typhus, and typhoid; see and often remove internal tumors in their early stages; and identify in general early warning signs of oncoming illnesses. To a large extent, they had acquired this knowledge through the techniques of auscultation, percussion, microscopy, and chemical analysis, aided by the use of such instruments as the ophthalmoscope, kymograph, laryngoscope, urometer, thermometer, and pleximeter.

Physicians' faith in the exact method derived thus in part from their diagnostic successes. But given the absence of therapeutic gains, this may not have sufficed had it not been for the gradual emergence of a new *Zeitgeist* characterized by a high veneration for the exact sciences. Between 1830 and 1860 German society had undergone major changes. Significant increases in manufacture and trade, advances in transportation and communication, and the founding of large banking establishments, mining companies, and industrial plants had all marked the first wave of industrialization in the period prior to the unification of Germany. These economic changes had not occurred without a corresponding shift in the values esteemed by society. Whereas knowledge of the classical languages had once defined the scholar [*Gelehrter*], facility with instruments, mastery of experimental techniques, and mathematical reasoning—in short, knowledge of an exact and precise nature—had slowly become the highly regarded traits. Should we thus be surprised at the faith of physicians that they had only to continue dissecting, weighing, and measuring to guarantee that medical practice would some day benefit as well? If nothing else, their armamentarium of instruments reassured them and their patients that they belonged to the new scientific elite.

Many changes had occurred since the 1830s. Laboratory training, then viewed by the state to be inappropriate for university education, had acquired a higher status as society became increasingly industrialized. The power of the knowledge acquired in the laboratory was already beginning to make itself felt in the modernization of agricultural techniques, transportation, and communication. This was, of course, only a beginning. A closer link between science and industry, as evidenced in the emergence of chemical-, pharmaceutical-, and electrical-based industries, would not occur until the last decades of the century. But by mid-century a strong faith existed that scientific knowledge, particularly the scientific method, would provide both the ideological and material backbone for the emergence of a modern society. And it was this faith that led to significant investments in the natural sciences during the 1850s and 1860s, well before the so-called institutional revolution that marked the period following the founding of the German Empire.

Notes

1. See Claudia Huerkamp, *Der Aufstieg der Ärzte im 19. Jahrhundert* (Göttingen, 1985), p. 58.

2. Reprinted in *Mittheilungen*, 10 February 1858 (Nr. 3), pp. 17–20. See also ministry of interior to state ministry, 8 January 1858, BGLA 233/31847.

3. *Mittheilungen*, 10 February 1848, pp. 18–19. I am not aware of any other state requiring laboratory instruction of their medical students at or before this time. In Prussia similar reforms in the state medical examination (the shift from the Tentamum philosophicum to the Tentamum physicum) did not occur until 1861. See Klaus Sczibilanski, *Von der Prüfungs- und Vorprüfungsordnung (1883) bis zur Approbationsordnung 1970 für Aerzte der Bundesrepublik Deutschland. Die Entwicklung der medizinischen Prüfungsordnungen, darg. an Aufsätzen aus der deutschen ärztlichen Standespresse* (Diss. Münster, 1977).

For a discussion of the reform proposals of 1848, see Chapter 6 of this book.

4. Wolfgang G. Bringmann, Gottfried Bringmann, David Cottrall, "Helmholtz und Wundt an der Heidelberger Universität 1858–1871," *Heidelberger Jahrbücher*, 20 (1976): 79–88, here pp. 81–85; Wilhelm Wundt, *Erlebtes und Erkanntes* (Stuttgart, 1920), p. 154.

5. "Wie sollen die Aerzte gebildet werden?" in *Mittheilungen*, 12 May 1852 (Nr. 9), pp. 65–69, here p. 66.

6. Wundt, *Erlebtes und Erkanntes*, p. 154.

7. Helmoltz to du Bois-Reymond, 29 October 1858, in Christa Kirsten, et al., eds., *Dokumente einer Freundschaft. Briefwechsel zwischen Hermann von Helmholtz und Emil du Bois-Reymond 1846–1894* (Berlin, 1986), pp. 193–94.

8. Gerhard Rudolph, "Julius Bernstein," *DSB*, 15 (1978): 20–22.

9. Bringmann, et al., "Helmholtz und Wundt," p. 83.

10. *BL,* s.v. "Mandelstamm, Emanuel;" "Woinow, M." (Woinow actually worked with Hirschberg in Berlin, not von Graefe); and "Knapp, Hermann Jakob."

11. *Anzeige,* 1858–1871.

12. For information on Volz, see Chapter 6.

13. Reprinted in *Mittheilungen,* 30 September 1858 (Nr. 18), pp. 137–141, here p. 137.

14. Ibid., p. 138.

15. Ibid., pp. 139–140.

16. Ibid., pp. 140–141.

9

The Triumph of the Ideology
of the Practical—the 1850s

Since the *Vormärz* period, the Baden government had been increasing its
support of the natural sciences, convinced that the success of the modern
state depended on an education in these subjects. A greater emphasis on
the *Realwissenschaften*, the establishment of trade schools and non-classical
secondary schools, and the expansion of the polytechnic institute had all
marked an attempt by the government to increase society's familiarity with
the natural sciences and provide individuals with the knowledge and skills
deemed necessary for rationalizing and improving the means of production. In this context the experimental sciences and laboratory training had
grown steadily in importance. In the laboratory students were introduced
to methods of analysis that permitted exact and critical investigation of the
phenomena at hand. Mastery of this method promised, in addition, the
ability to control and ultimately to manipulate natural forces. Faith in
the power of this knowledge, already present in the *Vormärz* period, increased in the years following the revolution of 1848 as Germany entered a
period of industrial and commercial prosperity. It was at this time as well,
as the link between the production of scientific knowledge and economic
growth was becoming more obvious, that the experimental sciences became firmly established in the German university system. In Baden, the
government actively sought professors capable of directing research laboratories where students would be introduced to the methods of exact
scientific investigation. Bunsen, Kirchhoff, and Helmholtz were all hired
for this reason. The government did not, however, limit its support of the
experimental sciences to faculty appointments; it also set out immediately

to construct research laboratories where these professors would not only conduct their own research but would also teach their students how to apply the exact method of investigation to the study of nature, health, and disease.

The Construction of Modern Research Laboratories— the 1850s

Between 1850 and 1871 Baden spent over 450,000 gulden on the construction of new scientific institutes, an exorbitant sum for a small state trying to recuperate from the financial setbacks of the previous decade.[1] The first institute built along the lines of a modern research and teaching institution—Bunsen's chemistry laboratory—was completed in 1854 at a cost of almost 70,000 gulden. With work space for fifty students, this institute permitted Bunsen to focus his chemistry courses on laboratory instruction. Here students learned analytic techniques that qualified them in later years for laboratory positions in the German chemical industry. In the thirty-two years Bunsen taught at Heidelberg, he trained 3450 students in such techniques, lending his laboratory international fame, and contributing significantly to the emergence of chemistry as a profession.[2]

In the 1850s parliament also invested large sums in the polytechnic institute, allotting 68,000 gulden in 1858/59 specifically for a school of mechanics, and another 150,000 during the next three years to permit expansion of the physical premises, necessary to accommodate the rapid increase in enrollment as more and more individuals became aware of career possibilities associated with a technical education.[3]

It was within this context that the government also began in the late 1850s to revive its earlier plans for an institute for the natural sciences.[4] Catalyst for this renewed interest was Helmholtz's insistence that a new physiology institute be placed at his disposal. On his arrival in 1858 he had agreed to set up a temporary laboratory in a rented building (*"Haus zum Riesen"*) along with physics and part of the mineralogy collection, but he had requested that funds for a new institute be included in the budget for 1860/61.[5] The government building and economics commission, given the task of drawing up plans for the new physiology institute, decided to investigate the condition of all the natural sciences at the University of Heidelberg. It soon recognized that physics needed a new laboratory as well, and that something also had to be done for the remaining sciences. At the time, mathematics (with its instruments), part of the mineralogy collection, a second chemistry laboratory for organic chemistry, and a collection of technological and agricultural models were all sharing cramped quarters in the old and now dilapidated Dominican cloister. The commission favored the construction of a new institute that could accommodate all these subjects, and it suggested the site of the old cloister as the most appropriate place to begin construction. The remainder of the report elaborated on the specific needs of each of the sciences involved.[6]

The commission had worked together with the respective professors to draw up the following plans, with physiology taking precedence. High on the list of Helmholtz's demands were two large student work areas (each for roughly thirty students), one specifically for physiological investigations and the other most likely for microscopical research. In addition, he requested a large auditorium (1290 sq. ft.), a chamber for frogs, two small stalls (perhaps for dogs?), a number of rooms for equipment, books, and storage space, and live-in quarters for an assistant and a servant. For himself, he requested an office, private work space, and an apartment.

Kirchhoff's demands for the physics institute were similarly elaborate, including a medium-sized laboratory (480 sq. ft.), somewhat smaller rooms specifically for optics and magnetics (400 sq. ft.), a small chemical kitchen, a large hall for instruments (1680 sq. ft.), a large auditorium (70 to 80 seats), private work space for the director, and two apartments, one for a servant and the other for himself.

The last institute was a laboratory for the professor of organic chemistry in the medical faculty, Wilhelm Delffs. This was to include an auditorium (50 seats), one laboratory for at least twelve students, a smaller laboratory specifically for chemical investigations of a forensic nature, and a series of rooms for apparatus and chemical preparations, for study purposes, and for combustible materials. The remaining natural sciences— mineralogy, agricultural science, mathematics, technology, and archaeology—required large spaces for displaying collections, and auditoriums for holding lectures.

The building and economics commission submitted these plans to the members of the ministry of interior on 25 February 1859. The ministry responded by making a few suggestions for curtailing expenses. It favored, for example, omitting the chemistry laboratory for Delffs, reducing the allotted space for most of the other sciences, and cutting back on some of the live-in apartments. The building and economics commission, backed by the faculty senate, rejected these proposals, and a battle ensued. In December the ministry sent a report to von Stengel describing the two sides of the disagreement and elaborating on the differences in expense.[7] The commission's plan, intended to accommodate physiology, physics, mathematics, technology, agriculture, and chemistry, was estimated at 165,000 gulden, whereas the ministry proposed cuts that would save 38,000 gulden. One week later von Stengel, speaking for the Grand Duke, ordered the ministry to adopt the more expensive institute. Early in 1860 parliament granted the necessary funds: 165,000 gulden.[8]

"Friedrichsbau," as this institute came to be called, was completed in 1863. It was a massive structure, including three laboratories, work space for roughly 100 students, numerous science collections, and private apartments. Standard accounts of the construction of German science laboratories omit mention of this building because of its inclusion of several different disciplines under one roof, an arrangement that was, even for the time, unusual.[9] Nevertheless, none of its inhabitants objected to this setup.

Helmholtz's own interest in physics may even have led him to welcome proximity to Kirchhoff's laboratory. What is certain is that the Grand Duke favored this particular form, for he saw in the unification of the sciences a symbol for the unification of Germany, something he desired since his university days when he had attended the lectures of such liberals as Ludwig Häusser and Friedrich Christoph Dahlmann. For Friedrich, the inclusion of all the natural sciences in one building fit in well with a plan he had developed together with his friend, Heinrich Gelzer, to try and bring about the unification of Germany through education.[10] Opposed to Bismarck's blood and iron politics, but convinced that unification under Prussian hegemony would benefit Baden economically and protect it from the territorial aspirations of France, Friedrich favored the establishment of a school for German princes where, through a modern education, traditions of particularism would be broken and feelings of German consciousness awakened. One can see here the influence of his liberal education, particularly his conviction that education was the best tool for bringing about political and economic change. Friedrichsbau had, thus, symbolic character for the Grand Duke. Asked by the ministry of interior to suggest an appropriate inscription for the building, Friedrich's personal secretary responded:

> The new building in Heidelberg that has been constructed for the natural sciences distinguishes itself fundamentally from the isolated institutes of other universities in that it strives to unite within itself exact sciences that stand by nature in intimate union with one another. . . .
> His Royal Highness believes that an inscription in the following form would capture this meaning:
>
> Friedrich
>
> the Grand Duke of Baden wanted this edifice, built under his direction in MDCCCLXIII, to be dedicated to the unified efforts of the natural sciences.[11]

Friedrichsbau stood, thus, for unification, and the Grand Duke hoped (in vain, as we know) that the efforts of the German states would prove to be as successful as the joint efforts of the natural sciences had been. It is significant that Friedrich turned to a research laboratory when he sought an appropriate symbol of unification, power, and prestige. Nothing demonstrates more clearly the extent to which familiarity with experimental techniques and sophisticated instruments had increased in status. The laboratory, like the telegraph and railroad, had become a symbol of the new era. Much had changed since the first half of the century. Large student laboratories and faculty apartments distinguished the new science institutes from those in which Tiedemann and Henle had held classes and conducted research. The contrast Ludwig Winter had made in the 1830s between universities and polytechnic schools, in which one had a scientific, the other a practical goal, could now only be maintained with great difficulty. To be sure, the narrowing of the gap had occurred in part because of changes within the technical institutes themselves. Desirous of acquiring university status (a battle they did not win until late in the century), technical institutes continued to raise their standards and expand their curriculum to include general courses in the humanities.[12] But university education had also moved in the direction of more practical training. Although university professors often denied the narrowing of this gap, emphasizing the *"wissenschaftliche"* orientation of their institutions as opposed to the more utilitarian goals of the technical schools, in reality the kind of education provided at the universities no longer warranted such grandiose claims. There, too, facility with instruments and experimental techniques had become the standard by which a professor's talents were judged, something he himself acknowledged through his express desire to live in immediate proximity to his instruments and laboratory. He was expected, moreover, not only to be skilled in these methods and techniques himself, but also to teach them to his students. As in the polytechnic institutes, it had become part of the standard university curriculum to complement theoretical courses with practical instruction in the laboratory.

The exact method of the experimental sciences had grown in importance because of its association with the ability to control and manipulate natural phenomena. Whether one engaged in research for direct utilitarian ends was, in some ways, irrelevant. The exact method, much like computer techniques today, represented first and foremost a particular way of approaching and dissecting a problem, one that had begun to show successes in such areas as communication, agriculture, and even medical diagnostics. It promised, more than any other analytic method, to be a powerful tool for the acquisition of new knowledge. There is perhaps no better expression of this faith than the inaugural speech Helmholtz gave in 1862 on the occasion of his election to the office of university rector. Choosing as his topic the relationship of the natural sciences to other branches of knowledge, Helmholtz, who intended to treat all forms of knowledge equally, ended up praising the experimental sciences above all else.

The Power of Knowledge

"It is not enough to know facts," claimed Helmholtz. "Science first begins when the laws and causes are revealed."[13] And the more general the law— that is, the more phenomena for which it could account—the more sophisticated the science. Helmholtz used this dictum to generate a hierarchy of the sciences: the humanities, where judgment was based on "psychological insight," and generalities (and ultimately predictions) were difficult to make, ranked low on the scientific totem pole. Mathematics, on the other hand, capable of deriving laws of unconditional validity from a very small number of observations, occupied the highest position.[14]

Helmholtz held the importance of laws to be manifold. Beside permitting one to combine seemingly disparate facts under one overarching principle, laws provided a source of creativity, leading to the expansion of knowledge through their application to totally new situations. Of perhaps greater importance, they symbolized for him a liberalizing and anti-authoritative principle. For these reasons Helmholtz criticized the *Gymnasia* for favoring grammar over mathematics as a tool for teaching logic. Grammatical rules, he argued, have too many exceptions, thus keeping students from learning to "trust the certainty of a legitimate consequence derived from strictly universal laws."[15] Consequently, he continued, students rely too heavily on authority, even in situations where they could well form their own opinions. This he also blamed on philological studies, arguing that they required a sophisticated aesthetic appreciation for language, and thus many years of training, before the students could make their own judgments. "These two shortcomings," Helmholtz concluded,

> are owing to a certain sluggishness and uncertainty in the way of thinking that will be damaging not only for later scientific studies. Mathematical studies are, however, certainly the best medicine for both; here there is absolute certainty of inference and the only authority that rules is that of one's own reason.[16]

Mathematical studies thus taught the kind of critical thinking necessary not only for scientific work, but for the success of constitutionalism, in which an educated population participated in, and even defined, the political and economic affairs of the state. Nor was mathematics the only branch of knowledge capable of imparting such independence of thought to students. Indeed, not too far below mathematics in Helmholtz's scientific hierarchy were the experimental sciences. Because they could arbitrarily alter the conditions under which certain effects were produced, they too were capable of deriving general laws of nature from a relatively small number of observations, thus also teaching students how to work independently. But Helmholtz's praise for the method of the experimental sciences had an additional source, for he pointed out as well that it alone had granted scientists the ability "to exploit the powers of nature for our benefit and make them subservient to our will."[17]

Thus the exact method of the experimental sciences provided an ideal tool for training the critical faculties of the mind, at the same time that it led to tangible results. Helmholtz emphasized this last point in his speech, yet he stopped short of identifying too closely the power of scientific knowledge with utilitarian gains. Although inspired by science's increased powers to control and manipulate the environment, he emphasized the need to have freedom of choice in research. He did not deny the importance of producing knowledge that would enhance industry, wealth, and the fitness of life, but he refused to judge scientific knowledge according to its immediate utility. Who, he asked, would have thought that eighty years after Galvani observed frog legs contract on contact with various metals that Europe would be interlaced with wires capable of transmitting information from Madrid to Petersburg with the speed of light![18] In short, an emphasis on direct practical gains would prove less fruitful in the attempt to gain control over nature.

"Knowledge is power," Helmholtz argued, power that one could see in the application of steam, which had increased the physical power of human beings a million times over, in weaving and spinning machines, in transportation and communication. It should be emphasized that for Helmholtz, all branches of knowledge contributed to the intellectual superiority of a nation; all strove to "give the intellect [*Geist*] power over the world."[19] Yet only the natural sciences increased both the material and intellectual power of the nation. Thus, despite his attempt to grant equal status to all branches of knowledge in this endeavor, the natural sciences occupied for him a privileged position. They alone adhered strictly to the inductive method, uncovering thereby general laws of nature; and, most important, they alone converted this knowledge into tangible products that were totally transforming the shape of society. Certainly if the goal of knowledge was to acquire control, then no branch of knowledge had a better history of success than the experimental sciences.

CONCLUSION
The 1860s and Beyond: An Institutional Revolution?

Helmholtz's speech, delivered in 1862 to the entire university (and most likely some government officials as well), gave expression to ideas that had been actively defended by German liberals for several decades. As in the countless articles in Brockhaus's *Conversations-Lexikon der Gegenwart* and Rotteck's and Welcker's *Staatslexikon,* the picture painted here was of a world in which the symbols of an advanced civilization were no longer Latin, Greek, and classical literature, but railroads, steam engines, telegraphs, electricity, and the scientific laboratory.[20] The anxiety that this transition unleashed among humanists who sensed the diminution of the power of their knowledge in a slowly industrialising economy has been well documented in Fritz Ringer's book, *The Decline of the German Mandarins.*[21] But humanists did not make up the whole of the German academic elite, and, for obvious reasons, members of the natural science and medical faculties responded quite differently to the social and economic changes occurring around them. Indeed, many actively encouraged this transformation, joining hands with the growing number of engineers and industrialists, and helping, as Helmholtz did, to define a "culture of science" that provided an ideological basis for the new world order.[22] For this branch of the academic intelligentsia, the laboratory may well have been the most potent of all the new symbols, for whereas the railroad or telegraph, impressive as they may have been, were finished products, the laboratory, where scientific activity took place, stood for the creative act itself. There the next generation gained familiarity with the techniques and analytical tools of the experimental sciences, while learning—at least in principle—to think critically and independently as well. Helmholtz and other German liberals viewed the latter as by far the most important of all educational goals, for only a well-educated population could ever hope to replace the landed gentry as the natural ally of the monarch and the backbone of the nation. The laboratory, then, came laden with symbolic meaning. The site both of scientific and technological innovations and of instruction in critical methods of analysis, it represented par excellence the place where higher education and modernity joined hands.

The government in Baden had proven particularly receptive to this image of the laboratory, pursuing a more coherent science policy in the 1850s than any other German land. Only Bavaria came close during this decade in its support for the natural sciences, spending over 100,000 gulden on a new institute for anatomy and physiology, and another 21,000 gulden on improving a chemistry laboratory, both at the University of Munich.[23] Prussia, on the other hand, consistently viewed by German historians as the pacesetter in educational reforms, sorely neglected its universities during this decade. We have already mentioned both the difficulties Helmholtz had at the University of Bonn, and the deplorable situation at the University of Berlin, where the professors of physics, physiology, and chemistry all sought in vain to convince the Prussian government to finance new institutes.[24] Repeatedly they were told that funds were unavailable; and indeed Prussia's military ventures absorbed a substantial portion of the state's budget, claiming funds that might well have gone to the construction of university-based scientific laboratories. But, as I have been arguing, the political climate in the 1850s worked against this marriage of university and state as well: the conservative minister, Karl Otto von Raumer, showed little inclination to support liberal-minded university professors in furthering their cause.

In the 1850s and early 1860s, Baden was clearly a trailblazer. Yet by the time Helmholtz gave his speech he had reason to believe that support for the natural sciences would soon spread. Throughout Germany the period of reaction had ended and a "New Era" had begun, fueling the hopes of liberals that their time had come.[25] As far as the natural sciences were concerned, their dreams were soon realized. In Saxony, for example, the liberal minister of education, Johann Paul Freiherr von Falkenstein, worked together with parliament to finance the construction of large teaching and research institutes at the University of Leipzig, the most famous being Ludwig's physiology laboratory. Bavaria, moreover, escalated its support, spending one million gulden alone on the Munich polytechnical institute. Even Prussia began slowly to heed the wishes of its professors. In the 1860s it constructed two substantial institutes, one in anatomy and the other in chemistry, at the University of Berlin.[26]

Nowhere, however, was the excitement among liberals greater than in Baden itself, where Grand Duke Friedrich had appointed a liberal ministry in 1860, thus turning the traditional party of opposition into the ruling party of the land.[27] The liberals had come to power by taking advantage of tensions between the Catholic Church and the state government. For a brief period in the 1850s they had actually defended representatives of the Church against state encroachment, thereby acquiring enough popular support to bring about the downfall of the conservative ministry. But the union between liberals and the Church ended almost immediately following the change of government; indeed, Baden was one of the first states to become embroiled in the *Kulturkampf* (literally, the "battle of civilizations"). This battle, traditionally conceived as a church-state conflict, was at a deeper level a struggle between competing social and cultural systems.[28] In the eyes of the liberals, the Catholic Church—and the rural population it came to represent—stood for everything against which they had been struggling for decades: a pre-industrial, agriculturally based social and economic order, dominated by clerical tutelage and marked by popular prejudice and superstition. Most of the measures adopted by Baden's new ministry in the 1860s aimed specifically at transforming this way of life and furthering the economic and political modernization of the state. Under the leadership of August Lamey (ministry of the interior), Anton Stabel (state ministry), and Franz Freiherr von Roggenbach (as of 1861, ministry of foreign affairs) the new government immediately created an independent ministry of trade, whose task was to enhance the state's "material interests";[29] it removed school affairs from the churches, centralizing all educational affairs under a single state-run supervisory board [*Oberschulrat*], answerable directly to the ministry of interior;[30] and it continued unabated its support for the sciences and medicine. Indeed, even before Friedrichsbau was completed, parliament approved 200,000 gulden for the purchase of a site for a new academic hospital; in every budget period thereafter (parliament met every two years) it approved the necessary funds without any debate. Only the war prevented the hospital from being completed before 1876, by which time total costs had increased to 1,130,500 gulden, or 1.9 million marks. The finished hospital was an expansive structure, with a total of 360 beds for internal medicine and surgery alone, laboratory facilities for carrying out chemical and microscopical investigations, an out-patient clinic, and a pathological institute. And this was only the beginning. Two years later (1878), two more clinics, one in ophthalmology and the other in psychiatry, were added to the hospital; and in 1884 a women's clinic with 120 beds was founded as well.[31] Baden continued, moreover, to continuously improve its institutes for scientific research. Between 1870 and 1900, for example, it spent exorbitant sums on new laboratories for physiology, botany, and zoology, as well as expanding the existing structures for chemistry and physics.[32]

By this time, of course, Baden was by no means alone. In the years following the founding of the German Empire in 1871, each and every university poured millions of marks into the construction of large-scale laboratories and modern academic hospitals, helping to turn the newly created nation into a leading industrial power. During this second phase of institute building, governments had proof of the economic advantages of scientific research, and support for the sciences no longer depended on the presence of a politically liberal atmosphere. What better evidence of this than Prussia's emergence as a leader in institute building in the final decades of the nineteenth century. Historians of German higher education have traditionally pointed to the unprecedented expansion of scientific and medical institutes in Prussia during the period when Friedrich Althoff headed the Higher Education Section of the Prussian Culture Ministry (1882–1907)—and rightfully so. Althoff alone was responsible for the creation at the nine Prussian universities of eighty-six institutes, laboratories, and clinics in the medical sciences, and seventy-seven institutes and seminars in the philosophical faculties, where the natural sciences had their home.[33] Some of these institutes were, moreover, nothing short of spectacular. Helmholtz's new physics institute, for example, completed in 1878, cost over 1.5 million marks—more than the combined costs of physics institutes at eleven other universities![34]

Nevertheless, the tendency to focus on Prussia to the near exclusion of other German states has led to several distortions. It has, first and foremost, contributed to an almost complete neglect of the connection between support for the natural sciences and political liberalism in the period prior to the unification of Germany. As we have seen, the older historiographic tradition emphasized continuity between the Humboldtian-inspired philological seminars and the research laboratories built during mid-century, denying any link between the construction of science institutes and the more immediate economic and social needs of the state. More recent revisionist work has challenged this picture of continuity, emphasizing instead the radical differences between the late nineteenth-century laboratories and the early anatomical museums and scientific cabinets, yet the political context, at least for the pre-1871 period, is still absent. David Cahan, for example, in his study of German physics institutes, argues that an "institutional revolution" swept through Germany between 1870 and 1920.[35] Cahan's claim is based on an analysis of all the major German states, not just Prussia. Nevertheless, I wish to suggest that the term "revolution" may turn out to be most appropriate for the Prussian case, where something close to a major change in science policy seems to have occurred. Indeed, of those German states with major universities, Prussia participated most reluctantly in the first wave of institute building in the 1850s and 1860s, making all the more spectacular its heavy investments in the 1870s, and even more so during the Althoff ministry. But Prussia was not Germany; indeed, it is debatable whether anything as simple as a single German path existed.[36] Certainly the relationship between science education and political and social reform followed a different course in Baden than in Prussia; and it was one marked by greater harmony and continuity than radical breaks.

Events as they unfolded in Baden thus suggest an alternative model to those currently in use for interpreting the relationship between science, the universities, and the state. It is not, of course, unusual for historians of

German science to argue for continuity, but I am not subscribing here to the image of the research laboratories as natural outgrowths of the philological seminars, removed from the social and economic needs of the state until late in the century. Germany's rapid emergence as a world leader in science and technology did not occur because industrialists were fortunate enough to have at their disposal science institutes that had been created for an entirely different purpose. On the contrary, this model proposes that the research and teaching laboratories had their origin in the 1830s, when government administrators, parliamentarians, and professors alike began voicing an interest in involving students more actively in the educational process. By the 1840s university curricula had changed to accommodate these concerns, offering an increased number of courses dedicated to practical exercises in scientific and medical techniques; and by the 1850s and 1860s laboratories able to accommodate such instruction were appearing in several German states, particularly those where liberal ministers showed a willingness to work together with parliament and the universities to encourage the material interests of the state. What this model suggests is that the science laboratories, and indeed the universities themselves, were always integral parts of society, constantly adapting to the very same forces that ultimately transformed Germany into a modern industrial power.

Notes

1. See "Vergleichung der Budgets-Sätze mit den Rechnungs-Resultaten für die Etats-Jahre 1850–71," in *Verhandlungen,* usually but not always in Beilagenheft 2. Also Horst Werner Kupka, *Die Ausgaben der süddeutschen Länder für die medizinischen und naturwissenschaftlichen Hochschul-Einrichtungen, 1848–1914* (Diss. Bonn, 1970), pp. 136–139.

2. See Peter Borscheid, *Naturwissenschaft, Staat und Industrie in Baden (1848–1914)* (Stuttgart, 1976), pp. 50–71.

3. Budget Commissionsbericht in *Verhandlungen,* 2. Kammer, 1859/60, Beilagenheft 5, pp. 409–411. See also the "Vergleichung der Budgets-Sätze mit den Rechnungs-Resultaten für die Etats-Jahre 1858–63," in *Verhandlungen,* usually but not always in Beilagenheft 2.

4. See Chapter 4.

5. Building and economics commission to the ministry of interior, 25 February 1859, BGLA 235/352.

6. Ibid. The following description of the various laboratories is from this source.

7. Ministry of interior to the building and economics commission, 16 July 1859; building and economics commission to the ministry of interior, 26 August 1859; ministry of interior to the faculty senate, 2 September 1859; faculty senate and building and economics commission to the ministry of interior, 19 October 1859; ministry of interior to the state ministry, 1 December 1859; all in ibid.

8. Von Stengel to the ministry of interior, 9 December 1859, ibid. See also the budget commission's report in *Verhandlungen,* 2. Kammer, 1859/60, Beila-

genheft 4, pp. 277–278, and Beilagenheft 5, pp. 406–408. The budget is printed in "Vergleichung der Budgets-Sätze mit den Rechnungs-Resultaten für die Etats-Jahre 1860–63," in *Verhandlungen,* 1860–63, usually but not always in Beilagenheft 2.

9. Hans-Heinz Eulner, for example, cites 1874 as the date of the construction of a laboratory for experimental physiology at the University of Heidelberg. See his *Die Entwicklung der medizinischen Spezialfächer an den Universitäten des deutschen Sprachgebiets* (Stuttgart, 1970), p. 508.

10. Alfred Girlich, *Die Grundlagen der Innenpolitik Badens unter Großherzog Friedrich I. Entwicklung und Verwirklichung der Idee einer Volkserziehung* (Diss. Heidelberg), 1952. See also Hermann Oncken, ed. *Großherzog Friedrich I. von Baden und die deutsche Politik von 1854–1871. Briefwechsel, Denkschriften, Tagebücher,* 2 vols. (Stuttgart, 1927), vol. 1, p. 46; and Karl Stiefel, *Baden, 1648–1952,* 2 vols. (Karlsruhe, 1977), vol. 1, pp. 290–298.

11. Großh. Geheimes Cabinet to the ministry of interior, 29 March 1863, BGLA 235/352.

12. See Karl Heinz Manegold, *Universität, Technische Hochschule und Industrie* (Berlin, 1970).

13. Hermann von Helmholtz, "Ueber das Verhältnis der Naturwissenschaften zur Gesamtheit der Wissenschaft," Akademische Festrede gehalten zu Heidelberg am 22 November 1862 bei Antritt des Prorectorats. In Helmholtz, *Vorträge und Reden,* 5th ed., 2 vols. (Braunschweig, 1903), vol. 1, pp. 157–185, here p. 169.

14. Ibid., pp. 172–179.

15. Ibid., p. 179.

16. Ibid., pp. 179–180.

17. Ibid., p. 177.

18. Ibid., pp. 181–182.

19. Ibid., p. 183.

20. See Chapter 5 of this book.

21. Fritz Ringer, *The Decline of the German Mandarins. The German Academic Community, 1890–1933* (Cambridge, 1969).

22. See Timothy Lenoir, "Social Interests and the Organic Physics of 1847," in E. Ullmann-Margalit, ed., *Science in Reflection* (Dordrecht, 1988), pp. 169–181. This picture of German academics as actively involved in redefining the social and economic structure of the state fully supports the work of David Blackbourn, in which he, too, challenges the image of the "overly abstract, academic and unworldly German liberal, at home in a comfortable pre-industrial world and anxious about 'modernity'." See, especially, Blackbourn's article, "Progress and Piety: Liberals, Catholics, and the State in Bismarck's Germany," in his *Populists and Patricians: Essays in Modern German History* (London and Boston, 1987), pp. 143–167. The quotation is from p. 151.

23. See Kupka, *Die Ausgaben der süddeutschen Länder,* pp. 156–57.

24. See Chapters 5 and 7 of this book.

25. James J. Sheehan, *German Liberalism in the Nineteenth Century* (Chicago, 1978), p. 95.

26. On Saxony, see Timothy Lenoir, "Science for the Clinic: Science Policy and the Formation of Carl Ludwig's Institute in Leipzig," in William Coleman and Frederic L. Holmes, eds., *The Investigative Enterprise. Experimental Physiology in Nineteenth-Century Medicine* (Berkeley, 1988), pp. 139–178. On Bavaria, see

Kupka, *Die Ausgaben der süddeutschen Länder,* p. 157. On Berlin, see Max Lenz, *Geschichte der königlichen Friedrich-Wilhelms-Universität zu Berlin,* 4 vols. in 5 (Halle, 1910–1918), vol. 3, pp. 129–141, 296–306.

27. Lothar Gall, *Der Liberalismus als regierende Partei* (Wiesbaden, 1968).

28. Lothar Gall, "Die partei- und sozialgeschichtliche Problematik des badischen Kulturkampfes," *Zeitschrift für die Geschichte des Oberrheins,* 113 (1985): 151–196; Blackbourn, "Progress and Piety;" and Helmut Walser Smith, *Nationalism and Religious Conflict in Germany, 1887–1914* (Ph.D. diss., Yale, 1991), esp. pp. 90–94.

29. Cited in ibid., p. 176.

30. Ibid., pp. 192–198. Before this centralization occurred, a multitude of school boards existed; elementary schools, middle schools (*Gymnasia* and non-classical secondary schools), and universities each had their own supervisory committees. Moreover, at the level of the elementary schools, Catholic, Protestant, and Jewish groups each had responsibility for their own schools. In 1862, the government strengthened its control over educational affairs by replacing all these groups with a single state-run supervisory board. Protests came almost immediately from the various churches, which fought to maintain their influence over elementary school education, but at the level of the universities, little opposition was heard.

31. On the plans to construct a new academic hospital, see BGLA 235/676, 235/677, 235/681, 235/696, and 235/697. See also Otto Weber, *Das akademische Krankenhaus in Heidelberg, seine Mängel und die Bedürfnisse eines Neubaus* (Heidelberg, 1865).

32. Reinhard Riese, *Die Hochschule auf dem Wege zum wissenschaftlichen Großbetrieb* (Stuttgart, 1977), p. 366.

33. Charles E. McClelland, *State, Society and University in Germany, 1700–1914* (Cambridge, 1980), p. 281.

34. David Cahan, "The institutional revolution in German physics, 1865–1914," in *Historical Studies in the Physical Sciences,* 15, 2 (1985): 1–65, here p. 22.

35. Ibid. See also Timothy Lenoir, "Science for the Clinic."

36. See David Blackbourn, Geoff Eley, *The Peculiarities of German History. Bourgeois Society and Politics in Nineteenth-Century Germany* (Oxford, 1984); Richard Evans, *Rethinking German History. Nineteenth-Century Germany and the Origins of the Third Reich* (London, 1987).

Bibliography

Archival Material

Badisches Generallandesarchiv Karlsruhe

File Number:	Title:
76/8137:	Personalakte Robert Volz
205/255:	Personalakte Professor Leopold Gmelin
205/524:	Personalakte Professor Friedrich Tiedemann
233/31847:	Die Prüfung der Aerzte, Wundärzte, Zahnärzte und Apotheker
235/352:	Der Neubau für die naturwissenschaftlichen Institute der Universität Heidelberg—"Friedrichsbau"
235/354:	Die Lokalitäten für die naturwissenschaftlichen Institute, nebst Wohnung für die Professoren der Physik und Chemie
235/559:	Das anatomische und physiologische Institut, respective Sammlung, 1807–65
235/571:	Betr. den Neubau des Anatomie- und Zoologiegebäudes, 1847
235/576:	Das anatomische Institut
235/604:	Das physiologische Institut
235/607:	Die II. Klinik des Hofrats Pfeufer
235/676:	Das academische Krankenhaus, hier dessen Gebäude, 1835–38, 1841–47
235/3113:	Die Lehrkanzel der Chemie, so wie die Stelle eines Directors des chemischen Laboratoriums, 1836–1923
235/3133:	Die Lehrstellen bei der medicinischen Facultät und deren Besetzung
235/3141:	Die Lehrstellen der medicinischen Facultät. Der Lehrstuhl für Pathologie, Therapie und die Direktion der medicinischen Klinik
235/4131:	Der Entwurf einer neuen Medicinalordnung, 1839–43
235/27692:	Die Sanitäts-Commission in objectiver Hinsicht
235/29867:	Die Lehrstellen der medicinischen Facultät. Der Lehrstuhl für pathologische Anatomie
235/29872:	Die Lehrstellen der medicinischen Facultät. Der Lehrstuhl für Physiologie
236/15027:	Die Constituirung der Sanitäts-Commission für das Großherzogthum Baden

Universität Heidelberg, Handschriftenabteilung [Manuscript Division]
Correspondences
    Robert Bunsen
    Philipp Jolly

Universitätsarchiv Heidelberg
Acten der medizinischen Fakultät zu Heidelberg

Universitätsarchiv Göttingen
Personalakte Professor Jakob Henle

Staatsbibliothek Preußischer Kulturbesitz, Handschriftenabteilung
Darmstaedter Collection

Geheimes Staatsarchiv Preußischer Kulturbesitz Merseburg
Ministerium der Geistlichen-, Unterrichts- und Medicinal Angelegenheiten

Printed Sources

Primary Sources

Allgemeine deutsche Biographie, 56 vols. Leipzig, 1875–1912.
Annalen der Staatsarzneikunde
Anon., "Unsere Aufgabe im neuen Jahr," in *Mittheilungen,* 1 January 1845 (Nr.1), pp. 1–8.
Anon., "Revolution," *Mittheilungen,* 14 July 1849 (Nr.13), pp. 93–95.
Anon., "Ein Wort über die Betheiligung der Aerzte an der Revolution," *Mittheilungen,* 24 November 1849 (Nr.20), pp. 149–156.
Anon., "Wie sollen die Aerzte gebildet werden?" in *Mittheilungen,* 12 May 1852 (Nr.9), pp. 65–69.
Anzeige der Vorlesungen auf der Großherzoglich Badischen Ruprecht Karolinischen Universität zu Heidelberg
Arnold, Friedrich. *Die physiologische Anstalt der Universität Heidelberg von 1853 bis 1858.* Heidelberg, 1858.
Bidder, Friedrich. (Report on his visit to the University of Berlin in 1834), reprinted in "Vor hundert Jahren im Laboratorium Johannes Müllers," *Münchener Medizinische Wochenschrift,* 82 (1934): 60–64.
Billroth, Theodor. *Ueber das Lehren und Lernen der medicinischen Wissenschaften an den Universitäten der Deutschen Nation, nebst allegemeinen Bemerkungen über Universitäten.* Vienna, 1876.
Bischoff, Theodor. *Gedächtnißrede auf Friedrich Tiedemann. Vorgetragen in der öffentlichen Sitzung der königlichen Akademie der Wissenschaften am 28. November 1861.* Munich, 1861.
Brockhaus, F. A. *Conversations-Lexikon der Gegenwart,* 4 vols. Leipzig, 1838–41.
    [The *Conversations-Lexikon der Gegenwart* is a supplement to the eighth edition

of the larger Brockhaus *Conversations-Lexikon,* 12 vols. Leipzig, 1833–39.]

Diez, C. A. *Zusammenstellung der gegenwärtig geltenden Gesetze, Verordnungen, Instructionen und Entscheidungen über das Medicinalwesen und die Stellung und die Verrichtungen der Medicinalbeamten und Sanitätsdiener im Großherzogthum Baden.* Karlsruhe, 1859.

Ehlers, E. "Carl Theodor Ernst von Siebold. Eine biographische Skizze," *Zeitschrift für wissenschaftliche Zoologie,* 42 (1885): i–xxxiv.

"Einrichtung einer landwirthschaftlichen Schule zu Karlsruhe," *Karlsruher Zeitung,* 17 September 1851.

"Erfahrung," in *Staatslexikon oder Encyclopädie der Staatswissenschaften,* ed. Carl von Rotteck, Carl Welcker, 15 vols. Altona, 1834–1843, vol. 5 (1837), pp. 253–263.

Gräfe, Albrecht von. "Vorwort," *Archiv für Ophthalmologie,* 1 (1854): v–x.

Greeff, Richard. "II. Historisches zur Erfindung des Augenspiegels," *Berliner klinische Wochenschrift,* 38,48 (2 December 1901): 1201–02.

Grimm, "Commissionsbericht über die Mittelschulen," *Verhandlungen,* 2. Kammer, 67. Sitzung, 26 September 1833, Beilagenheft 5, pp. 303–343.

Großherzogliche badische Sanitäts-Commission, *Entwurf einer neuen Medicinalordnung für das Großherzogthum Baden.* Karlsruhe, 1840.

Großherzoglich Badisches Staats- und Regierungsblatt

Guttstadt, Albert. *Die naturwissenschaftlichen und medicinischen Staatsanstalten Berlins. Festschrift für die 59. Versammlung deutscher Naturforscher und Aerzte.* Berlin, 1886.

Helmholtz, Hermann von. *De Fabrica Systematis nervosi Evertebratorum.* Med. diss., Berlin, 1842.

———. "Ueber den Stoffverbrauch bei der Muskelaktion," *Archiv für Anatomie, Physiologie und wissenschaftliche Medicin,* 1845: 72–83.

———. *Ueber die Erhaltung der Kraft.* Berlin, 1847.

———. "Ueber die Wärmeentwicklung bei der Muskelaction," *Archiv für Anatomie, Physiologie und wissenschaftliche Medicin,* 1848: 144–164.

———. *Beschreibung eines Augen-Spiegels zur Untersuchung der Netzhaut im lebenden Auge.* Berlin, 1851.

———. "Ueber eine neue einfache Form des Augenspiegels," *Vierordt's Archiv für physiologische Heilkunde,* 11 (1852): 827–852.

———. "Ueber die Accommodation des Auges," *Graefe's Archiv für Ophthalmologie,"* 2 (1856): 1–74.

———. "Ueber das Verhältnis der Naturwissenschaften zur Gesamtheit der Wissenschaft," Akademische Festrede gehalten zu Heidelberg am 22 November 1862 bei Antritt des Prorectorats. In his *Vorträge und Reden,* 5th ed., 2 vols. Braunschweig, 1903, vol. 1, pp. 157–185.

———. "Das Denken in der Medizin" (1877), in his *Vorträge und Reden,* 5th ed., 2 vols. Braunschweig, 1903, vol. II, pp. 167–190.

———. "Erinnerungen (1891)," in his *Vorträge und Reden,* 5th ed., 2 vols. Braunschweig, 1903, vol. 1, pp. 1–21.

———. *Vorträge und Reden,* 5th ed., 2 vols. Braunschweig, 1903.

Henle, Jacob. "Ueber Schleim- und Eiterbildung und ihr Verhältnis zur Oberhaut," *Journal der practischen Arzneykunde und Wundarzneykunst (Hufelands Journal),* 86,8 (1838): 3–62.

———. *Pathologische Untersuchungen.* Berlin, 1840.

———. *Allegemeine Anatomie.* Leipzig, 1841.

————. "Medizinische Wissenschaft und Empirie," *Zeitschrift für rationelle Medizin*, 1 (1844): 1–35.

————. *Handbuch der rationellen Pathologie*, 2 vols. Braunschweig, 1846–53.

————. "Theodor Schwann. Nachruf," *Archiv für mikroscopische Anatomie*, 21 (1882): i–xlix.

Hertwig, Richard. *Gedächtnißrede auf Carl Theodor von Siebold gehalten in der öffentlichen Sitzung der königlichen Akademie der Wissenschaften zu München am 29 März 1886*. Munich, 1886.

Heymann, F. "Die Augenspiegel, ihre Construktion und Verwendung," *Schmidt's Jahrbücher der In- und Ausländer gesammten Medicin*, 89 (1856): 105–122.

Hufeland, C. W. "Nachrichten von der Medizinisch-Chirurgischen Krankenanstalt zu Jena, nebst einer Vergleichung der klinischen und Hospitalanstalten überhaupt," *Journal der practischen Arzneykunde und Wundarzneykunst*, 3,1 (1797): 528–566.

"Ideen, politisch, und Ideologie; ideele und materielle Interessen," in *Staatslexikon oder Encyclopädie der Staatswissenschaften*, ed. Carl von Rotteck, Carl Welcker, 15 vols. Altona, 1834–43, vol. 8 (1839), pp. 283–295.

Kerschensteiner, Josef. *Das Leben und Wirken des Dr. Carl von Pfeufer*. Augsburg, 1871.

Kölliker, Albert von. *Erinnerungen aus meinem Leben*. Leipzig, 1899.

Kröll, "Commissionsbericht über die Errichtung von höhern Bürger- und Gewerbeschulen," *Verhandlungen*, 2. Kammer, 66. Sitzung, 24 September 1833, Beilagenheft 5, pp. 235–251.

Kurfürstliche Badische General-Sanitäts-Commission, *Badische Medicinal-Ordnung*. Karlsruhe, 1807.

Kussmaul, Adolf. *Memoirs of an Old Physician*, transl. by the Journal Program for Scientific Translation. India, 1981.

"Materielle Interessen," in F. A. Brockhaus, *Conversations-Lexikon der Gegenwart*, (Leipzig, 1838–41), 3 (1840): 557–564.

"Die materiellen Interessen," *Karlsruher Zeitung*, 25 August 1852.

Medicinische Centralzeitung

Mittheilungen des badischen ärztlichen Vereins

Nebenius, C. F. *Ueber technische Lehranstalten in ihrem Zusammenhange mit dem gesammten Unterrichtswesen und mit besonderer Rücksicht auf die polytechnische Schule zu Karlsruhe*. Karlsruhe, 1833.

"Die neuesten Verordnungen über das Volksschulwesen," *Karlsruher Zeitung*, 6 November 1851.

Oncken, Hermann, ed. *Großherzog Friedrich I. von Baden und die deutsche Politik von 1854-1871. Briefwechsel, Denkschriften, Tagebücher*. Stuttgart, 1927.

Otto, A. W. *Einige geschichtliche Erinnerungen an das frühere Studium der Anatomie in Schlesien, nebst einer Beschreibung und Abbildung des jetzigen königlichen Anatomie-Instituts*. Breslau, 1823.

Pfeufer, Carl. "Ueber den gegenwärtigen Zustand der Medizin. Rede gehalten bei dem Antritt des klinischen Lehramts in Zürich den 7 November 1840," reprinted in *Annalen der städtischen allgemeinen Krankenhäuser in München*, 1 (1878): 395–406.

Regenauer, "Commissionsbericht über die Adresse der ersten Kammer, die Revision der Mittelschulen betreffend," in *Verhandlungen*, 2. Kammer, 65. Sitzung, 25 July 1831, Beilagenheft 6, pp. 77–106.

Rotteck, Carl von; Carl Welcker, eds. *Staatslexikon oder Encyclopädie der Staatswissenschaften,* 15 vols. Altona, 1834–43.

Dr. Schickert, *Die militärärztlichen Bildungsanstalten von ihrer Gründung bis zur Gegenwart.* Berlin, 1895.

Schmetzer, C. "Erinnerungen an die letzte Prüfung im Lyceum zu Heidelberg," *Heidelberger Journal,* 15 and 16 October 1843.

Tiedemann, Friedrich. *Zoologie.* Landshut, 1808, 1810, 1814.

———. *Anatomie der kopflosen Mißgeburten.* Landshut, 1813.

———. *Anatomie und Bildungs-Geschichte des Gehirns im Foetus des Menschen, nebst einer vergleichenden Darstellung des Hirnbaues in den Thieren.* Nuremberg, 1816.

———. (Opening speech held at the meeting of the Deutschen Naturforscher und Ärzte in 1829), in *Amtlicher Bericht über die Versammlung der Deutschen Naturforscher und Ärzte in Heidelberg,* September 1829.

———. *Physiologie,* 3 vols. Darmstadt, 1830–36.

Tiedemann, Friedrich; Leopold Gmelin. *Versuch über die Wege, auf welchen Substanzen aus dem Magen und Darmkanal in's Blut gelangen, über die Verrichtung der Milz und die geheimen Harnwege.* Heidelberg, 1820.

———. *Die Verdauung nach Versuchen,* 2 vols. Heidelberg, 1826.

Verhandlungen der Stände-Versammlung des Großherzogthums Baden

Virchow, Rudolf. "Ein alter Bericht über die Gestaltung der pathologischen Anatomie in Deutschland, wie sie ist und wie sie werden muss," *Archiv für pathologische Anatomie und Physiologie und klinische Medizin,* 159 (1900): 31.

"Die Volksschule in Hinsicht auf die Landwirthschaft," *Karlsruher Zeitung,* 19 February 1852.

Waldeyer, W. "J. Henle. Nachruf," *Archiv für mikroscopische Anatomie,* 26 (1886): i–xxxii.

Weber, Otto. *Das akademische Krankenhaus in Heidelberg, seine Mängel und die Bedürfnisse eines Neubaus.* Heidelberg, 1865.

Weech, Friedrich von, ed. *Badische Biographieen,* 6 vols. Heidelberg, 1875–1935.

———. *Baden in den Jahren 1852 bis 1877.* Karlsruhe, 1877.

———. *Badische Geschichte.* Karlsruhe, 1890.

Wunderlich, Carl. "Einleitung," *Archiv für physiologische Heilkunde,* 1 (1842): xvi.

Wundt, Wilhelm. *Erlebtes und Erkanntes.* Stuttgart, 1920.

Zeitschrift für rationelle Medizin

Ziemssen, H. von. "Feuilleton. Karl Ewald Hasse," *Münchener medicinische Wochenschrift,* 44,1 (1897): 282–283.

Secondary Sources

Ackerknecht, Erwin H. "Beiträge zur Geschichte der Medizinalreform von 1848," *Sudhoffs Archiv,* 25 (1932): 61–109, 113–183.

———. *Rudolf Virchow. Arzt, Politiker, Anthropologe.* Stuttgart, 1957.

———. *Therapeutics. From the Primitives to the Twentieth Century.* New York, 1973.

Andreas, Willy. "Sigismund von Reitzenstein und der Neuaufbau der Universität Heidelberg," *Ruperto-Carola,* 9/10 (1955): 29–32.

Angermann, Erich. "Karl Mathy als Sozial- und Wirtschaftspolitiker (1842–48)," *Zeitschrift für die Geschichte des Oberrheins,* 103 (1955): 499–622.

Artelt, Walter. "Jacob Henle," in Hugo Freund and Alexander Berg, eds., *Geschichte der Mikroskope. Lehren und Werk grosser Forscher*, 3 vols. Frankfurt a. M., 1963–66, vol. 2 (1964): Medizin, pp. 147–159.

Ben-David, Joseph. "Scientific Productivity and Academic Organization in Nineteenth Century Medicine," *American Sociological Review*, 25,2 (1960): 828–843.

———. "Review Article. Scientific Growth: A Sociological View," *Minerva*, 2,4 (1964): 455–476.

———. *The Scientist's Role in Society: A Comparative Study*, with a new introduction. Chicago, 1984.

Blackbourn, David, "Progress and Piety: Liberals, Catholics and the State in Bismarck's Germany," in his *Populists and Patricians: Essays in Modern German History*. London and Boston, 1987, pp. 143–167.

Blackbourn, David; Geoff Eley. *The Peculiarities of German History. Bourgeois Society and Politics in Nineteenth-Century Germany*. Oxford and New York, 1984.

Bleker, Johanna. *Die Naturhistorische Schule, 1825–1845. Ein Beitrag zur Geschichte der klinischen Medizin in Deutschland*. Stuttgart, 1981.

Borscheid, Peter. *Naturwissenschaft, Staat und Industrie in Baden, 1848–1914*. Stuttgart, 1976.

Bradbury, S. *The Evolution of the Microscope*. Oxford and New York, 1967.

Bringmann, Wolfgang G.; Gottfried Bringmann; David Cottrall. "Helmholtz und Wundt an der Heidelberger Universität 1858–1871," *Heidelberger Jahrbücher*, 20 (1976): 79–88.

Broman, Thomas Hoyt. "University Reform in Medical Thought at the End of the Eighteenth Century," in *Osiris*, 2nd series, 5 (1989): 36–53.

Cahan, David. "The institutional revolution in German physics, 1865–1914," in *Historical Studies in the Physical Sciences*, 15,2 (1985): 1–65.

———, ed. *Letters of Hermann von Helmholtz to his Parents 1837–1855*. Stuttgart, forthcoming, 1993.

Coleman, William. *Georges Cuvier, Zoologist. A Study in the History of Evolutionary Thought*. Cambridge, 1964.

———. *Biology in the Nineteenth Century: Problems of Form, Function, and Transformation*. Cambridge, 1977.

———. "Experimental Physiology and Statistical Inference: The Therapeutic Trial in Nineteenth-Century Germany," in Lorenz Krüger, et al., eds. *The Probabilistic Revolution*, 2 vols. Cambridge, Mass., 1987, vol. 2, pp. 201–26.

———. "Prussian Pedagogy: Purkyne at Breslau, 1823–1839," in William Coleman and Frederic L. Holmes, eds., *The Investigative Enterprise. Experimental Physiology in Nineteenth-Century Medicine*. Berkeley, 1988, pp. 15–64.

Cranefield, Paul F. "The Organic Physics of 1847 and the Biophysics of Today," *Journal of the History of Medicine*, 12 (1957): 407–423.

Diepgen, Paul. *Geschichte der Medizin*, 3 vols. in 2. Berlin, 1951.

Eulenberg, Franz. *Die Frequenz der deutschen Universitäten von ihrer Gründung bis zur Gegenwart*. Leipzig, 1904.

Eulner, Hans-Heinz. *Die Entwicklung der medizinischen Spezialfächer an den Universitäten des deutschen Sprachgebiets*. Stuttgart, 1970.

Eulner, Hans-Heinz; Hermann Hoepke, eds. *Der Briefwechsel zwischen Rudolph Wagner und Jacob Henle, 1838–1862*. Göttingen, 1979.

Evans, Richard. *Rethinking German History. Nineteenth-Century Germany and the Origins of the Third Reich*. London, 1987.

————. *Death in Hamburg: Society and Politics in the Cholera Years, 1830–1910.* Oxford and New York, 1987.

Fischer, Alfons. *Geschichte des deutschen Gesundheitswesens,* 2 vols. Berlin, 1933.

Fischer, K. "Die Utrechter Mikroskope," *Zeitschrift für Instrumentenkunde,* 55 (1935): 239–300.

Fischer, Wolfram. *Der Staat und die Anfänge der Industrialisierung in Baden 1800–1850. Vol.1: Die staatliche Gewerbepolitik.* Berlin, 1962. (Other volumes were never written.)

————. "Staat und Gesellschaft Badens im Vormärz," in Werner Conze, ed. *Staat und Gesellschaft im deutschen Vormärz, 1818–1848.* Stuttgart, 1962, pp. 143–172.

————. "Wissenschaft, Technik und wirtschaftliche Entwicklung in Deutschland seit dem 18. Jahrhundert," *Berliner wissenschaftliche Gesellschaft e.v. Jahrbuch,* 1 (1977/1978): 107–128.

Foucault, Michel. *The Birth of the Clinic.* New York, 1975.

Freidson, Eliot. *Professional Powers: A Study of the Institutionalization of Formal Knowledge.* Chicago, 1986.

Gall, Lothar. *Der Liberalismus als regierende Partei. Das Grossherzogtum Baden zwischen Restauration und Reichsgründung.* Wiesbaden, 1968.

————. "Gründung und politische Entwicklung des Großherzogtums bis 1848," in Landeszentrale für politische Bildung Baden-Württemberg, ed. *Badische Geschichte. Vom Großherzogtum bis zur Gegenwart.* Stuttgart, 1979, pp. 11–36.

————. "Liberalismus und 'bürgerliche Gesellschaft'—zu Charakter und Entwicklung der liberalen Bewegung in Deutschland," *Historische Zeitschrift,* 220 (1975): 324–356.

Gorin, George. *History of Ophthalmology.* Delaware, 1982.

Gozzi, Guido. *Jakob Henles Zürcher Jahre, 1840–1844* (Zürcher medizingeschichtliche Abhandlungen, Neue Reihe Nr. 103). Zurich, 1974.

Gregory, Frederick. "Kant, Schelling, and the Administration of Science in the Romantic Era," in *Osiris,* 2nd series, 5 (1989): 17–35.

Hall, Thomas S. *History of General Physiology,* 2 vols. Chicago, 1969.

Hamerow, Theodore S. *Restoration, Revolution, Reaction. Economics and Politics in Germany, 1815–1871.* Princeton, 1958.

Henning, F.-W. *Die Industrialisierung in Deutschland, 1800–1914.* Paderborn, 1973.

Hintzsche, E. "Das Mikroskop," *Ciba Zeitschrift,* 115 (1949): 4238–4268.

Hoepke, Hermann. "Der Streit der Professoren Tiedemann und Henle um den Neubau des anatomischen Institutes in Heidelberg (1844–1849)," *Heidelberger Jahrbücher,* 5 (1961): 114–127.

————. "Jakob Henles Briefe aus Berlin 1834–1840," *Heidelberger Jahrbücher,* 8 (1964): 57–86.

————. "Jakob Henles Briefe aus seiner Heidelberger Studentenzeit (26 April 1830–Januar 1831)," *Heidelberger Jahrbücher,* 11 (1967): 40–56.

————. "Jakob Henles Gutachten zur Besetzung des Lehrstuhls für Anatomie an der Universität Berlin 1883," *Anatomischer Anzeiger,* 120,8 (1967): 221–232.

————. "Der Bonner Student Jakob Henle in seinem Verhältnis zu Johannes Müller," *Sudhoffs Archiv,* 53 (1969): 193–261.

————. *Der Briefwechsel zwischen Jakob Henle und Karl Pfeufer, 1843–1869* (Sudhoffs Archiv. Beihefte 11.) Wiesbaden, 1970.

———. "Zur Geschichte der Anatomie in Heidelberg," *Sonderdruck aus Ruperto Carola*, 67/68 (1982): 115–122.

Holmes, Frederic L. *Claude Bernard and Animal Chemistry*. Cambridge, 1974.

———. "The Formation of the Munich School of Metabolism," in William Coleman and Frederic L. Holmes, eds., *The Investigative Enterprise. Experimental Physiology in Nineteenth-Century Medicine*. Berkeley, 1988, pp. 179–210.

Holzl, Josef; et al. "Simon Plössl—Optiker und Mechaniker in Wien," *Blätter für Technikgeschichte (Wien)*, 31 (1969): 82.

Huerkamp, Claudia. "Ärzte und Professionalisierung in Deutschland. Überlegungen zum Wandel des Arztberufs im 19. Jahrhundert, *Geschichte und Gesellschaft*, 6 (1980): 349–382.

———. *Der Aufstieg der Ärzte im 19. Jahrhundert*. Göttingen, 1985.

Jarausch, Konrad H. "Higher Education and Social Change," in Jarausch, ed., *The Transformation of Higher Learning, 1860–1930*. Stuttgart, 1982, pp. 9–36.

Kaiser, Wolfram; Reinhard Mocek. *Johann Christian Reil* (Biographien hervorragender Naturwissenschaftler, Techniker und Mediziner, Band 41) Leipzig, 1979.

Keller, Gottfried. *Das Leben des Biologen Johannes Müller, 1801–1858* (Grosse Naturforscher, Bd. 23) Stuttgart, 1958.

Keller, Richard August. *Geschichte der Universität Heidelberg im ersten Jahrzehnt nach der Reorganisation durch Karl Friedrich (1803–1813)*. Heidelberg, 1913.

Kirsten, Christa, et al., eds. *Dokumente einer Freundschaft. Briefwechsel zwischen Hermann von Helmholtz und Emil du Bois-Reymond 1846–1894*. Berlin, 1986.

Koenigsberger, Leo. *Hermann von Helmholtz*, 2 vols. Braunschweig, 1902.

Langewiesche, Dieter. *Liberalismus in Deutschland*. Frankfurt am Main, 1988.

———, ed. *Liberalismus im 19. Jahrhundert: Deutschland in europäischen Vergleich: dreissig Beiträge*. Göttingen, 1988.

Larson, Magali Sarfatti. *The Rise of Professionalism. A Sociological Analysis*. Berkeley, 1977.

Lee, Loyd E. *The Politics of Harmony. Civil Service, Liberalism, and Social Reform in Baden, 1800–1850*. Newark, 1980.

Lenoir, Timothy. "Kant, Blumenbach, and Vital Materialism in German Biology," *Isis*, 7 (1980): 77–108.

———. *The Strategy of Life. Teleology and Mechanics in Nineteenth-Century German Biology* (Studies in the History of Modern Science, 13). Dordrecht, 1982.

———. "Social Interests and the Organic Physics of 1847," in E. Ullmann-Margalit, ed., *Science in Reflection*. Dordrecht, 1988, pp. 169–181.

———. "Science for the Clinic: Science Policy and the Formation of Carl Ludwig's Institute in Leipzig," in William Coleman and Frederic L. Holmes, eds., *The Investigative Enterprise. Experimental Physiology in Nineteenth-Century Medicine*. Berkeley, 1988, pp. 139–178.

———. "Morphotypes and the Historical-genetic Method in Romantic Biology," in Andrew Cunningham and Nicholas Jardine, eds., *Romanticism and the Sciences*. Cambridge, 1990, pp. 119–129.

Lenz, Max. *Geschichte der königlichen Friedrich-Wilhelms-Universität zu Berlin*, 4 vols. in 5. Halle, 1910–18.

Lesch, John. *Science and Medicine in France. The Emergence of Experimental Physiology, 1790–1855*. Cambridge, Mass., 1984.

Lockemann, Georg. *The Story of Chemistry*. New York, 1959.

Lundgreen, Peter. *Bildung und Wirtschaftswachstum im Industrialisierungsprozess des 19. Jahrhunderts.* Berlin, 1973.
———. *Sozialgeschichte der deutschen Schule im Überblick, Teil I: 1770–1918.* Göttingen, 1980.
Manegold, Karl Heinz. *Universität, Technische Hochschule und Industrie.* Berlin, 1970.
McClelland, Charles E. *State, Society and University in Germany, 1700–1914.* Cambridge, 1980.
———. *The German Experience of Professionalization. Modern Learned Professions and their Organizations from the Early Nineteenth Century to the Hitler Era.* Cambridge, 1991.
Merkel, Friedrich. *Jacob Henle. Ein deutsches Gelehrtenleben.* Braunschweig, 1891.
Merkel, Gerhard. *Wirtschaftsgeschichte der Universität Heidelberg im 18. Jahrhundert.* Stuttgart, 1973.
Nipperdey, Thomas. *Deutsche Geschichte, 1800–1866. Bürgerwelt und starker Staat.* Munich, 1983.
———. "Probleme der Modernisierung in Deutschland," in his *Nachdenken über die deutsche Geschichte. Essays.* Munich, 1986, pp. 44–59.
Numbers, Ronald L. "The Fall and Rise of the American Medical Profession," in Judith Walzer Leavitt, Ronald L. Numbers, eds., *Sickness and Health in America,* 2nd ed. Wisconsin, 1985, pp. 185–196.
O'Boyle, Lenore. "Klassische Bildung und soziale Struktur in Deutschland zwischen 1800 und 1848," *Historische Zeitschrift,* 207 (1968): 584–608.
Ott, Hugo. "Die wirtschaftliche und soziale Entwicklung von der Mitte des 19. Jahrhunderts bis zum Ende des Ersten Weltkriegs," in Landeszentrale für politische Bildung Baden-Württemberg, ed. *Badische Geschichte. Vom Großherzogtum bis zur Gegenwart.* Stuttgart, 1979, pp. 103–142.
Ottnad, Bernd. "Politische Geschichte von 1850 bis 1918," in Landeszentrale für politische Bildung Baden-Württemberg, ed. *Badische Geschichte. Vom Großherzogtum bis zur Gegenwart.* Stuttgart, 1979, pp. 65–85.
Patzelt, Viktor. "Die Bedeutung des Wiener Optikers Simon Plössl für die Mikroskope," *Mikroskopie,* 2 (1946): 1–64.
Paulsen, Friedrich. *Geschichte des gelehrten Unterrichts auf den deutschen Schulen und Universitäten,* 2 vols. Leipzig, 1897.
Pfetsch, Frank R. *Zur Entwicklung der Wissenschaftspolitik in Deutschland, 1750–1914.* Berlin, 1974.
Pinson, Koppel S. *Modern Germany. Its History and Civilization,* 2nd ed. New York, 1966.
Puschmann, Theodor. *A History of Medical Education,* facsimile of 1891 edition. New York, 1966.
Rabl, Marie, ed. *Rudolf Virchow. Briefe an seine Eltern 1839 bis 1864.* Leipzig, 1907.
Reiser, Stanley Joel. *Medicine and the Reign of Technology.* Cambridge, 1978.
Richter, Günter. "Revolution und Gegenrevolution in Baden 1849," *Zeitschrift für die Geschichte des Oberrheins,* 119 (1971): 387–425.
Riese, Reinhard. *Die Hochschule auf dem Wege zum wissenschaftlichen Großbetrieb.* Stuttgart, 1977.
Ringer, Fritz. *The Decline of the German Mandarins. The German Academic Community, 1890–1933.* Cambridge, 1969.
Risse, Guenter. "Health and Disease: History of the Concepts," in Warren T. Reich, ed. *Encyclopedia of Bioethics,* 4 vols. New York, 1978, vol. 2, pp. 579–85.

Bibliography

Rosen, George. "Jacob Henle: On Miasmata and Contagia," *Bulletin of the Institute of the History of Medicine,* 6 (1938): 907–983.
Rosenberg, Charles. "Toward an Ecology of Knowledge: On Discipline, Context, and History," in Alexandra Oleson and John Voss, eds. *The Organization of Knowledge in Modern America, 1860–1920.* Baltimore, 1979.
Rothschuh, Karl. "Von der Histomorphologie zur Histophysiologie unter besonderer Berücksichtigung von Purkinjes Arbeiten," in Vl. Kruta, ed. *J. E. Purkyne 1787–1869. Centenary Symposium, Prague, 8–10 September 1969.* Brno, 1971, pp. 197–212.
———. *History of Physiology.* New York, 1973.
Schelsky, Helmut. *Einsamkeit und Freiheit. Idee und Gestalt der deutschen Universität und ihrer Reformen,* 2nd ed. Düsseldorf, 1971.
Schnabel, Franz. *Sigismund von Reitzenstein. Der Begründer des badischen Staates.* Karlsruhe, 1927.
———. *Deutsche Geschichte im 19. Jahrhundert,* 3rd ed., 4 vols. Freiburg, 1934.
Schneider, Franz. *Geschichte der Universität Heidelberg im ersten Jahrzehnt nach der Reorganisation durch Karl Friedrich (1803–1813).* Heidelberg, 1913.
Schöler, Walter. *Geschichte des naturwissenschaftlichen Unterrichts im 17. bis 19. Jahrhundert.* Berlin, 1970.
Schröer, Heinz. *Carl Ludwig. Begründer der messenden Experimentalphysiologie.* Stuttgart, 1967.
Schubring, Gert. "The Rise and Decline of the Bonn Natural Sciences Seminar," in *Osiris,* 2nd series, 5 (1989): 57–93.
Sheehan, James J. "Liberalism and Society in Germany, 1815–48," *Modern History,* 45 (1973): 583–604.
———. *German Liberalism in the Nineteenth Century.* Chicago, 1978.
Simmer, Hans H. "Principles and Problems of Medical Undergraduate Education in Germany during the Nineteenth and Early Twentieth Centuries," in C. D. O'Mally, ed. *History of Medical Education.* Berkeley, 1970, pp. 173–200.
Stiefel, Karl. *Baden 1648–1952,* 2 vols. Karlsruhe, 1977.
Stübler, Eberhard. *Geschichte der medizinischen Fakultät der Universität Heidelberg, 1326–1925.* Heidelberg, 1926.
Stürzbecher, Manfred. "Zur Berufung Johannes Müllers an die Berliner Universität," *Jahrbuch für die Geschichte Mittel- und Ostdeutschlands,* 21 (1972): 184–226.
Teich, Mikulás. "Purkyne and Valentin on Ciliary Motion: An Early Investigation in Morphological Physiology," *British Journal for the History of Science,* 5 (1970/71): 168–177.
Temkin, Owsei. "Health and Disease," in Philip Wiener, ed. *Dictionary of the History of Ideas,* 4 vols. New York, 1973–74, vol. 2, pp. 395–407.
———. "The Scientific Approach to Disease: Specific Entity and Individual Sickness," in his *The Double Face of Janus.* Baltimore, 1977, pp. 441–454.
Tennstedt, Florian. *Sozialgeschichte der Sozialpolitik in Deutschland.* Göttingen, 1981.
Tipps, Dean C. "Modernization Theory and the Comparative Study of Societies: A Critical Perspective," *Comparative Studies in Society and History,* 15 (1973): 199–226.
Tipton, Frank B. "The National Consensus in German Economic History," *Central European History,* 7,3 (1974): 195–224.
Tuchman, Arleen Marcia. "Experimental Physiology, Medical Reform and the

Politics of Education at the University of Heidelberg: A Case Study," *Bulletin of the History of Medicine,* 61 (1987): 203–215.

———. "From the Lecture to the Laboratory: The Institutionalization of Scientific Medicine at the University of Heidelberg," in Frederic L. Holmes and William Coleman, eds., *The Investigative Enterprise,* Berkeley, 1988, pp. 65–98.

———. "Helmholtz and the German Medical Community," in David Cahan, ed., *The Borders of Science: Essays on Hermann von Helmholtz.* Berkeley, forthcoming, 1993.

Turner, R. Steven. "The Growth of Professorial Research in Prussia, 1818–1848—Causes and Context," *Historical Studies in the Physical Sciences,* 3 (1971): 137–182.

———. "University Reformers and Professorial Scholarship in Germany, 1760–1806," in Lawrence Stone, ed., *The University in Society,* 2 vols. Princeton, 1974, vol. 2, pp. 495–531.

———. "The *Bildungsbürgertum* and the Learned Professions in Prussia, 1770–1830: The Origins of a Class," *Histoire sociale. Social History,* 13 (1980): 105–135.

———. "The Prussian Universities and the Concept of Research," *Internationales Archiv für Sozialgeschichte der deutschen Literatur,* 5 (1980): 68–93.

———. "The Prussian Professoriate and the Research Imperative," in N. H. Jahnke and M. Otto, eds., *Epistemological and Social Problems of the Sciences in the Early Nineteenth Century.* Dordrecht, 1981, pp. 109–121.

———. "Justus Liebig versus Prussian chemistry: Reflections on early institute-building in Germany," *Historical Studies in the Physical Sciences,* 13,1 (1982): 129–162.

Vollmer, Franz X. "Die 48er Revolution," in *Badische Geschichte,* ed. Landeszentrale für politische Bildung Baden-Würtemberg. Stuttgart, 1979, pp. 37–64.

Weisert, Hermann. "Die Verfassung der Universität Heidelberg, Überblick 1386–1852," *Abhandlungen der Heidelberger Akademie der Wissenschaften. Philosophisch-historische Klasse,* 1974: 1–168.

Wolgast, Eike. *Die Universität Heidelberg, 1386–1986.* Berlin, 1986.

Zehntner, Hans. *Das Staatslexikon von Rotteck und Welcker. Eine Studie zur Geschichte des deutschen Frühliberalismus.* Jena, 1929.

Zloczower, Avraham. *Career Opportunities and the Growth of Scientific Disciplines in Nineteenth-Century Germany.* New York, 1981.

Dissertations and other unpublished manuscripts

Broman, Thomas Hoyt. *The Transformation of Academic Medicine in Germany, 1780–1820.* Ph.D. diss., Princeton University, 1987.

Dreher, Astrid. *Briefe von Carl Ludwig an Jacob Henle aus den Jahren 1846–1872.* Diss. Heidelberg, 1980.

Genz, Axel. *Die Emanzipation der naturwissenschaftlichen Physiologie in Berlin.* Diss. Magdeburg, 1970.

Girlich, Alfred. *Die Grundlagen der Innenpolitik Badens unter Großherzog Friedrich I. Entwicklung und Verwirklichung der Idee einer Volkserziehung.* Diss. Heidelberg, 1952.

Goth, Werner. *Zur Geschichte der Klinik in Heidelberg im 19. Jahrhundert.* Diss. Heidelberg, 1982.

Kläß, Konrad. *Die Einführung besonderer Kurse für Mikroskopie und physikalische Diagnostik (Perkussion und Auskultation) in den medizinischen Unterricht an deutschen Universitäten im 19. Jahrhundert.* Diss. Göttingen, 1971.

Kupka, Horst Werner. *Die Ausgaben der süddeutschen Länder für die medizinischen und naturwissenschaftlichen Hochschul-Einrichtungen 1848–1914.* Diss. Bonn, 1970.

Lenoir, Timothy. "The Politics of Material Interests" (unpublished manuscript).

Mehlen, Willi. *Das Werk von Friedrich Tiedemann und Leopold Gmelin "Die Verdauung nach Versuchen."* Diss. Bonn, 1976.

Sczibilanski, Klaus. *Von der Prüfungs- und Vorprüfungsordnung (1883) bis zur Approbationsordnung 1970 für Aerzte der Bundesrepublik Deutschland. Die Entwicklung der medizinischen Prüfungsordnungen, darg. an Aufsätzen aus der deutschen ärztlichen Standespresse.* Diss. Münster, 1977.

Smith, Helmut Walser. *Nationalism and Religious Conflict in Germany, 1887–1914.* Ph.D. diss., Yale, 1991.

Wenig, H.-G. *Medizinische Ausbildung im 19. Jahrhundert.* Diss. Bonn, 1969.

Index

Index

Ludwig, Carl, 127
  Heidelberg's interest in, 114, 116, 133 n.13, 143, 152, 153
  and Henle, 81, 116–18, 150
  and kymograph, 115
  laboratory of, 4, 108. *See also* Saxony, and its universities
  and organic physics, 87, 114, 142
  teaching style, 161
Ludwig Wilhelm August, Grand Duke of Baden, 37
Lundgreen, Peter, 13 n.11

Magendie, François, 64
Magnus, Gustav, 107
Mai, Franz Anton, 19
Mandelstamm, Emanuel, 161
Marcus, Adalbert, 30 n.18
Marstallhof, 43
Material interests, 9, 45, 100, 105–7, 132, 175, 177
Mathy, Karl, 55, 94, 96
Meckel, Johann Friedrich, 19
Medical faculty
  political makeup, 114, 127, 139
  reform of, 18–19, 54–55, 138
  structure of, 18–19
Medical licensing. *See* Medical reform
Medical reform, 120–22
  Baden's regulation of 1858, 158–60
  and licensing, 27, 120, 158, 165 n.3
Medical society. *See* Baden medical society
Meier, Emmanual, 37
Merk, Josef, 45
Meyer, August, 56
Microscope, 55, 62, 86
  improvements in, 57
  as symbol, 83
Microscopical exercises. *See* Practical exercises, in microscopy
Mitscherlich, Eilhardt, 107
Mittermaier, Karl, 43, 123
Modernization. *See also* Liberalism, and science education
  and educational reform, 5–6, 34

  35, 39–41, 44–47, 72, 96–109, 179 n.30
  and universities, 6–7, 11–12, 13 n.10, 99–100, 107–8, 175–77
Mohl, Robert von, 108
Montgelas, Maximilian von, 18
Müller, Johannes, 24, 144–45
  research style, 32 n.31, 44, 86
  teaching style, 25, 55, 57, 58, 160

Nägeli, Franz Josef, 76, 127, 139
Nassau, 48
Nature philosophy, 17, 78–79
Nebenius, Karl Friedrich, 55, 75, 92, 95
  author of Baden's constitution, 36
  director of ministry of interior, 38
  education and early career, 36
  educational philosophy, 39–41
  on technical institutes, 11, 40–41
  and University of Heidelberg, 43
Neohumanism, 4, 5, 17, 28
Non-classical secondary schools. *See* Secondary schools, non-classical
Numerical method, 78, 79

Oberhäuser, Georg, 57
Oken, Lorenz, 162
Ophthalmoscope, 10, 143, 146–49
  Helmholtz's invention of, 146–47
  medical community's response to, 147–48
Organic physics, 87, 114–15
  compared to morphology, 117, 118

Parliament, *See* Baden parliament
Pathological anatomy, 10, 125, 142
Pathological physiology, 64
Percussion. *See* Diagnostics
Pestalozzi, Johann Heinrich, 40
Pfeufer, Karl
  departure from Heidelberg, 123–24
  education and career before Heidelberg appointment, 64–66
  Heidelberg's interest in, 67–68, 72
  on importance of clinical instruction, 74